W9-BLV-825
3 3013 00002 7569

BF
38
.M35
Mandler, George
Language of
psychology.
BRADNER LIBRARY
SCHOOLCRAFT COLLEGE
LIVONIA, MICHIGAN 48152

The language of psychology

New York · John Wiley & Sons, Inc.

London · Chapman & Hall, Ltd.

GEORGE MANDLER

Harvard University

The language of psychology

WILLIAM KESSEN

Yale University

Library of Congress Catalog Card Number: 59–10997

Printed in the United States of America

Wovon man nicht sprechen kann, darüber muss man schweigen.

——— ***Ludwig Wittgenstein***

A word to the wise is not sufficient if it doesn't make any sense.

——— ***James Thurber***

For
Jean and Marion

Preface

THROUGH THE PAST SEVERAL DECADES BEHAVioral scientists have devoted a good deal of professional attention to talking about the language of science. Psychologists in particular seem addicted to the discussion of definitions and constructs, theories and the deductive method. Against this conversation about philosophical analysis can be heard the protestations of empiricists, who want to "get back to work," and philosophers, who decry the "methodolatry" of the social scientist. To write a book about the language of psychology under this crossfire seemed to us a dangerous undertaking. In examining our persistence through the last four years, we have come up with two justifications for this book—one substantive, the other subjective.

At the substantive level, we can say best what this book is *not*. It is neither an exhortation to the practicing scientist to spend the next few weeks thinking about the assumptions and presuppositions of his research before he is allowed to handle his data again, nor is it intended to be a new philosophy of science for psychologists. Both of us are familiar enough with the way research proceeds not to advise the first, and too much aware of the profound contributions of contemporary philosophers of science to attempt the second. Rather, we set out with the belief that an attempt to combine empirical and logical considerations of the language of psychology might be useful to researchers in the behavioral sciences.

Professor C. G. Hempel first aroused our interest in philosophical analysis and provided an insight into its limitations. His continuing interest in our explorations, as well as his commanding knowledge of philosophy, were the sharpest spurs to our effort. As psychologists, however, we were unable to think and talk about the language of science without relating it to what we knew about the psychology of scientists. This book is intended to be a compound of the analytic and the behavioral view of science, presenting as reasonable a reconstruction of the scientific behavior of the psychologist as can be built with the logical and empirical tools at our command.

Our subjective justification was the desire to write down what has been the subject of extended conversations over several years between us and with many colleagues. Once this commitment was undertaken, we were more and more attracted by the possibilities of a behavioral analysis of the scientific enterprise. We were encouraged to proceed by an increasing appreciation of the work of two men whose influence will be apparent in the following pages—B. F. Skinner and W. V. Quine. Their unyielding rejection of nonsense, whether psychological or metaphysical, stands as a model to students of human behavior.

One of the decisions involved in writing this book—to determine the audience we were addressing—was taken out of our hands by its progress. What was at first a personal expression of some notions about the language of psychology soon included explications of some traditional psychological and philosophical problems, considerations in the history of psychology, and comments on classical solutions in the philosophy of science. The end result is addressed primarily to psychologists and other behavioral scientists who share an interest in the science-making behavior of their colleagues and in the analysis of their language. To philosophers we submit these pages as an addendum to the logical analysis of science. For the student, this book will provide an introduction to the language of science in psychology and the social sciences.

The writing of this book has been a truly joint venture. At this stage it has become difficult to assign priority for any specific ideas contained in it, and each of us willingly assigns any ambiguities or erroneous notions to the other one. The required decision about the order of names on the title page could not be made on any rational grounds; even as this preface is written chance has not determined who will be "first" author.

William Kessen
George Mandler

New Haven, Connecticut
Cambridge, Massachusetts
September 1, 1958

Acknowledgments

THE WRITING OF THIS BOOK WAS SO MUCH A result of our interactions with our teachers, colleagues, and students that whatever merit it may have must be shared with them. Our special debt is to the teachers who first made us think about the underpinnings of psychology—Gregory A. Kimble and Bernard Mausner. We also want to express our appreciation to the many friends who patiently served as soundingboards and critics during the preparation of the book, particularly to H. D. Aiken, D. Bakan, G. N. Bower, R. W. Brown, C. G. Hempel, C. I. Hovland, G. Lindzey, F. A. Logan, R. D. Luce, G. A. Miller, T. E. Shipley, and the late Katherine M. Wolf. Mrs. Susan R. Henry spent many hours deciphering our drafts to provide us with a clean manuscript.

We are indebted to the Laboratory of Social Relations, Harvard University, and to the Harvard Foundation for grants-in-aid which provided research and clerical assistance.

Some of the drive, many of the cues, and all of the important reinforcement to our writing this book must be assigned to our wives, Marion Kessen and Jean Mandler.

Acknowledgment is made to the following publishers for permission to quote from their publications: American Association for the Advancement of Science; American Psychological Association; Appleton-Century-Crofts, Inc.; The Athlone Press; Basic Books, Inc.; Basil Blackwell; Cambridge University Press; Constable and Company, Ltd.; E. P. Dutton and Company; George Allen and Unwin, Ltd.; Harcourt, Brace and Company; Harvard University Press; Houghton Mifflin Company; The Journal Press; Little, Brown and Company; The Macmillan Company; Oxford University Press; The Philosophical Review; Routledge and Kegan Paul, Ltd.; University of Chicago Press; University of Kansas Press; Williams and Wilkins Company; Yale University Press.

W. K.
G. M.

Contents

part II Theory in psychology

Introduction

THE ANALYSIS OF LANGUAGE HAS LONG BEEN an occupation of major interest to scholars, but in recent years the study of linguistic forms, of meaning, and of communication has burgeoned to new size. No longer does the grammarian or the literary critic dominate the area of language analysis, for the philosopher, the linguist, and the psychologist have entered the investigation of man's use of words. The past several decades have seen the development within traditional academic disciplines of several lines of study which are related by their concern with language, and a long list of books and specialized journals attests to the thesis that the proper study of man is through his vocabulary.

For the philosopher, this is not an altogether new role—he has for centuries been held either in awe or in contempt as a dealer in words—but the contemporary trader in "philosophical analysis" has an aversion to other-worldliness which sets him apart to a substantial degree from his metaphysical ancestors. Perhaps the most striking instance of this development is the growth of the philosophy of science, which sets as its explicit goal the understanding of the activities of practicing scientists or, somewhat more accurately, the analysis of scientific languages. The intense scrutiny by philosophers of science has forced an almost revolutionary reappraisal of the nature of scientific activity. The classical view, both popular and academic, of the scientist has had its focus on his manipulation of the world, not on his language. Whether in pursuit of microbes, atoms, or genes, the True Scientist has been surrounded by paraphernalia, busily pouring something into something else, or cutting something out, or at least looking intensely at something. From the day that a legendary scholar actually looked into the horse's mouth to determine the number of his teeth, the mark of the scientist has been his investment in *things,* in reality, coupled with a sometimes arrogant disdain for arguments about metaphysics, semantics, or methodology. This consuming devotion to manipulation, prediction, and control remains the primary tenet of any laboratory scientist, and the new entry of the philosopher as overseer and critic of his efforts has not always been greeted with applause. Nonetheless, the twentieth century has become the age of the self-conscious scientist, and his basic apparatus of logic, mathematics, the formation of a vocabulary, and the elaboration of theories is being subjected to continuing examination by the philosophers of science and by the scientists themselves.

To understand this shift in emphasis, it is necessary to recognize that any scientific activity depends on successful communication. The latitude in meaning which is possible in common speech and laudable in poetry is not permitted to science. The difference between "the bigger they come, the harder they fall" and "$M = mv$" is enormous, encompassing not only part of the history of physics, but a good deal of language clarification as well. Even so, such an example only hints at the problems of adequate scientific communication, which stands with one foot in the everyday vernacular and the other in the specialized language of theoretical abstraction. The theme of the chapters to follow is an examination of these two footholds and the steps connecting them in the empirical science of psychology.

It is important to note at the outset that any treatment of psychological language is necessarily timebound. A century ago the psychological vocabulary would have included "will," "intellect," "conation," and so on, while somewhat later it would have included "recency," "association-bond," and "instinct." Despite its relative youth, psychological science has produced a prolixity and variability of technical terms which rivals that of more ancient disciplines. Moreover, there is little sign that a winnowing is in progress, with a hardier variety of words surviving the onslaught of new theories. This diversity raises the important issue of whether a strict specification of the vocabulary of psychology can be advanced. A number of attempts to define psychology have been made and enshrined in introductory texts, turning successively on consciousness, experience, and behavior, with remarkably little disagreement among the definers until some Wundt, James, or Watson broke stroke. Perhaps the lesson here is that no empirical science reaches an end point; it is in recognition of this developing character of the science that we will outline rather than define the language of psychology as *the language of psychologists,* or more precisely, of contemporary psychologists.

There are other difficulties in the way of an analysis of psychological language. Clearly, there is some difference between the language the psychologist uses in hiring a secretary and the language he uses to present his empirical findings and his theories. The distinction underlying this case is an important one and its elaboration will be detailed later; for now, some crude characterization of the several languages of psychologists must be set out as a guideline.

Genetically the psychologist's first language is the one learned from and shared with his cultural community, and it is in this communication mode—English for most readers of this book—that he hires secretaries, tells jokes, defends his political party, and writes books. The English language has an elaborate set of rules which govern its proper application, and these rules are taught willy-nilly to children, together with a set of ambiguities and exceptions that result in arguments academic as well as political. Presumably, an intensive study of the psychologist's use of this *common language* would not show striking differences from its use by other members of his social and educational community. It is on the relatively rare occasions when he shifts to *system language* that the psychologist's professional color shows, and he can be identified as a scientific specialist. In the mid-twentieth century, the system language of psychologists includes words such as "anxiety," "dissonance," "function of," "significant at .05 level," "$_{S}H_{R}$," "ego syntonicity," "ascending reticular tracts," and "retroactive inhibition," plus rules for combining such expressions into grammatically proper statements. This vocabulary with its combination rules—the system language of psychologists—is the subject of the present enquiry.

Were the specification of intention left at this point, however, this version of psychology would have all the relevance of a crossword puzzle. Scientific psychology is more than a word game; its vocabulary, however vague and limited, is *about something,* and the relation between the words psychologists use and the appropriate somethings is the heart of what is usually meant in calling a discipline empirical.

We have no desire to become enmeshed in epistemological subtleties, and therefore propose the most limited statement with regard to this issue that will permit us to proceed. It can be said (in the common language!) that there are *objects* and *events* to which rats, psychologists, and poets react, and that responses to these events are possible without words.

The system language of psychology must grow from non-verbal behavior and the archaic language of common use, both of which deal with the everyday world of objects and events. But in its refined form, the vocabulary of a system language must be precise and invariant, its grammatical rules explicit and shared by the scientific community. Basic to these requirements are the notions of publicity and communicability. The scientific genius who labors in linguistic isolation from his predecessors and his successors may grace our planet, but he is necessarily as unknown to his colleagues and as uninfluential in the development of a science as an Alpha Centaurian physicist.

From this first-order approximation of the range of psychology, the tentative distinction between common and system language, and the necessity for communicability of scientific statements, a host of questions arise for further consideration:

As a science develops from its philosophical groundings and from the generalizations of common sense, how does it maintain its ties to the vernacular? In what ways does it break away from the vague and ambiguous formulations of the common language?

How does a relatively new science like psychology develop its basic vocabulary? What rules or tests can be applied to decide upon the acceptability of its terms?

Why do scientists, and psychologists in particular, engage in theorizing? How are theories and hypotheses developed and codified?

To what use are theories put? How are they tested? What is the relation between the "real world" and the psychologist's statements about it?

These questions are not restricted to the science of psychology. In one form or another they have appeared throughout the history of Western science. They have also generated two antagonistic sets of answers. On the one hand the questions have been treated as superfluous and as interfering with the ongoing business of science; on the other hand the position has been taken that science should not, and possibly cannot, proceed without first examining its logical foundation and the sources of its language.

Arguments have been proposed in philosophy and in science, ancient and modern, in defense of both extreme positions. Whatever labels may be applied to the exposition in the pages to follow, we will attempt to steer clear of extreme positivism and extreme negativism. The workaday scientist must maintain a strict adherence to the canons of empirical investigation and evidence, but an analysis of his assumptions about logic and language may turn out to be useful to him.

A major premise underlying our analysis of psychological language is that science, like any other human activity, can be studied fruitfully even with the limited knowledge we have about the organism which makes science.[1] To assert the human character of science goes beyond the merely trivial comment that scientists are human, not lower organisms. An attempt to understand the making of science by studying the maker commits us to an examination of the empirical generalizations about behavior which will illuminate this specialized kind of human activity. How do people at large use words, state generalizations, test their hunches? Wherein does the scientist's activity differ from this everyday behavior of men?

Before settling in to a study of these questions, we must enter two disclaimers. There will arise throughout the treatment of science which is developed in the following chapters problems which cannot easily be resolved by an appeal to data about behavior. At such points, the only alternatives to arrant speculation are the confession of ignorance and the proposal of a best guess. The study of the scientist as a behaving organism must start with whatever material is available and make changes as the analysis proceeds and better generalizations, laws, or logics come along. There are many missing data about the behavior of scientists, but a first approximation is more likely to indicate the lacunae than will a resigned shrug.

The second disclaimer concerns the peculiar status of logic and mathematics as somehow "nonempirical." This has long been an intricate problem for philosophers and mathematicians; in the context of talking about the development of science, we will perforce touch on it again. For now, it will clarify our intention to remark that no attempt will be made to "reduce" the complexities of logical and mathematical expression to simple laws of human behavior. Rather, we will be concerned with an examination of the relationships among lan-

---

[1] We will anticipate a later discussion to note that seeing science as human behavior does not entail the assertion that psychology is the fundamental or propaedeutic science (see Chapter 9).

guage systems of this elevated order, the mundane language of everyday discourse, and the in-between language of the psychologist.

In the following pages, a distinction will be made between the vocabulary and the grammar of psychology. This distinction is primarily of heuristic and didactic value, for neither words nor sentences can be investigated independently. Little would be gained by learning either vocabulary or grammar in isolation; skill at using the complete system marks the successful scientist. The use of words depends on the context in which they appear and a list of words is not particularly useful unless we know grammatical rules for their connection.

With these general conventions and reservations agreed upon, we will deal first with the basic vocabulary of psychology. Several attempts to define classes of acceptable scientific terms will be examined—and found wanting. A behavioral criterion for the basic vocabulary will be suggested, but it will be found that any satisfactory examination of the language of psychology requires in addition an analysis of rules for the formation of sentences.

The rules for sentence formation and the collection of sentences which results from their application are the subject of the second major section of this book—the theory language of psychology. After a general discussion of the place of theories in an empirical science, we will turn to a closer examination of the ways in which theories have been constructed and used in psychology.

part I

The vocabulary of psychology

chapter one

The common language and the language of science

THE ASSERTION THAT SCIENCE CAN BE VIEWED as a special language system does not imply that scientific languages are independent of everyday language or that the scientific language can be investigated without reference to the *vernacular*—the common language of ordinary use. All men come to the scientific enterprise with a highly elaborated system for ordering events and perceptions. As adult human beings they have acquired an ingrained way of looking at the world—a cultural patterning of the environment which all of us use as the basic framework for making statements about the world of objects and events. This archaic view of the world, a protopsychology and protophilosophy, is the initial source of statements and generalizations in science. It does not magically disappear in the laboratory or in the library. The scientist does not approach his scientific universe in a linguistic vacuum, and for this reason the usefulness of the vernacular vocabulary for scientific activity must be examined. If the common language is found wanting, then the requirements for a special scientific language must be defined.

Dissatisfaction with the vernacular is not a modern worry. Francis Bacon, in the early seventeenth century, discussed the shortcomings of the "vulgar" or the "idols of the market-place." His two major criticisms of the common language have a modern ring to them:

> The idols imposed by words on the understanding are of two kinds. They are either names of things which do not exist (for as there are things left unnamed through lack of observation, so likewise are there names which result from fantastic suppositions and to which nothing in reality corresponds), or they are names of things which exist, but yet confused and ill-defined, and hastily and irregularly derived from realities. Of the former kind are Fortune, the Prime Mover, Planetary Orbits, Elements of Fire, and like fictions which owe their origin to false and idle theories. . . . But the other class, which springs out of a faulty and unskillful abstraction, is intricate and deeply rooted. Let us take for example such a word as *humid,* and see how far the several things which the word is used to signify agree with each other; and we shall find the word *humid* to be nothing else than a mark loosely and confusedly applied to denote a variety of actions which will not bear to be reduced to any constant meaning. For it both signifies that which easily spreads itself round any other body; and that which in itself is indeterminate and cannot solidize; and that which readily yields in every direction; and that which easily divides and scatters itself; and that which easily unites and collects itself; and that which readily flows and is put in motion; and that which readily clings to another body and wets it; and that which is easily reduced to a liquid, or being solid easily melts. (Bacon, 1620, p. 68.)

What is it in language that makes for such confusion? While Bacon's irritation with the word "humid" may not be relevant to its much-distilled use today, similar confusions arise over other frequently used terms. An exhaustive logical and semantic analysis of natural and artificial languages is beyond the scope of this investigation, but some psychological aspects of common languages and their relation to the requirements of scientific languages must be treated here.[1]

The dominant medium of assertions about the world is linguistic.

---

[1] The distinction between grammar and vocabulary, suggested in the Introduction, will be abandoned at various points in this discussion. Both semantic and grammatical aspects of the vernacular must enter into the analysis of any language. For extensive discussions of logical and semantic analysis, see such basic works as Wittgenstein's *Tractatus Logico-Philosophicus* (1922), Carnap's *Logical Syntax of Language* (1937), and Ryle's *The Concept of Mind* (1949).

It is language that carries the burden of communicating observations, generalizations, and inferences. The leading role of this particular mode of behavior is such an essential part of our protopsychology that any description of its importance may become a series of commonplaces: Language is the primary mode of communication—Language is acquired by the developing organism—Language is often vague or ambiguous—and so forth. On occasion, communication can proceed without the apparatus of spoken or written language. Nevertheless, psychologists, physicists, and suburban commuters all talk and write, and an examination of the linguistic aspects of psychology, or physics, or suburbia will afford a comprehensive view of these fields of human activity.

What are these spoken or written assertions about the world? What do they communicate?

When a suburban resident gets out of bed on a wintry morning, he may say to his sleepy wife: "Look, it's snowing" or "You never get up on time." While such interchanges may seem far removed from the language of science, they have several characteristics in common with scientific sentences: Both statements "communicate," they are verbal responses, and neither needs much elaboration in order to produce some specific behavior on the part of the individual to whom it is addressed. The scientist's sentences and generalizations may be more effective and valid, but they have a history very similar to these vernacular assertions. The two modes of discourse share another important characteristic; they both can be fruitfully studied as a function of the occasions of their occurrence. The important language responses of all men are elicited by some antecedent conditions, and the satisfactory understanding of any language requires the examination of these occasions. The statement "It is snowing" may be elicited by such diverse antecedents as a look out the window or a call to the weather bureau, and the study of verbal behavior must take into account such diversity as well as the reliability of the subsequent response. Our analysis of language behavior will be concerned primarily with the way in which various means of acquiring or using language may help or hinder communication. Such an investigation will deal with spoken or written words and sentences, with the utterances of names and the relations among them.

The study of the conditions for language behavior—the antecedents of names and sentences—will be particularly helpful in the development of a language which makes contact with the world of objects and events that surrounds laymen and scientists alike. To say "It is snowing" or "There is a table" is not just a fortuitous occurrence of sounds; unless one is lying, these statements assert at the common-sense level that it is *in fact* snowing and that there *really* is a table. In scientific discourse similar assertions are made, and we will have repeated occasion to examine the import of "in fact" and "really" in the language of science. As a first approximation such assertions are assumed to indicate that there are objects and events which are the occasions for these utterances. Science comes down to earth in this contact between the events of our surroundings and the words we use; it is in this sense that scientific statements will be seen to be about empirical events.

One of the ways in which language brings order into both life and the laboratory is by means of its equivalence function. Two occasions for talking about snowfall were indicated above; at a simpler level, names such as "lady," "table," or "rat" may serve the purpose of indicating equivalence between two or more females, pieces of furniture, or mammals. Whatever else these objects may be, the equivalence function of naming tells us to treat them as ladies, tables, or rats.[2]

People could not communicate equivalence among objects if they had learned their language in radically different ways. We can therefore conclude that most people in our culture learn English in pretty much the same way and use it quite consistently. But the fact that variations occur and that members of the same social community sometimes have difficulty in communicating will be seen to be typical of the common language and worthy of special attention when we consider scientific languages.[3]

The human being may learn about his environment in terms of either verbal or nonverbal behavior. These two ways of distinguishing important aspects of the surroundings may function independently or conjointly. Thus the child may learn that peanuts are edible and that buttons are not by learning the nonverbal eating response to only

---

[2] We may note at this point that a distinction will have to be made between two kinds of names, *generic names,* which are applied to various instances of a class and which serve to indicate equivalence of objects or events belonging to that one class, and *proper names,* which are the names of single objects or individuals equivalent over various instances of time. The present discussion is primarily concerned with generic naming; a more extended discussion of this distinction and its relation to the problem of denotation will be found in Chapter 3.

[3] Several important issues in the psychology of language will not be considered here. Two excellent introductions to the psychology of language have been provided by Miller (1951) and Brown (1956).

one of the two sets of objects. Or he may learn the verbal response "Teddy" to a particular toy. The point to be made here is that both the eating response and the "Teddy" response differentiate the environment. Both types of responses may be considered to be attributes of environmental objects or events.

The use of the concept of attribute to include all responses elicited by an object differs in breadth from classical uses of the term. Historically it has been used to name the "different ways in which sensations may vary" (Pillsbury, 1916). Our use of the term includes these different aspects of sensations, although in modern dress, but we will extend it to all verbal expressions which name some single or complex aspect of an event or object. So-called nonverbal attributes will be useful only to the extent that they in turn are tied to a verbal response.

Much of our primary differentiation and categorization of objects relies on the use of nonverbal, or nonlinguistic, attributes. But an object or event may frequently be categorized by the particular verbal response or category which it elicits, without any differentiation of the nonlinguistic attributes. As Brown has stated: "It is a functional attribute of [an object] to elicit a particular utterance from properly disposed and informed persons" (Brown, 1956, p. 279).

Traditionally, much has been made of the distinction between the attributes of an object and the words which somehow signify those attributes. It appears that while we may accept the distinction between nonverbal attributes and the terms which name them, *all* attributes serve to categorize events and thus depend on an active, differentiating organism. Since the name-in-use of an attribute implies the presence of some verbal or nonverbal category, we may for practical purposes dispense with this distinction and simply use the name.

For example, a package of cigarettes has many attributes, verbal ones such as "Chesterfield" and nonverbal ones such as being smooth to the touch and light enough to be lifted. These latter attributes of smoothness and relative weight are nonverbal in the sense that the primary responses involved are manual. However, in order to talk about them we must use verbal responses ("smooth," "light"). This use of language to label prior discriminations applies particularly to science. All attributes in science must in the long run be verbal; otherwise communication among scientists is severely restricted. Although much scientific activity consists of nonverbal behavior such as measuring responses, this behavior must eventually be translated into verbal units, just as the words "smooth" and "light" had to be used in describing the pack of cigarettes.

DIFFICULTIES IN THE COMMON LANGUAGE

There are a variety of characteristics of the common language which make the communication of observations or generalizations difficult. Misunderstandings and miscommunication arise from reification, vagueness, ambiguity, and the use of indicator words and tenses.

The first problem, that of *reification,* is intimately connected with the archaic notion that everything with a name exists "out there." This notion develops from the way in which language is first acquired. Some differentiations of objects and events are acquired by the use of verbal responses. In most cases, however, the initial learning is nonverbal and words and phrases are used to name previously established discriminations. Thus a child perceives colors and differences between colors and subsequently learns to name them. Such early language learning leads to the inevitable conclusion that language is a secondary apparatus for *talking about* prior discriminations. This protophilosophy creates occasional problems in subsequent language learning. It is apparent in the use of brand names. Two identical commercial products will be considered to have some distinguishable characteristic simply because they are differently named. The smoker who swears by Brand A will insist that he can tell his cigarette from Brand B in a blindfold test. Frequently this discrimination is based on labeling alone, and he cannot in fact distinguish between the two brands. In the case of tobaccos there is a possible discrimination to be made and some cigarette smokers can in fact distinguish reliably among different brands. In other cases, such as those of drugs which have a legally determined composition, no discrimination is even possible, yet many people insist that there are differences—a belief based only on the use of words such as brand names.

Complex language acquisition goes beyond simple naming behavior. It requires not only nonverbal discriminations but also a context of previously acquired words and sentences. The learning individual acquires new knowledge about his surroundings through language. The little girl who is told that her brother has been "bad" may enquire whether she too could be bad, and then whether Daddy is bad, and finally relate this verbally learned attribute to some particular nonverbal behavior such as stealing cookies. Similarly the college student first learns about semipermeable membranes from his chemistry textbook, which describes their characteristics in verbal terms. Later he may also make nonverbal contact with this new "entity" in his laboratory section, but for most of his new learning language is the primary vehicle.

There are then two processes: First, verbal responses are used to name external events, and second, new verbal units are learned through language. When these two blend into one another, the archaic notion prevails that language invariably refers to some nonverbal characteristic of the environment. Naming of previously established discriminations is the dominant, first-acquired mode. This use of language to talk about some independent reality generalizes to the second mode—the learning of words through language. This process has been called reification, the tendency to assume that words invariably make reference to some nonverbal reality.

In the course of these pages, the point will be made that science is not just a language game. Scientific generalizations are about something; they are about "traits of reality independent of language" (Quine, 1957, p. 7). But names like "mind" or "force" are used in the common language and sometimes in science as if their status were similar to that of names such as "red," "green," or "hot." This is not to deny the utility of such terms as "force," but it must be recognized that they owe their existence to elaborate theoretical and linguistic developments and not to the naming of a nonverbal discrimination.

A characteristic of the common language, closely related to the problem of reification, is that it often creates fanciful distinctions or discriminations which are based on little more than the juxtaposition of words. Just because the world of words may divide people into "good" and "bad," animals into "rational" and "irrational," behaviors into "willed" and "mechanistic," or even propositions into "analytic" and "synthetic," there is no guarantee that such dichotomies are useful or even possible within scientific languages, which must be tied to discriminable aspects of the world.

A second aspect of common language which concerns the scientist is its *vagueness,* or lack of specified usage. A brief examination of the following common-sense generalizations will illustrate this shortcoming:

"Fat men are jolly."
"Absence makes the heart grow fonder."

Consider the vagueness of some of the constituent terms of these expressions. Such words as "fat," "jolly," not to mention "heart," while probably quite specific for some people, will tend to elicit different specifications, expectations, and predictions from different individuals. The term "fat" suffers the additional indignity of being buffeted by changing concepts of fashion. Thus, it is sometimes hard to tell whether a particular instance is included under the generalization. Even if this problem of vagueness were not present, the generalizations still would be of limited usefulness. The range and scope of the jolliness principle is restricted. It applies only to "fat" men, i.e., individuals who reach a required degree of obesity. It says nothing about increments of obesity above that range; do fat men get jollier the fatter they are? Nor is any information supplied about the sense of humor of more diet-conscious persons. In contrast, as much as one may question the usefulness of a body-type psychology, such investigators as Kretschmer and Sheldon have approached a similar problem with concepts and statements of much more precise applicability. And their statements tend to be in the system language—the special language of science—rather than in the common language.

The problem of vagueness reappears when exceptions to these principles are considered. In the case of the second statement, the folklore of empirical generalizations provides a principle which legalizes the exception: "Out of sight, out of mind." This statement appears to be quite contradictory to "Absence makes the heart grow fonder." One solution might be to dismiss the possibility of any generalizations in this area of affective deprivation. Unfortunately, two such contradictory generalizations often provoke much psychological theorizing. It might be argued that "heart" in the original principle and "mind" in the contradictory statement refer to different things. The differences need an extensive and newly developed theory in order to explicate fully the differential predictions of the two statements. Adopting a novel definition of these two entities might resolve the conflict between the statements. But this is exactly the problem of vagueness: The lack of precision of the constituent terms of the two principles does not permit any precise prediction in the first place. Thus any usefulness of these two "laws" depends on the reconstruction of the terms of the two statements.

The rules of common languages do not determine usage in such a way that the use of a word or phrase is limited to a specific object or observation. Objects and characteristics which are given a particular designation or attribute are often only vaguely distinguished from those which are not so designated. In the example, the term "fat" has been given no fixed limiting characteristics. Habits of applying the term to people of different body weights vary from individual to individual because the rules of application have been left vague, and the acquisition and use of the term may differ. Frequently vagueness is not simply ascribable to a lack of proper discriminations among varying body weights. While the user of the common language may be able to discriminate between two people whose weights differ by 25 pounds, he often fails to use this "ability." This vagueness-in-use is part of the sloppiness of the common language; no strict insistence is made on the use of all possible discriminations, particularly when their presence or absence plays no important role in ordinary living. A housewife is likely to exert little effort in discriminating "large" or "small" portions of chocolate cake on her dinner table but will demonstrate much better discriminatory power when buying the cake at the local bakery. In a scientific language variation from occasion to occasion is inappropriate; scientists seem to be always buying cake.

An aspect of common languages which is related to vagueness is that of *ambiguity*. Ambiguity refers to the case in which the same sentence, unchanged in its linguistic structure, depends for its truth or falsity on the circumstances under which it is used. Thus the sentence "Children like you" may be construed as "Children similar to you" or as "Children prefer (love) you," depending upon the circumstance of usage. Even in the use of the common language ambiguities tend to be avoided because they lead too often to misunderstandings. Only some poets are happy about being ambiguous.

Two other characteristics of the vernacular deserve brief attention. One is the use of *indicator words,* the other that of *tense.* Indicator words include such terms as "I," "he," and "that." Tense is either expressed in verb forms or is introduced by indicator words such as "now" or "later." The difficulty with statements which include such terms is that their truth or falsity may vary from speaker to speaker, and from occasion to occasion. Specification is, of course, possible by the use of proper names and place names. Similarly the use of dates fixes an indicator of tense such as "now" to an invariable time dimension and leaves no question concerning the occasion of the particular occurrence. For example, the statement "He placed that rat over there yesterday" may be comprehensible if the occasion is observed, but general scientific usage requires the precision of "The experimenter placed rat No. 46 in the starting box on the 4th day of running."

BEYOND THE VERNACULAR

Our discussion has indicated some ways in which the common language is inadequate for scientific discourse. The first task in building a scientific language is to set up rules of usage which eliminate these shortcomings. A language built on such new foundations will at least cause less trouble than the vernacular. However, the scientist does not, and indeed cannot, start his investigations without some language. His primary identification and description of the world is couched in archaic forms. The scientist, like all other adult human beings, reports his observations primarily in words of the vernacular, and his native language determines to a large extent the form and content of these communications.

It is not the task of the scientist to construct a new language without any ties to his vernacular vocabulary. Rather it is to reformulate common language structures, to eliminate vague terms, to avoid reified concepts, and to reconstruct step by step *on the basis of his common language* a new language which avoids the problems and difficulties presented by the vernacular. This approach is not just a program or suggested method, but to a large extent a description of the history of the different sciences. Science does not abandon the vernacular but rather changes its objectionable features, using the common language as it rebuilds it from within. Thus the common language is not only a prerequisite for science, but in effect the very basis on which scientific language is built. This is the case not only for the development of a more appropriate vocabulary and grammar, but also for the initial categories and generalizations from which the scientist proceeds.

Requirements for Scientific Languages

Given the shortcomings of the common language, some solutions to these problems can now be discussed. The avoiding of indicator words, both of names and places, has already been described. By the use of proper names, particulars, and time terms such as dates and hours, scientists can avoid that source of confusion. This renovation provides one group of terms acceptable to the language of science.

A second class of terms which presents no difficulties comprises words and symbols from the language of logic. These supply connectives such as "and", "or", "if . . . then", and so forth. The language of logic, and by corollary, of mathematics, has been extensively reconstructed from its vernacular origins; modern symbolic logic provides the scientist with a rich notational and grammatical vocabulary. This vocabulary, by dint of its long history of analysis and reconstruction, permits little vagueness and has been taken over into the language of all sciences.

The third and last class of words in the language of science is the class of constructs—universal terms which characterize properties and relations. It is toward this class of words that the main effort to eliminate vague and diverse usage is aimed. The object of reconstructive activity in scientific language is the establishment of precise usage of terms which previously have been vague. It is probably the case that vagueness of usage cannot be entirely eliminated; the goal, more properly, is one of reducing vagueness.

It has already been shown that the vague usage and the indeterminacy of verbal habits in the vernacular are not necessarily ascribable to a lack of relevant knowledge. The scientific language is particularly concerned with making these language habits precise in order to assure uniformity of usage from speaker to speaker. In the use of "fat," constancy of usage is only a problem because the weight continuum might be cut differently by different users. Since the differentiation of body weight might be empirically important, the term "fat" could be replaced by a continuum of body weights in pounds. This new specification, while including all cases which fall under the old term, has the advantage of little variation in usage. However, in the course of increasing precision new terms are introduced. It is not particularly useful, indeed it is often hampering, to maintain that the old concept "fat" is still included as the class of weights of 250 pounds and more. The increase in precision has precisely the advantage of excluding the previously vague notion. If there is still reason to refer to the class of people whose body weight is above a certain figure, they can be characterized as such.

The continued use of the old term also carries with it the excess baggage of the associations and expectations which that word has acquired historically; the vagueness would still be an implicit characteristic of the redefined concept. It is the very purpose of these refinements to reduce associations and overtones of meaning which have accrued to a term in the course of its linguistic and pragmatic history. There is no doubt that this process deprives terms of much of their richness and vividness. But it is precisely this richness which prevents a communality of usage. The language of science differs in a large degree from the language of art and poetry in that it must have terms which carry no overtones; it will perforce be unfaithful to any vivid natural experience of reality.[4]

To this point the discussion has been concerned with terms which are primarily used in response to objects or relations occurring in the environment. We must not neglect, however, another important part of the scientific vocabulary—higher-order theoretical terms. While the former terms must be free from vagueness in their application to objects or directly observable events, the latter do not always make such reference. These higher-order concepts, such as "force," "habit," or "libido," function primarily *within* the language of science. Vagueness in this class of terms is usually a function of vagueness in the theoretical structure itself, and rules of usage for these words will eliminate their vagueness. Such rules insure that terms will be precise because they prevent imprecision in their application in purely verbal contexts. These two types of precise usage are not different in kind; for the time being it will suffice to say that precision is a goal both for lower-order and higher-order terms. In both cases precision is achieved by a rigorous explication of the rules of usage, whether in response to nonverbal events or within language units.

Artificial Languages for Science

The notion that a successful science must be based on a well-made language (Condillac, 1780) has led to repeated attempts in modern analytic philosophy to create an entirely new language. Although it represents an important aspect of scientific activity, such a dictum is not easily followed. However, the attempts to build a scientific language *de novo* deserve close inspection. The argument is straightforward and extremely appealing in its simplicity:

1. The common language has certain disabilities which are difficult to repair.
2. A language is essential for science.
3. Therefore, it might be best to construct a scientific language which will not have the defects of the vernacular.

---

[4] There are stages in the *development* of a science and of scientific hypotheses when these overtones are useful. The present statement represents a goal for scientific language.

Such an enterprise would involve agreement on an unequivocal, basic vocabulary, a system of logical connectives, and a grammar which permits the construction of theoretically and empirically meaningful sentences. Although this may sound like an impressive order, it would be an effort of incalculable value if it succeeded in circumventing the problems raised on the preceding pages. For the present, only the initial problem, the restriction to a basic vocabulary, will be examined in detail. It will become evident that even this limited goal is not attainable. Nevertheless, the attempt is worthwhile and its failure will have one important consequence; it will bring the difficulties in constructing any scientific vocabulary into sharper focus.

A vocabulary of a new language must bear some relation to common observation. The artificial language must perforce start with terms which can be used in sentences describing the world of events, and therefore the initial terms or words will have to be adopted from the common language. The basic vocabulary must furthermore contain all the terms that are necessary to build up the rest of the scientific language. All other terms can then be constructed from this vocabulary. Ambiguity and vagueness are eliminated by introducing only those relatively simple terms from the vernacular which admit little vagueness, and by reconstructing more complex terms by reference to these fundamental terms and these terms only. Such a procedure requires that all scientific terms must "have a bearing upon, and thus [be] conceptually connected with, statements reporting in . . . everyday language what has been established by immediate observation" (Hempel, 1952, p. 21).

In order to develop an artificial language, therefore, there must be found a set of vernacular terms which have two characteristics: First, they must refer to events or objects that permit "immediate observation"; and second, they must be free from vagueness and ambiguity.

Whenever scientific terms are directly connected with such basic units taken from the common language, e.g., by definition, they will be admissible to the new vocabulary. The class of basic terms is an inescapable requirement; language cannot be developed in a vacuum. The reconstructive activity in developing a language of science requires some class of immediately observable properties and relations, i.e., undefined concepts (Bergmann, 1951).

The single most influential suggestion in the search for an acceptable basic vocabulary comes from Carnap, who introduced the notion of the *physical thing-language.*[5] This language, and its vocabulary, is taken over from the prescientific common language and is used in "speaking about the properties of the observable (inorganic) things surrounding us" (Carnap, 1938, p. 52). It contains such terms as "hot," "heavy," "red," and "large," but not such terms as "temperature" and "weight" which require the application of apparatus and other scientific procedures to determine their use. Carnap notes that these basic terms can be determined by direct observation. This characteristic of the thing-language, its availability to "direct observation," appears to be the primary and possibly only criterion for the class of basic terms.

Other terms of the thing-language are so-called disposition terms and designations of substances. Disposition terms refer to the tendency of things to exhibit certain characteristics under certain specified conditions. Such terms as "elastic," "soluble," and "transparent" can be introduced by specifying the conditions under which they occur. The conditions and the expected reactions can be described in terms of the thing-predicates indicated above. Substances are introduced by definition in terms of the thing-predicates and the disposition terms.

Carnap's thesis was that all terms of the language of physics can be reduced by chains of definitions to the thing-language.[6] This statement for physics can be expanded to other sciences. Thus, while biologists, for example, may use some specialized biological terms in their language, these terms must still fulfill the requirement of reduction to the thing-language "because the determination of the term in question in a concrete case must finally be based upon observation of concrete things, i.e., upon observation statements formulated in the thing-language" (Carnap, 1938, p. 54).

Some of the difficulties encountered by positing the vocabulary of a thing-language as the primitive vocabulary of science will be discussed in the next chapter in relation to the vocabulary of psychology. However, let us assume for the moment that such a language is available and well enough defined to provide the basic vocabulary for the reconstructed language of science.

What about the requirement that all scientific concepts must be

---

[5] The position ascribed to Carnap has since been generally repudiated by him. Few philosophers of science today subscribe to this particular approach to an artificial language. However, it provides the best didactic example in this area.

[6] This "reduction" of all terms to the thing-language is the first of four uses of "reduction" to be discussed (see Chapters 6, 9, and 14).

reducible to observation terms, or specifically to predicates of the thing-language? This requirement has been called the *narrower thesis of empiricism* (Hempel, 1952). In its simplest form it states that scientific terms can be analyzed or reconstructed so that all terms other than observation terms can be defined by means of the latter. Bergmann (1951) has specifically stated that the only meaningful terms in science are either those definable in terms of the basic vocabulary, or else the final terms in a chain of definitions containing only undefined words or words previously defined in basic terms.

Such a requirement seems eminently reasonable. All the vagueness residing in the concepts of science could be avoided, since all terms would be reduced to the precise and unambiguous terms of the observation language—the thing-predicates. Unfortunately this requirement fails on several counts. Some of these shortcomings will be mentioned here; the problem of reduction sentences will be discussed later at length.[7]

The advantage of reduction of scientific terms resides in the resultant statements which can be couched exclusively in observation terms and the vocabulary of logic. No other terms would be needed for the basic vocabulary. However, when the form of these basic sentences is examined it is apparent that such a reduction is not possible. Let us assume that the spatial and temporal location of an event can be fixed by the use of three geographic dimensions (*x*, *y*, and *z*) and one time dimension (*t*). Then the basic thing-language sentence using only thing-predicates (or basic terms) would read:

> "Thing-predicate p is at *x*, *y*, *z*, *t*. For example: Blue is at 20° N, 50° E, at sea level, 5:30 P.M., June 27, 1956."

However, the reduction to thing-predicates and logical terms is still not reached. The expression "is at" is apparently not eliminable in terms of either of these two classes of terms. And there may be other such expressions which defy full reduction. While this objection might appear trivial for practical purposes, it must be remembered that this sentence represents the basic type to which all other sentences and terms must be reduced. Thus its failure to eliminate all terms other than thing-predicates is crucial (Quine, 1951b).

In addition, there is a whole set of theoretical terms which defy

---

[7] For a fuller discussion of some of the problems inherent in this reductionist position, the reader is referred to Quine's *Two Dogmas of Empiricism* (1951b) and to Hempel's *Fundamentals of Concept Formation in Empirical Science* (1952).

complete reduction, namely the metric terms. Statements which use metric terms are usually of the form "The weight of the physical object x is n pounds." Now, the value which n can assume is any real (non-negative) number. Theoretically it follows that there are an infinite number of possible cases. Each such case would be represented by one real number. The reductionist thesis requires, therefore, that for each of this infinite number of cases there should be a possible statement in terms of observables. This is patently impossible. The limits of the discriminatory power of the human organism are empirically such that in direct observation there can be made only a finite number of observations. It is obvious that the discriminatory power of any observer will break down at some definite point where he will no longer be able to distinguish between smaller and smaller subdivisions of the weight scale. Such a finite array of discriminations can only result in a finite set of observation terms which will be inadequate to handle the infinite range of values theoretically posited. This difficulty is in no sense trivial. If the reductionist position limits science to discrete sets of metric values, then it deprives the scientist of the use of the powerful tools of mathematics. The concept of limit as well as the use of differential and integral equations could not be introduced if such a limitation were maintained.

A final point may be made against the reductionist position. The growth of scientific languages does not proceed from simple to more complex terms; observation terms do not flower into theoretical constructs. Rather, whole systems or theories are set up which often involve the use of vague or vernacular terms. Such terms as "mass," "force," "pressure," or "drive" are not introduced in a piecemeal fashion, but are entered into the body of the theory without obvious reference to observation terms. The explicit observational import of these terms can be only slowly developed. Connections among theoretical terms are built up, and some of these constructs are finally connected with terms which are given observational interpretation. This process will be described in Chapter 12. For present purposes it should be stressed, however, that these theoretical constructs often carry their scientific import not by direct connections with observation terms, but by their role within the theory. Their precision of usage lies in the clarity of their connection with other theoretical terms. All constructs in a theory must be seen as having a multiplicity of relationships to observation terms and to the other terms and sentences of the theory. No construct can be viewed solely in a context of relationships to observables. Such a consideration holds even for the basic terms of a theory. While the physical thing-language has been primarily considered here, other basic vocabularies can be used for the construction of observation terms. The higher-order constructs of one science or theory may become the basic terms of another. In that case even the "observables" may not be assigned an "existence" independent of theoretical or systematic relationships to other terms.[8]

The rejection of a strict reductionist position does not imply the abandonment of a set of basic terms. The adequacy of the thing-predicates has yet to be investigated. The language of science must continually press for the elimination of vague concepts, and such a vocabulary could provide a good starting point. The problems to be raised in the next chapter concern the vocabularies and classes of terms that have been specifically used or advocated for a language of psychology. Once these suggestions have been examined desirable criteria for such a language and some general rules for a scientific vocabulary may be postulated.

SUMMARY

The investigation of the language of science proceeds within the framework of the common language of everyday use. Among the characteristics of the common language are its insistence on being about "real" events independent of language, its ability to summarize different events under one label, and its somewhat surprising constancy from user to user. These aspects may be related to the process of language acquisition—the way in which verbal behavior is learned. This process also produces some undesirable characteristics. The user of the common language tends to reify its words; he uses them as if words and things were interchangeable. Furthermore, vagueness and ambiguity arise out of the sometimes variable conditions of verbal learning. One of the first tasks imposed on the builder of a scientific language is to find ways of avoiding these debilitating characteristics. Apart from piecemeal attacks on such problems, a solution has been examined which would build artificial languages for science. How-

[8] We can anticipate a further objection to a simple reductionist position. Disposition terms were to be introduced by stating the conditions for their application solely in terms of thing-predicates. They would thus be reduced to the basic vocabulary. It will be seen in Chapter 6 that reduction sentences which introduce dispositional constructs require empirical and theoretical statements for their use as well as purely reductive observation statements.

ever, it does not appear to be possible to reduce the scientific vocabulary by means of explicit definitions to a single class of words, such as thing-predicates. But even without a complete reduction to one particular vocabulary, we still need a basic vocabulary of words with which the psychologist can talk about the objects and events of his universe.

chapter two

The search for a psychological vocabulary

PSYCHOLOGY, WHETHER THE STUDY OF THE soul, of minds, or of behavior, has played a somewhat deviant role in its scientific childhood and adolescence. While one by one the other sciences successfully broke away from the mother discipline of philosophy, psychology and the empirical study of man tarried until the nineteenth and twentieth centuries. The reasons for this late weaning appear to be threefold. A general notion has prevailed that the pyramid of sciences extends from mathematics at the apex through physics and chemistry to physiology and finally to psychology and other behavioral sciences at the base. Further, philosophy in general has had a particular preoccupation with the behavior and thought of man. And finally, there are specific problems posed by the relation between the subject matter of psychology and the psychologist as a human organism.

The pyramid of science may for the present purposes be accepted as a fact of life. However, psychologists have often bemoaned their lowly status as newcomers, and welcomed any position which made them seem less immature. The unity-of-science movement which proclaimed the equality of all sciences found its most vocal advocates among psychologists or psychologically oriented philosophers. Alternatively psychologists have tried to turn the pyramid upside down by asserting the primacy of psychology in all scientific activity. No claim will be made here that psychology is the propaedeutic science, the *sine qua non* of scientific activity (see also Chapter 9). If thousands of years of scientific and prescientific thinking and behaving have established a hierarchy of sciences, this archaic notion may well be accepted without further shedding of tears for lost youth. The genealogy of this hierarchy is properly studied by historians, philosophers, sociologists, and anthropologists of science, and only marginally by psychologists.

The second reason for the relatively late appearance of a psychology independent of philosophy deserves closer attention. The investigation of man has always been the preoccupation of philosophers. Some of them may have focused attention on astronomy or botany, but philosophers, whether during the Golden Age of Greece or the days of the Vienna Circle, were primarily concerned with the mind, the behavior, or the language of man. Thus, the loss of physics or of astronomy as they split away from a general body of knowledge was not crippling to the development and continuing existence of philosophy as a discipline. However, in the nineteenth century all the children had grown up and only the study of man remained without a separate scientific home. It was not until then that psychology, sociology, and anthropology made their first independent steps. This development does not make philosophy in the twentieth century an empty shell; rather it is once again becoming an encyclopedic discipline. It combines the studies of man's appreciation of the world around him and of the logic and presuppositions of his language and science.

The persistent concern with the activity of man has made much of philosophy a part of psychology's past. Even in its scientific beginnings, psychology was said to have a long past and a short history (Ebbinghaus, 1908). What distinguishes the persistent and ancient concern with man from the history of scientific psychology? Both Aristotle and Freud wrote "On Dreams," both Descartes and Lashley were concerned with the relation between physiology and behavior; yet, Freud and Lashley belong to modern scientific psychology, while Aristotle and Descartes are prescientific philosophers of man. The continuity of philosophical and empirical psychology is not to be questioned any more than the continuity from Democritus to modern atomic theory. The beginning of modern physics, however, is usually dated from the seventeenth century with the advent of Galileo and Newton. What gave rise to modern psychology in the nineteenth century, and how did this development differ from its past?

One of the answers to this question is embedded in the third reason for a late emergence of scientific psychology—the relation between the subject matter and the investigator. The study of man, whether in mental or behavioral terms, is carried out by man. This assertion, trivial as it may seem, sets psychology apart from the other sciences. Atoms do not study atoms, stars do not investigate planets, paramecia presumably do not have a general theory of the behavior of paramecia; but man studies, investigates, and theorizes about man. He does not engage in this sort of activity through any special effort; it comes all too naturally. He talks about his fellow men and women, describes their behavior to others when he gossips, predicts the thoughts and behaviors of his boss, his teacher, his spouse, and his children. In addition to all this psychologizing, he watches himself; his own thoughts and actions are his first laboratory. He may ignore atoms, stars, or paramecia, but he is never able to ignore either himself or other human beings. In this sense every person is his own psychologist, as any psychologist who has ever been cornered in a bar or railroad diner can attest. The common language is full of quasi-psychological assertions, and the inadequacy of the language in which these are framed has already been discussed. But the fact that man studies himself and that he has archaic notions which persist in the daily behavior of all men puts a major stumbling block in the path of a scientific psychology. Somehow two states of affairs must be separated; the subject matter of psychology and the behavior of its students. The appearance of scientific psychology seems based on a recognition, in fact if not in words, of this distinction.

SOME HISTORICAL GUIDEPOSTS

In 1874 a German philosopher began the preface to a book on "Principles of Physiological Psychology" with the following words:

> The work which I here present to the public is an attempt to mark out a new domain of science. (Wundt, 1874, p. iii.)

This curtain raiser to the "new" psychology, against the background of Helmholtz's and Fechner's experimental work in vision and psychophysics, has remained a major milestone of modern scientific psychology. In what way did Wundt see the new psychology as different from the old? His own words best convey the spirit of this revolution.

> As an experimental science, physiological psychology seeks to accomplish a reform in psychological investigation comparable with the revolution brought about in the natural sciences by the introduction of the experimental method. . . . It is only with grave reservations that what is called "pure self-observation" can properly be termed observation at all, and under no circumstances can it lay claim to accuracy. On the other hand, it is of the essence of experiment that we can vary the conditions of an occurrence at will and, if we are aiming at exact results, in a quantitatively determinable way. . . .
>
> For all accurate observation implies that the object of observation (in this case the psychical process) can be held fast by the attention, and any change that it undergoes attentively followed. And this fixation by the attention implies, in its turn, that *the observed object is independent of the observer.* (Wundt, 1904, pp. 4–5; translated by E. B. Titchener. Our italics.)

It appears that one of Wundt's major concerns, in addition to the use of experimental methods and controls, was the achievement of independence of the observed and the observer. The processes observed may well be part of the observing organism, but the new psychologists attempted to spell out this distinction in detail. By controlling the conditions under which the psychical processes occurred they hoped to be better able to observe and describe them.

The control and observation of psychical processes continued to be the major concern of psychology for forty years. Whether in a structuralist or functionalist framework, mind rather than action or movement was the subject matter of psychology. And whether the mind was described as a collection of processes which were to be analyzed into the smallest constituent units or as an important biological function of the organism, the vocabulary of psychology was restricted to words which seemed best suited to describe these mental processes or functions.

The introspective method did not, of course, originate with Wundt and his contemporaries. They only introduced controlled conditions to a method which was already well established in the days of early British empiricism. But in both cases the vocabulary depended on language units freely available to the subject, who was often the same person as the observer. However, the distinction between man the object and man the observer remained confused because the report of introspective experiences and the words in which it was couched became the language of psychology. Since these reports depended primarily on the subject's vocabulary, the common language and the scientific language became almost identical. All the difficulties of the common language were inextricably included in psychology. The vagueness of the introspective report was largely due to the vagueness of the language that was used to communicate it, and even the most ardent defender of the introspectionist method decried the inadequacy of everyday language.

One attempt to evade this problem involved the introduction of a basic unit of analysis—the sensation. It "resists analysis, just as do the chemical elements oxygen and hydrogen" (Titchener, 1896). Sensations were such things as "cold," "blue," "salty," which "cannot be divided up into any simpler modes of experience" (Titchener, 1896). This new vocabulary and the difficulties in its usage paved the way for the next upheaval in psychology. By analyzing experiences into constituent sensations, two major weaknesses appeared. First, the resulting analysis was rejected as esoteric and untrue to "real" experience, and second, it did not stand up to intersubjective criteria. Two different observers might analyze the same external stimulus into widely different constituent sensations. These observers were highly skilled and their training consisted primarily in practicing the vocabulary of sensations, the basic phenomenological vocabulary. But it was just this vocabulary, and particularly the attempt to force the analysis of complex experiences into the same constituent elements, which made progress impossible. Such an analysis failed to be invariant from one individual to the next; the content of the experience varied from subject to subject. The analysis of "feelings" in particular provided a stumbling block for this mental chemistry—the language and history of the observer were inherent parts of the processes observed.

Apart from phenomenology, the only contemporary remnant of the method and language of late-nineteenth-century psychology is its first concern—the lusty field of psychophysics. Sensory experiences expressed in simple, and if possible unitary, dimensions can be usefully related to the dimensions of physical events. Yet even this latter-day sensationalism appears to be possible only after extended training of the observer in the particular language dimension to be used, such as loudness or brightness.

The revolution of the early twentieth century, the "newer" psychology, traveled two widely divergent paths. Gestalt psychology took as its point of departure the "unrealistic" aspects of sensationist introspections. Behaviorism, on the other hand, grew out of dissatisfaction with the unreliability of the findings of the introspective method.

Wertheimer articulated the dissatisfactions of the Gestalt group in these words:

> One turned from a living experience to science and asked what it had to say about this experience, and one found an assortment of elements, sensations, images, feelings, acts of will and laws governing these elements—and was told, "Take your choice, reconstruct from them the experience you had." Such procedure led to difficulties in concrete psychological research and to the emergence of problems which defied solution by the traditional analytic methods. Historically the most important impulse came from von Ehrenfels who raised the following problem. Psychology had said that experience is a compound of elements: we hear a melody and then, upon hearing it again, memory enables us to recognize it. But what is it that enables us to recognize the melody when it is played in a new key? The sum of the elements is different, yet the melody is the same; indeed, one is often not even aware that a transposition has been made. (Wertheimer, 1938, p. 4.)

Gestalt theory not only denied the empirical utility of an analysis into sensations, but it also emphasized that experience as communicated by the observer defied such analysis since it contained objects with thing-character, wholes, and transposable structures. The Gestalt group restored the more readily available terms and sentences of the common language to the subject; they adopted what Brunswik has called "the thing-language of daily life." Important to our present interest in the distinction between the observer and the observed is the treatment of observer reports as data, as initial steps in a psychological investigation of experience. The reports of observers were analyzed in terms of the principles of Gestalt theory. These principles were stated in a language quite distinct from the common language, and observer reports were seen as evidence for Gestalten, closure, and so forth. The report of the subject was used as the basic datum in talking about an *inferred* experience; these reports were not thought to *be* psychological variables.

The structuralists' evidence for taking the sensation as the basic unit of experience consisted of putting these sensations into the subject by training him to make discriminations in these and no other units, whereas the Gestalt theorists accepted whatever vocabulary was readily available to the subject as their initial data.

The behaviorist attack was much broader, and in its breadth it proceeded to throw out the baby with the bath water. All introspective report was to be eliminated as not relevant to psychological science. In the summary to his first published paper on behaviorism, Watson wrote:

> Psychology, as the behaviorist views it, is a purely objective, experimental branch of natural science which needs introspection as little as do the sciences of chemistry and physics. It is granted that the behavior of animals can be investigated without appeal to consciousness. Heretofore the viewpoint has been that such data have value only insofar as they can be interpreted by analogy in terms of consciousness. The position is taken here that the behavior of man and the behavior of animals must be considered on the same plane; as being equally essential to a general understanding of behavior. (Watson, 1913, p. 176.)

Previously in the same paper he had said:

> There is no longer any guarantee that we all mean the same thing when we use the terms now current in psychology (p. 163).

The vagueness of the introspective vocabulary was to be remedied by abandoning it altogether. For the description of man the same vocabulary was to be used as had been used for the description of animal behavior. It was certainly the most drastic suggestion possible for the separation of the language of the subject (which was to be abandoned) and the language of the scientist. At about the same time the general availability of results from Pavlov's laboratory encouraged such a step. The language of conditioned reflexes also was descriptive of animal behavior and independent of the language used by a human subject.

During the succeeding forty years the behaviorist dicta concerning the uselessness of introspection were slowly abandoned, but the return of introspective report did not bring with it the implication that its vocabulary describes psychological variables. Rather, the introspective report of the human subject was part of the data of psychology, about which generalizations were to be developed. More recent methods, such as content analysis, in both academic psychology and in the psychoanalytic movement, have regarded introspection and the data of consciousness as something to be observed and to be described in another language, the system language of psychology.

Psychology appears to have come of age during the past eighty years. Psychologists argue a great deal about theories and findings, but little about the subject matter of the field. In eighty years that problem seems to have been settled. In part, this resolution has been achieved by a developing distinction between the psychologist's scientific behavior on the one hand and human behavior, including that of the psychologist, as his subject matter on the other.

THE PSYCHOLOGIST AND HIS SUBJECT MATTER

Science may be viewed as an organized system of statements about objects and events. Just as other scientists look at and listen to slides, stars, and whooping cranes, the psychologist looks at and listens to the behavior of organisms. As a scientist he makes statements about the events which he has observed. In this respect he does not differ from the bacteriologist, astronomer, or ornithologist. The psychologist, however, soon faces a confusion not normally shared by his scientific colleagues, a confusion derived from the fact that he also happens to belong to the universe of objects which he is observing. But once recognized the confusion need not be maintained. Psychologists can continue to talk *about* people without being paralyzed by the recognition of kinship with the objects of their enquiry any more than by the recognition that rats too are mammals, or that their own brain cavities contain nerve cells. In this regard the language of psychology is no different from the language of astronomy; one is largely about the behavior of organisms, the other about the behavior of stars and galaxies.

Whether about stars or men, all scientists use a set of basic sentences, the *protocol statements.* These sentences have variously been called "observation sentences" or "statements of raw data or observables." Protocol statements are phrased in the protocol language of the psychologist and are the basic sentences about the events which concern him. We will have occasion repeatedly to return to the role of these sentences in psychological science, but for the present our concern is with the function of such protocol statements in their relation to the distinction between the psychologist and his subject matter.

The distinction between man as a scientist and man as an object of science creates relatively few problems when the psychologist deals with nonverbal behavior. The basic requirement of the scientific enterprise is a system of unambiguous verbal statements, and the nonverbal behavior of organisms can be described and communicated in sets of such statements. For example, the observation of a subject's response to a tone of 12,000 cycles per second may be phrased in protocol statements such as:

"Rat A ran around the cage in circles."
"Infant B turned his head 45° to his right."

However, psychology also deals with the *verbal* behavior of man and thus assertions *in* language have to be made *about* language. It is at this point that the subject-scientist distinction needs affirmation. Consider the sentences:

"Subject A said 'I have a pain in my back.' "
"I have a pain in my back."

The latter is not a protocol statement in psychology. Nor does it lead to the protocol statement "The subject has a pain in his back," unless the defining statement for back pains is:

"x says 'I have a pain in my back.' "

This statement might be acceptable, but it leads to other sentences such as "x is Napoleon" defined as "x says he is Napoleon," or "x is happy" defined as "x says that he is happy."

Neither the delusion implied in the first statement nor the private experience asserted in the second will be readily accepted as statements of fact by an observing psychologist. In other words, an assertion by a human subject about himself is not readily transformed into a parallel assertion in the psychological system language. To assert "x is Napoleon" or "x is happy" will require other evidence in addition to the verbal statement. This other evidence may include information about Napoleon's death on St. Helena which would contradict the subject's assertion.

One further example, borrowed from Bergmann (1951), will illustrate that the language of the subject and the language of the psychologist must be kept strictly separate. In an investigation of the discrimination of two shades of green the scientist is concerned with protocol statements of the order "Subject sees two different shades of green." "Sees" in this case is part of the system language of psychology and differs from the verb as used in the phrase "I see."

Broadly, the definition of the *technical* term "sees" might be introduced into the system language in the following way:

> "S *sees* two different shades of green" is defined as "When the subject is presented with these two areas he says 'I see two shades of green.' "

Or one might define "see" as any evidence of discrimination between the two areas, even when the subject reports: "In this area I sense a blue-green sensation, while in this other my experience is more yellow." Stated generally, *"the behavior scientist and his subjects do not, in principle, speak the same language"* (Bergmann, 1950, p. 485).[1] This is not a trivial assertion, particularly in the light of modern personality theory. Any therapist knows that the patient's statement "I am not angry" is not only not equivalent with the statement "The patient is not angry" but may in fact be used as a datum for the conclusion that the patient *is* angry. Therapist and patient are using the word "angry" differently, the former presumably in a usage like that of other psychologists—within the system language.

There is a clear distinction to be made between the analysis of verbal behavior in general and the analysis of statements in the system language. The investigation of verbal behavior might be concerned with the antecedent conditions which give rise to such behavior, or with the linguistic analysis of the constituent phonemes and morphemes, or with characteristics of the subject which are correlated with his verbal behavior. A statement in the system language on the other hand must be analyzed in terms of its precision and reliability in communicating from scientist to scientist. Its structure and semantics are the concern of the investigation of the language of science.

As a behavioral datum the subject's report "I have a pain in my back" presents a variety of problems in psychology. However, the protocol statement about a subject exhibiting that verbal behavior happens to be fairly precise and reliable and little confusion is likely to result in communicating the subject's behavior from scientist to scientist. All one psychologist tells the other is that the subject said something; the protocol statement as such is not concerned with the

---

[1] It must be stressed, incidentally, that the difference between the two languages does not necessitate a physical distinction between the subject and the scientist. Thus, if the scientist were to look at the laboratory situation just described and to say "I see two shades of green," such a statement could serve as the basis for a protocol statement.

antecedent conditions for exhibiting such behavior any more than a protocol statement about a rat running a maze is concerned with the antecedent conditions for making a particular turn. Both the turn and the report of a pain may be unreliable behavioral indices, but that unreliability is investigated by the psychologist using precise terms *about* such behavior. What is important for our subsequent discussion is that the behavior of the subject, verbal or not, is an event in the external world of the scientist, just as is the behavior of a rat, the construction of a maze, or the composition of a list of nonsense syllables. The investigation of the protocol language of the psychologist deals with his acquisition and use of a *precise* vocabulary which names such events, including the intricate verbal behavior of his human subjects.

The distinction between the language of the subject and that of the scientist does not deny that psychologists, as human beings, acquire their language in the same manner as their human subjects do. On the contrary, the language of the scientist must be examined as human behavior if we want to state the conditions for the development of a precise vocabulary. If there are variations of usage from word to word and from occasion to occasion, it might well be that different terms are learned under different conditions, and that only some conditions lead to a vocabulary which has the high consistency and precision of usage necessary for scientific discourse. As in any scientific enquiry such an examination must be based on current knowledge, in this case about the acquisition of language. In this manner the study of the language of science makes use of all available knowledge in order to approach its empirical problems. Such knowledge is, of course, timebound and subject to change and refinement. It is no more timebound, however, than any other statement about the activities of the scientist, or about a cloud, a rock, or a neuron. As contemporary psychologists we can investigate the language of the psychologist in his psychological warren, and make statements about such behavior.

THE REJECTION OF PHENOMENOLOGY

The subject-scientist distinction, particularly in respect to verbal behavior, is germane to an examination of one of the major positions regarding the basic language of scientific psychology—the advocacy of phenomenology.

In contrast to the physicalistic reduction examined earlier, which required a basic vocabulary based on the physical thing-language, phenomenology proposes a reduction to immediate experience. It asserts the necessity of an elementary analysis of appearances and perceptions, "a descriptive phenomenology of inner experience, which is the basis of empirical psychology" (Husserl, 1913). Phenomenology is an introspectionism *ne plus ultra* which aims at the pure description of phenomenal experience. Unashamedly subjective, phenomenologists assert that raw experience, prior to any translation, is necessarily the basis of all science, and particularly of psychology. The final testing ground of all knowledge lies in the immediate experience of the scientist-observer.[2]

Even the phenomenal experience, however, must be communicated through language. What constitutes the vocabulary of such a language? Presumably it tells of perceptions or appearances free of the restrictions of an externally imposed language.

The phrases of a phenomenological language may include such expressions as "blue feeling," "sensation of hardness," "perception of green," and so forth. These terms are not used as applying to a particular object, but rather represent qualities or attributes as somehow present without objective reference. Phenomenological terms refer to experiences which are private, and which the subject reports as having occurred in his visual, auditory, or kinesthetic field.

This language must and does vary from subject to subject; it cannot, therefore, be subjected to public tests. In other words, the particular terms a subject uses in this language are not to be questioned; his idiosyncratic vocabulary must be accepted at face value as directly descriptive of raw experience. The phenomenologists accept this point of view, and as a matter of fact use it as a major argument for one of the basic postulates of phenomenology, i.e., the phenomenal field does indeed vary from individual to individual. But any language hinders the complete communication of the phenomenal experience. Words and sentences, socially acquired, are found to be inadequate for a satisfactory expression of the true experience.

The inability to find a suitable *utterance* provokes word frenzy.
Language unfailingly reveals its derivation from, and indissoluble

---

[2] The phenomenology of Gestalt psychology uses phenomenal report to *reconstruct* the experience of its subjects; it attempts to talk *about* experience. For the strict phenomenologist, experience must be made available because it is the *true* structure of reality for both subject and scientist.

> attachment to, the observed world. When transcendency attempts to reject this world it must reject language or else do violence to it. The various devices are familiar. Words are undefined, continuously redefined, or definition as well as logic are rejected; words may be italicized or spelled with capital letters; new words are coined abundantly; metaphors are substituted for more precise statement; familiar words are used for their affective connotation but their meaning denied; etc. In the effort to attain sublimity, the linguistic turmoil continually turns on itself until the outline of all that is *non-linguistic,* the only thing that can give meaning to language, is blotted beyond effective recognition. (Bucklew, 1955, p. 295.)

Notwithstanding these difficulties, the phenomenologist argues that the private experience of different subjects, even in identical physical situations, varies greatly. Implicit in the phenomenologist's plea is the mirror image of the reification of words, which was discussed in relation to natural languages. Where the vernacular implies that for every word (or noun) there is a thing, the phenomenologist seems to argue that for every private experience there is, or should be, a word. But the responses of a person are frequently not derived from verbal learning experiences—they are not analogous to words. Often they consist of complex groups of autonomic, skeletal, and vague imaginal responses. To expect a subject to have words available which are invariantly related to these responses flies in the face of current psychological knowledge. It was this insistence on a one-to-one correspondence between language and other responses or experiences which probably undid the introspectionists. If the assumption of a one-to-one relationship between private experience and vocabulary is untenable, then a phenomenological vocabulary is not only difficult but empirically impossible.[3]

The rejection of a phenomenological language for the basic vocabulary of a scientific psychology does not argue against the *use* of a sub-

---

[3] Apart from the difficulty of communicating private experience or private language from scientist to scientist, phenomenal experience does play an important part in the development of a field of knowledge. However, this role is in the field of theory and hypothesis formation. Prediction in a phenomenological psychology based on such questions as "Now why did he do that?" and "Under what circumstances would I have done that?" (Snygg, 1941) leads to the development of tentative hunches and generalizations. It will be seen that these hunches form an important part of the presystematic stage of theory construction in all of psychology.

ject's idiosyncratic report or of his private language. Modern personality theory, and in particular the psychoanalytic school, depend to a large extent on the examination of the relationships among a subject's reports of private events. Reports of experiences or perceptions, without direct reference to physical stimuli, are legitimate subject matter for science. When the clinician relates free associations to a prediction about the perception of some future environmental situation, he is making statements *about* a subject's behavior, or even about inferred private responses. Idiosyncratic reports of fears, goals, and the attributes of the environment can be classified and used for predictive purposes. But the predictions and generalizations must be presented in terms which seek intersubjective (interscientist) reliability and communicability.

PSYCHOLOGY AND THE THING-LANGUAGE

With the rejection of the phenomenological language as one alternative for a psychological vocabulary, the possibility of using another, the thing-language, may now be examined. We have already seen that a *complete* reduction of the language of science to the terms of a thing-language is not feasible. What remains to be discussed is whether or not the physicalistic solution meets the requirement of providing a vocabulary for the *protocol language* of psychology.

The basic terms of the thing-language are the thing-predicates, such as "cold," "red," and "hard"; they are "terms signifying certain directly observable characteristics of physical objects" (Hempel, 1952, p. 22). The term "thing-language" is used here in the narrow sense in which it was presented in Chapter 1. Carnap (1938) suggested that this language is used in speaking about the properties of observable things. He specifically defined it as "the common part of . . . prescientific language and the physical language."

This kind of language not only was advocated by the behavioristic schools of the 1920's, but has also recently found its way into Gestalt-psychological points of view. The language of the Gestalt school depends to a large extent on the "thing-language of daily life." Such a thing-language is adapted from the vernacular to take "its rightful place in the inventory of immediately given experience" (Brunswik, 1952, p. 6). It is also a language for speaking about the things surrounding us; it contains in addition to physical thing-predicates such as "hot" or "red," such terms as "table" or "man," i.e., names of common objects. Brunswik insists that such a language is to be used only for the responses of the subject, and not to describe the stimulus situations that are under experimental control. Such a distinction between vocabularies must, however, be rejected. Any bifurcation of subject and environment for the purposes of psychological science weakens the subject-scientist distinction. In the development of a psychological vocabulary, the subject must be considered as environment; he is one of the environmental objects about which the psychologist makes scientific statements. Brunswik's thing-language of daily life is a proposal for a vocabulary to be used *by* his subjects; that vocabulary in turn can then be discussed and analyzed by the psychologist in protocol statements.

Brunswik's proposal to have his subjects talk in the terms of a freely available thing-language as they respond to their environment suggests that this kind of language may be suited for environmental descriptions by the scientist. But any hope that such a thing-language might prove to be useful for a *precise* vocabulary about events "out there" Brunswik finds to be empty, as in the case in which a subject gives two or more different thing-language labels to the same environmental situation.

> A picture first seen as two profiles facing each other may suddenly shift in perception to give the radically different impression of a goblet formed by the same outlines. Both the terms "profile" and "goblet" designate "thing-predicates" in the naive-realistic language of perceptual units. Although the figure-ground reversals like the one described may play a minor role when it comes to the description of physical apparatus in the laboratory, they are nonetheless significant enough in principle to upset the unique constancy required in a truly physicalistic language (Brunswik, 1952, p. 7).

In this case, any attempt to use the physical thing-language becomes difficult. If the use of two terms in that language can vary so radically, how is the psychologist to describe the physical antecedents of behavior and predict the behavioral consequents? It is at this point that Brunswik argues for a strict distinction between stimuli and responses. While the latter, extended to "perceptual thing-impressions or their physiological counterparts—or the ensuing overt verbal or behavioral manifestations," are to be employed as they are displayed by the subject, the former cannot be left to such intersubjective vagaries. This argument states that what the psychologist manipulates are always stimuli, and that the description of these stimuli must become invariant and precise from scientist to scientist in order to insure maximal communicability. The subject's language may still vary and is to be further examined, but the scientist must be able to describe the conditions of its occurrence in invariant terms.

What Brunswik has shown is that the thing-language, of which terms like "goblet" and "profile" are a part, is inadequate for such a description of stimuli. Thus the Gestalt thing-language is rejected as the language of the psychologist. Names of objects do not always satisfy scientific requirements, and errors such as the one illustrated here may always interfere with an adequate description of experimental conditions.

It will be recalled that Carnap's physical thing-language depends on thing-predicates as basic units. However, terms such as "hot" or "red" are also subject to perceptual confusion, depending for their use on particular sets and states of the person using them. The predicate "hot" will be differentially applied depending on the immediately preceding temperature stimulation applied to the perceiving organism. Should such judgments depend on the scientist's ownership of fur gloves on a cold winter day? Similarly, light of a 700-millimicron wavelength may be called "red" but so may light of a wavelength of 650 millimicrons. Thus, even thing-predicates in the "physical" thing-language are subject to the same vagaries as Brunswik's profiles and goblets.

The description of light in terms of measurable wavelengths already indicates one solution to the dilemma. Abandoning the thing-language, Brunswik suggests that descriptions of stimuli might be restricted to the forms of measurements only. Physical measurements (such as wavelengths) represent a class of observations which show the highest degree of agreement among different observers (intersubjectively) and from one observation to another for the same observer (intrasubjectively). Coincidence of points in space-time (as in pointer readings) can be easily delimited from other experiences or introspections. These geographic elements presumably yield maximal reliability coefficients within or between individuals facing a common geographic situation.

Having accepted Brunswik's argument and rejected the thing-language as inadequate for the communication of *stimulus* events, a reminder is necessary that Brunswik's distinction between stimuli and responses violates the subject-scientist distinction. Therefore, his suggestion that the vocabulary for *response* events may be taken from the thing-language must also be rejected. It must be remembered that for the scientist Brunswik's stimuli and responses are both environmental (or stimulus) events. The subject's response, in the thing-language, may be quoted and we shall see shortly that such "quotation" provides useful protocol statements for psychological science. However, such protocol statements will not, in principle, read: "The subject alternately saw a profile and a goblet," but rather: "At time t_1 the subject said: 'Now I see a profile,' and at time t_2 he said: 'Now I see a goblet.' "

We can now summarize the criteria that have been advanced for various basic vocabularies. The major criteria for the physicalistic thing-language were its availability to direct observation and its supposed lack of vagueness. A similar claim was made for the language of point-space-time coincidences, when it was found that the thing-language did not live up to expectations. No new criteria were advanced; rather a new class of terms was proposed to take the place of one that was found deficient. It might now be profitable to look for general criteria for scientific terms, criteria which will admit *any* term that satisfies them. This approach will indicate that no class of terms need be wholly accepted or wholly rejected; some of the terms of the thing-languages have good reasons to remain as part of the basic vocabulary. The only general guide still available to us is the search for some "objective" language about the world of objects and events. Such objectivity will be found to reside in the intra- and inter-subjective consistency of verbal responses.

THE REQUIREMENT OF RESPONSE CONSISTENCY

The criterion of inter- and intra-subjective consistency states that the same objects or events will be described (or responded to) in the same way by different investigators and by the same investigator at different times. Obviously the same object can be described in different ways and different degrees of inter- and intra-subjective consistency may be obtained. Given a particular stimulus, such as a Rorschach card, a person may respond "bat" whenever it is presented to him. However, different people respond to the same stimulus with such phrases as "rabbit's leg," "man with a beard," "butterfly," as well as with the response "bat." Here then is a case with apparently high intrasubjective consistency but low intersubjective consistency. What is the most useful way to describe this particular stimulus situation?

The choice of the language to be used is related to the distinction between the psychologist's language and the subjects' responses. In scientific discourse when communication from one psychologist to another is desired, the response to be used must be consistent, both inter- and intra-subjectively. Thus the term "Card 5 of the Rorschach" will be used, not "the card which sometimes looks like a butterfly," or even "the bat card." The reference to the particular numbered card of the Rorschach set is given in terms which will show little, if any, variation from psychologist to psychologist, or from one instance to the next. The different responses obtained may then be a source of information about the subject, possibly about his particular mode of responding to his environment, his verbal reinforcement history, and so forth.

The same consistent language must be used in analyzing, describing, and classifying the behavior of the subject. The terms which the psychologist uses to describe behavior must fulfill the same conditions of inter- and intra-subjective consistency as those which describe the "physical" or environmental conditions. Some of these terms take the form of measurement, of highly reliable and consistent references to point-space-time coincidences. The numbers of a counter on a Skinner box which records an animal's bar-pressing behavior, an electronic timer which records an animal's traversal of a maze alley, a chronoscope which records a subject's reaction time to a visual stimulus, all fall into this category. Other measures used to describe an organism's behavior are less reliable and precise. Short of a complete recording via camera or recorder, these less precise terms will almost invariably enter into the description of behavior, just as terms like "precipitate," "suspension," or "viscous" enter into the description of some chemical "behavior." The psychologist might describe certain responses to the Rorschach as "animal response," others as "human movement," and so on. In all cases the requirement of maximal communicability must be achieved.

In other words, the only remaining requirement for the vocabulary of protocol statements is a high degree of intra- and inter-scientist consistency for all relevant events. These include both the conditions under which behavior is examined or elicited, and the behavioral events or characteristics of the organism which are observed.

The language of measurement is not restricted to stimulus events alone; it may also be used for response events. But behavior must often be described in terms other than temporal-geographic ones. Therefore a restriction to such terms is not acceptable.

The criterion for a basic vocabulary remains one of strict precision and reliability among scientists and from occasion to occasion. To the extent that science must develop a system of communication, any one investigator must be certain not only that other scientists will describe the same events in identical terms but also that they will respond to his terms with the same operations, methods, and manipulations. The criterion of consistency must be applicable to all terms, whether basic or not, whether descriptions of the environment or constructs used to order the behavior of organisms.

SUMMARY

The search for a psychological vocabulary is a search for a language that will permit precise protocol statements about the behavior and characteristics of organisms and about the conditions under which behavior takes place. Several historical factors have hindered the development of such a language, and chief among them is the confusion between man as the object of scientific enquiry and man as the scientific enquirer. We have said that men must talk *about* the behavior of human beings just as they talk *about* the behavior of metals, bridges, amebas, or anthills. The distinction between human subjects and human scientists is central to the historical development of psychological science, and it precludes a scientific vocabulary rooted in immediate phenomenal experience. At the other extreme, both a physicalistic and a common-sense thing-language fail to satisfy completely the requirement that all words in science must be used in the same fashion by all members of the scientific community. The only remaining criterion for a scientific vocabulary is that its words, from whatever source, must show a high consistency of usage from user to user and from occasion to occasion.

chapter three

A criterion for scientific terms

IN THE SEARCH FOR A BASIC VOCABULARY for psychology several classes of terms have been proposed and found wanting. The major criteria which have emerged are those of precision and reliability of usage. These criteria must be applied not only to the so-called observation terms of a science but also to its more complex, theoretical constructs. Even if a class of terms such as thing-predicates had been found to be adequate for a basic vocabulary, the precision of theoretical terms would still be in question since they cannot be completely reduced to the basic terms. Theoretical terms form an appreciable part of the scientific vocabulary, and criteria must be stated which apply to these as well as to more simple terms.

It will be argued here that such criteria must appeal to empirical evidence for their application. The earlier attempts at defining a basic vocabulary also claimed empirical justification, although that claim was often implied rather than asserted. A search for inter- and intra-subjective reliability must hinge on a test of consistency. If different users employ a term in the same fashion, then this observation confirms intersubjective reliability. A similar confirmation is sought for intrasubjective reliability. When such confirmations are absent the term is rejected. Acceptance of this empirical test for the scientific respectability of a term provides one leg upon which the criterion may stand. The other will be sought in a statement of the conditions under which reliability of usage can be achieved.

One other matter must be disposed of first. If the language of science depends entirely on the class of terms which are used in a precise, reliable, and public way, what has happened to the appeal to immediate experience?

SCIENCE AND EXPERIENCE

The notion that the ultimate testing ground for the confirmation of scientific statements lies in the appeal to subjective experience (as distinct from an objective reality) cannot be dismissed out of hand. It is intimately tied up with an archaic notion that factual statements are true or false to the extent that they are in accord with the way we see, perceive, or experience events and occasions.

In the classic view, experience is phenomenal, private, and not verbally communicable. This approach raised such hoary questions as whether two individuals, looking at a colored surface, are "really" experiencing the same color, even when the same verbal label is used by both. It asserts some antecedent private event, an experience which remains unspeakable, inexorably wedded to the perceiver. The utility of the phenomenal experience for science must be rejected on the same grounds on which a phenomenological vocabulary was rejected. It can be dispensed with for the purpose of the scientist without any commitments or conclusions concerning the questions posed by the phenomenological philosopher.

Notwithstanding this assertion, it can be argued further that all science deals with the report of experiences or perceptions. While the behaviorist might insist, probably mistakenly, that the term "experience" is meaningless because he can deal only with communicable observations, i.e., verbal reports, the phenomenologist says that something is indisputably occurring prior to this verbal report, and that he would rather deal with that occurrence. This argument (see Perkins, 1953) insists that some private response usually occurs prior to the report. It would be foolish to deny this state of affairs; it may be accepted at least for the sake of argument. But if correct, it is true of astronomers and chemists as well as of psychologists. The chemist in reporting a white precipitate uses the language of chemistry, whatever his private response might be antecedent to his report. He has learned to use some precise terms of the language of chemistry, and he has learned when and where to apply them. He does not use his phenomenological, private, or idiosyncratic vocabulary. He does not report a "cloudlike, ominous whiteness accompanied by a depressing sensation." Similarly, the psychologist-experimenter, even in the role of the subject, would be faced with the use of two languages in describing a figure-ground reversal. Using his phenomenal experience he might report a "shifting sensation, an indeterminacy of perceptual distinction" or he might use a sentence such as "At time t_1 the subject reported he saw a profile, and at time t_2 the subject reported he saw a goblet."

The latter language is the language of psychology, however "unreal" it might appear; it is precise and communicable. The "phenomenal" expressions lack these features. If the psychologist is interested in the particular words the subject uses to describe his figure-ground reversal, he may use the phenomenal language as a datum about the subject. These utterances might be referred to early learning experiences or to an idiosyncratic way of structuring the environment; they are data for a personality theory rather than for a perceptual theory. A similar argument was presented in the last chapter when the distinction between the phenomenal language of the subject and the psychologist's statements about that behavior was elaborated.

It can be argued that the elusive phenomenal experience is at least in part a function of the particular background and learning history of the observer. One's phenomenal experience will vary from someone else's to the extent that his history has structured his perceptions of his environment. How this process takes place is not at all clear to contemporary psychologists. Suffice it to say that many divergent theories of perception agree that the private phenomenal datum will vary from individual to individual, that the same environmental situation described in physical terms may give rise to different perceptions in different subjects. If it is further assumed that such differences are lawful, then their causal locus is often sought in the differential acquisition or availability of these perceptions. Both psychoanalytic theory (Rapaport, 1951) and the newer look in perception (Bruner, 1957a; Klein, 1954) as well as learning theory (Dollard and Miller, 1950) support such a point of view. Probably one of the more powerful determiners of such differential perception is the structure of the individual's language behavior. Different semantic and grammatical usage of language may well influence the phenomenal experience of the individual.[1]

If such a position is correct then the scientist's phenomenal experience as well as his language may diverge markedly from that of his naive subject. The chemist not only does not report a "cloudlike, ominous whiteness" which he "really" perceives, but he probably perceives "a precipitate." Well-established scientific terms are not just constructed artificialities but become part of the scientist's private, as well as public, vocabulary. The attribution of a well-learned system vocabulary to events "out there" is not restricted to the chemist and physicist; it has become part and parcel of any theoretically convinced psychologist. Thus the California rat-runner "sees" the vicarious trial and error behavior of his charges which his Yale or Iowa colleagues might not "see." Similarly the well-indoctrinated clinician will perceive a world full of libidinal cathexes which his laboratory colleagues may dismiss as nonexistent. This difference is not a function of the clinician's lechery but rather an inevitable outcome of a well-learned and well-assimilated vocabulary. The adequacy of these newly acquired perceptions is of course an empirical question and a function of the validity of the theoretical system of which this vocabulary is a part. Until these empirical questions are settled, the perception of different "facts" by differently reared psychologists may be an inevitable outcome of different theories structuring the experiences of their users.

The burden of the foregoing argument can be stated briefly. Everyone is "aware of" or "knows" his own private experience. But the public character of science forces the rejection of such idiosyncratic experience, however fundamental. The verbal report of that experience will not usually serve as a protocol statement; whatever the experience "is," it must always be communicated in public and reliable terms. If this reasoning is accepted, the experiential datum may be conveniently dropped from the language of science.

Once the phenomenal experience is rejected in favor of protocol statements, a final attempt could be made to reconstruct the concept of experience. For example, the term might be assigned to a class of inferences about private stimuli or private responses. Such private events are the occasions for public utterances, and "experience" is

---

[1] In its extreme form this point of view has been advocated by Whorf (1956). His position is that differences in linguistic structures among different cultural groups strongly influence their differential perception of reality.

used to name a class of events inferred from and antecedent to the public statements or behaviors of the organism. While such an approach is undoubtedly useful in investigating the phenomenal data of our subjects, it contributes little to the scientific endeavor. If the scientist must communicate his observational and confirmatory experiences to another scientist, he must perforce use public utterances. To infer some antecedent event from his public statements seems to offer little additional usefulness. Science might as well restrict itself to protocol statements as its basic unit of communication.[2]

Protocol statements are not confined to reports of observations. They obviously enter into the description of the conditions under which some other protocol statement, occurring at the end of an observational period, is made. However, it can be concluded that protocol statements in all fields of science consist primarily of verbal behavior which the scientist learns to make in response to public events. Responses to inferred events belong to the *subject matter* of psychology.

ACQUISITION OF THE VOCABULARY OF SCIENCE

A General Framework

The assertion that scientific words are learned in the same fashion as is the ordinary vocabulary necessitates a choice of a psychological theory which describes *the acquisition of verbal behavior.* Our analysis of choice is related to Skinner's (1957) reinforcement analysis. It is a simple and, for the present purposes, a very useful account of the processes of *vocabulary* acquisition and seems to present the fewest problems of interpretation and application. Skinner insists on the three-part framework of stimulus, response, and reinforcement, and he distinguishes five distinct types of verbal behavior that are under the control of stimuli. Of these, two are of particular interest here.

The *intraverbal* response is of special importance in scientific languages. This type of verbal response is under the control of a verbal stimulus. Its elicitation is often governed by complex sets of conditions, depending on elaborate rules of language structure. This class includes grammatical words and conventions, as well as constructs in

---

[2] A protocol statement need not be a statement in verbal form. Two investigators may agree concerning the use of hand signals, facial grimaces, and even, in practical use, sighs and sneers, to communicate the observation of an event.

relation to their behavior in theoretical networks and sentences. Intraverbal responses also occur in social conventions, word-association experiments, and multiplication tables.

Another class of verbal responses—*tacts*—includes most responses elicited by nonverbal stimuli, by the objects and events of our environment. This type is, of course, of special importance to the vernacular and the scientific language; it represents the most important link between external reality and the linguistic structures. Tacts name and label our environment.[3]

Verbal behavior can be described in terms of the antecedent conditions which elicit it. A person initially learns to make a verbal response whenever specific eliciting conditions are present in his environment. This statement involves the assumption that there are objects and events independent of the responding organism; it posits a reality of events independent of the language of the human observer. More will be said about this posited reality in connection with the empirical import of theories (see Chapter 9).

The learning process is dependent upon social reinforcement. Thus, for the child, the response "red" is the response reinforced by the social community in the presence of a red object. For present purposes the term "reinforcement" includes all events which increase the probability of a response. Whether a particular event is or is not a reinforcer is an empirical question. For the child reinforcers may be such adult behaviors as head-patting, candy-giving, or even saccharine smiles. For the adult they usually consist of verbal behaviors such as "That is right" or other indications of the correctness or suitability of a response.[4]

---

[3] This analysis of language behavior is probably congruent with other current theories in this area. The term "reinforcement," for example, is interchangeable with such terms as "confirmation." It is hoped that the reader whose sensibilities are outraged by this specialized vocabulary will make the appropriate substitutions.

In general, Skinner's terminology will not be used in these pages. For an extensive analysis, sensitive to the vagaries of natural usage, the reader is referred to *Verbal Behavior* (Skinner, 1957).

[4] Three kinds of verbal events may be reinforced: Rate of verbal behavior can be affected by appropriate reinforcement procedures; frequency of occurrence of particular verbal responses can be manipulated; and specific occasions appropriate for a particular response can be controlled by adequate correction procedures. (See Salzinger (1959) for a review of the manipulation of verbal behavior.) Of primary concern in these pages is the last type. We are obviously interested in the "proper use" of terms such as "bar press," "hoarding," and "shading response" rather than in the production of psychologists who talk incessantly whether about nothing or something.

The occasion for reinforcement is determined by the reinforcing community (the teacher), and the use of a word or phrase will become more and more precise and invariant to the extent that the occurrence of the stimulus (the antecedent conditions) is always the occasion for the reinforcement of the same response. Since the reinforcer usually is also a human organism, how does he determine the presence of such an occasion? Presumably by observing the response in himself. A father trying to teach his newly verbal child the response "table" will reinforce any approximation the child makes to the sounds which constitute "table" if and only if he himself is "seeing" a table, or somehow responding "That is a table." He is likely to reinforce any response when it is correlated with *his* performance of a similar response. The reinforcer has a long history of reinforcements for the term which he is now teaching, so that it has become precise and invariant in its usage. His response "table" has in the past been correlated with other people's use of the word, i.e., with his hearing the word, so that the occurrence of a reinforcement depends upon a complex set of learned responses. These include the verbal response "table," the response to the child, "He is saying 'table,' " and the availability of a reinforcing response.

Other instances of language learning follow a similar pattern. For example, some words are not used in the simple manner in which the names of objects or actions are employed. They occur within phrases and are learned within phrases, and include such classes as relative terms (e.g., "smaller than," "heavier than"). The learning of other words depends on their position within sentences, i.e., on the particular verbal units which they connect or which are connected by them (e.g., "and", "neither . . . nor", "or", "if . . . then", etc.). Some of the occurrences of these words can be described in terms of the particular conditions under which their use is reinforced by the parent, teacher, or other member of the reinforcing community. However, it will be seen in Chapter 11 that the analysis of highly organized or structured verbal behavior, e.g., meaningful sentences, becomes more complicated and will have to go beyond a simple reinforcement model.

An important distinction for any language, and particularly for a scientific one, is that between verbal and nonverbal eliciting conditions for verbal responses. In general those responses which are elicited by nonverbal events represent the very important link to events independent of the organism. There are things in the world which may elicit responses such as "table," "angry men," "geraniums," "morticians," and "pussycats." The importance of these terms in the basic vocabulary of a science will become increasingly apparent. On the other hand there are verbal responses which are elicited by other verbal responses, whether vocal or written. We may say that "Caesar is dead," or that "Borogoves are mimsy" without ever having "seen" Caesar or borogoves. These attributions have been learned intraverbally. They owe their existence largely to the fact that there is a language to begin with. Much of our verbal behavior is intraverbal and the occurrence of these responses is controlled by contextual contingencies and by the development of more-or-less invariant rules for their use. The important point is that they do not depend on any events outside the linguistic framework—nonverbal occurrences are not relevant to their use.

Intraverbal responses may be analyzed within the reinforcement history and the rules of the language. When the rules are invariant as in logic or mathematics, such an analysis reveals important characteristics of these responses. Apart from logical relationships, the language of science is replete with intraverbal terms in its high-level theoretical statements. Skinner has pointed out that the study of history is to a large extent dependent on intraverbal acquisitions. Much of our knowledge is acquired in intraverbal, linguistic contexts, even though many of the statements in our textbooks and encyclopedias were originally elicited by nonverbal conditions.

At this stage in our discussion we are primarily concerned with responses to nonverbal events. As more complex terms in psychology are considered, more and more intraverbal relationships will intrude. Finally, in discussing theory and theoretical terms, we will be primarily dealing with intraverbally acquired terms and the rules for their organization. Psychology has always been much concerned with such terms as "will," "libido," "habit strength," or "bits," and it will be useful to remember that these have different eliciting conditions from the names or labels of nonverbal events.

Proper Names and Generic Names

One distinction between two kinds of responses to nonverbal events needs to be examined in detail. In Chapter 1 we briefly noted the difference between generic names, such as "table" and "pussycats," and proper names, such as "Oedipus" and "St. Mary's Church." Traditionally, this difference has been ascribed to a distinction between terms which *name* a thing or object and terms which *denote* a thing or object. Thus, "Oedipus," "St. Mary's Church," and "Fido" are all names of objects or individuals, while certain of their characteristics are said to be designated by such terms as "Jocasta's son," "Roman Catholic church," "stone edifice," "dog," "shaggy," and so forth. These terms are said to denote the object. We have maintained in Chapter 1 that it is not particularly useful to assert the independent existence of denoted characteristics or inferred attributes of objects; a dog is "shaggy" because he elicits under specified conditions the term "shaggy." This avoidance of transcendental attributes or characteristics does not, however, avoid the distinction between naming and denoting. Traditionally, naming has been restricted to proper names and singular terms, while denoting refers to concepts, character words, and universal terms. We shall call these two kinds of terms proper names and generic names.

Behaviorally the difference between these two is easily demonstrated. If the proverbial Martian who has no acquaintance with earthly animal life is presented with 20 dogs and 20 cats and properly reinforced for saying "dog" whenever a canine appears and "cat" whenever a feline appears, he will presumably be able to say "dog" upon the appearance of the 21st instance of a dog. But assume that we have presented him with 40 dogs, half of whom are called "Fido" and half "Rex"; the 21st appearance of a Fido is not likely to elicit the proper response. "Fido" then is not a generic name; it is not under stimulus control of the class of animals called "Fido." On the other hand, 40 presentations of two dogs, one called "Fido" and one called "Rex" will produce the desired discrimination. In other words, "a proper noun is a tact in which the response is under the control of a single person or thing" (Skinner, 1957, p. 113).

Our example also suggests that the acquisition of proper names and generic names shows important similarities. These similarities are most apparent in the initial stages of acquisition. The child who learns to give the response "dog" to a particular quadruped is certainly not concerned with the proper-generic distinction. The verbal response may be learned to different instances of the class of dogs, or, whenever such an instance is romping around the house, it may be learned to repeated instances of the same animal. In part, the generic extension is determined by the *reinforcement history of the particular term*. Thus, if Fido is Johnny's own dog to whom he learns the response "Fido," then he will not be reinforced for saying "Fido" when the neighbor's Rex comes into the house. If the child, on the other hand, has learned the response "dog" rather than "Fido," the reinforcement will be readily forthcoming. In both cases, however, the child has in the first instance learned either "Fido" or "dog" as a generically neutral term. Generic extension will depend upon further instances. In our culture we prefer the term "dog" to come under the control of stimulus characteristics or criterial attributes which are common to all dogs. Names such as "Fido" or "Rex," on the other hand, are not to be brought under the control of these characteristics. In fact, they are to be brought under the stimulus control of a single object. The interesting point, however, is that stimulus control by a single object does not protect the term against generic extension at some time in the future. To say that it is possible to differentiate between three purebred fox terriers by giving them different proper names implies that these three dogs have stimulus characteristics or criterial attributes which are different from animal to animal. This particular process, the maintenance of response distinction between three members of a generic class, assures us that there are characteristics of this class which permit its subdivision. To give one member of a litter of fox terriers a name which can be maintained assures the presence of distinctive stimulus characteristics. Such a distinction may suggest genetic experiments which will produce new canine breeds, and thus a new generic name, e.g., "Rex-type terrier," is born. The specification of such differences and their experimental production is one of the endeavors of the scientist. New distinctions may at first only elicit a proper name, which may soon become a generic name as other instances (other objects or events) are discovered or produced which also elicit that name.

This characteristic of proper names—that they may develop generic properties—tends to obscure another aspect which counteracts the generic power of words. Proper names usually imply identity of the object from time to time. Fido is the *same* dog during both puppyhood and senescence. The use of a proper name implies assumptions about the consistency or identity of objects. Sometimes these assumptions have explicit theoretical status, as in the case of the sun—the same sun—which rises each morning. In most cases they are not verbalized but underlie the general notion of objects and proper names. Without such assumptions, the use of proper names in the strict sense is not possible. Thus, while proper names do have the characteristic of naming the same object from one instance of time to another, they depend on the prior notion of objects or events that maintain some kind of identity from time to time. Proper names usually indicate identity and class membership over time, while generic names usually indicate class membership over instances. Both kinds of names enter into scientific statements; statements about the sun rising each morning rely mainly on the proper-name function; statements about stars use the generic-name function.[5]

Our discussion of the approach to be used to the acquisition of verbal behaviors has been necessarily brief. Some of its implications will become apparent as more specific characteristics of a scientific language are discussed. However, the same basic acquisition process will be used as a model for the description of the development and usage of "observational" terms in any language of science. In particular, this analysis will permit a closer look at the requirements of precision and reliability which were found to be the prerequisites of a scientific vocabulary.

The demand for precision and reliability may be interpreted as a demand for response invariance. Scientific terms must be used invariantly from scientist to scientist, and from occasion to occasion. The relevance of the criterion of response invariance to the problem of a scientific vocabulary is best illustrated by reference to the psychological problems which make it necessary.

PERCEPTION, THE SCIENTIST, AND THE ENVIRONMENT

To the extent that psychology is concerned with a description of relationships among certain environmental and behavioral events, the language of psychology must develop invariant descriptions of all such events. A distinction between stimulus events and response events was indicated in Chapter 2. It should be noted again that the terms "stimulus" and "response" are used here as taxonomic classes in Brunswik's sense; they are not equivalent with the theoretical terms of S-R theories, nor does this categorization raise any questions as to the functional, interpreted character of the cognitive theorists' stimuli. Such notions as the stimulus characteristics of drives, response-pro-

---

[5] The characteristics of proper names have also been the subject of logical and syntactic investigations. Quine (1950, pp. 220 ff.) has presented a general solution for the elimination of, i.e., substitution for, proper names in logical notation by an extension from Russell involving explication of the identity notion as a logical relation (Russell, 1905). Bergmann (1957, p. 42) has also pointed to another syntactic property of proper names, namely that they always occur in the subject place of a sentence, never in the predicate place.

duced stimuli, or an assumed correspondence between the stimulus-response dichotomy and the antecedent-consequent distinction are not relevant to the present discussion. In short, we wish to make a heuristic distinction between two classes of events important to the empirical psychologist and to examine his perceptions of and responses to them.

We have already noted that for the scientist both kinds of events are "out there." It is now necessary to examine the basis on which the psychologist, or anybody else for that matter, distinguishes and specifies constancies or invariances in his environment.

Stimulus events are frequently described in the language of the physical sciences, or in invariant terms of the common language. Such descriptions include protocol statements like:

"Card 1 of the Rorschach was presented to the subject."
"A female in heat was placed in cage No. 47."
"The target was placed 12 inches in front of the subject."
"The standard color had a wavelength of 512 millimicrons."

Psychologists have, of course, been more concerned with the language of response events, and it is in this area that psychological terms emerge. For example,

"The animals in group A showed an average of 3.4 VTE's per trial."
"The latency of S's response to stimulus B was 5.5 seconds."
"The patient's attitude was hostile."
"The subject said: 'I'm depressed.' "

While our concern is primarily with response events, both classes properly belong to the language of psychology. Events acting upon the organism must be described within the psychological system language as precisely as the behavior or state of the organism is described within that language. For purposes of an independent description of the conditions under which an organism is observed, psychologists need a vocabulary which satisfactorily handles both stimulus conditions and response events. Such descriptions involve the psychologist as a perceiving organism.

The psychology of perception has long been concerned with "a discrepancy between sensory input and the finished percept" (Gibson and Gibson, 1955). This discrepancy can be described as an imperfect correlation between measurement of the stimulus by the scientist and the measurement of organismic response or activity. The same stimulus, with sameness defined in terms of physical measurement, may give rise to different responses by the same or by different individuals. This is obviously the problem discussed in the last chapter when the usefulness of a thing-language was considered. Attention was given to Brunswik's suggestion that physical measurement should be the only permissible realm of description for stimulus variables. This solution arose out of the finding that variability in a subject's response (and thus in the scientist's response) may occur when other terms are used. The important characteristic of a language which properly talks about physical stimuli, point-coincidences, and energy is that statements in it specify invariant stimulus conditions. When we move away from "physical" and "geographic" descriptions, verbal reports are often found to be highly variable. Given a particular physical situation in which a subject alternately reports the perception of profiles and goblet, how is the scientist to decide on the description of such a phenomenon? The thing-language was rejected just because it may lead the scientist, qua human being, to describe the situation in variable terms. Since he does not actually do so, but refers to other measurements instead, how does he decide on the choice of a better vocabulary for stimulus events?

Given only the description of a subject saying alternately "profiles" and "goblet," with no other measurement available, two possible alternatives suggest themselves. The situation might be described in terms of environmental variability such that the subject is stimulated at one time by a "real" goblet and at another by "real" profiles, or it can be described in terms of subject (response) variability such that the subject can respond at one time with one and at another with the alternate response. Either stimulus or response variability can be assumed. How is such a choice resolved? Typically it is resolved by additional observations by the scientist. The scientist is sent into the situation to check on stimulus variability. This waterboy represents the scientific community, or at least the language habits of that community. When the scientist returns from his exploration of the environment, he reports that the stimulus is invariant. He may well be asked how he knows that to be the case. His answer is likely to be that he set up his whole armamentarium of measurement devices and found that whether the subject gave one or the other response, the pointer readings on his devices did not change. He may even report stimulus invariance without any elaborate instrumentation, simply stating that the same sheet of paper was facing the subject, that the subject never took his eyes off the paper, that the illumination appeared to be constant, and so forth. If no doubt exists concerning the scientific training of the messenger, his report will be accepted and with it the "reality" of stimulus invariance. Even more certainty, though without qualitative changes, might be achieved if an additional number of trained communicators were to come back with reports identical with those of the first reporter.

What has the scientific observer done that differs from the actions of the subject? Has he transported himself into some transcendental scientific state so that his perceptions of the situation reflect "real" reality? Is the subject merely a lay mortal who has not reached that exalted stage, who cannot be trusted because only subjective perceptions and experiences are available to him? Obviously not. Both individuals have looked at (or in some other situations listened to, smelled, felt) a particular environmental constellation and have given verbal responses to it. On the basis of the description given by one individual the inference has been made that the stimulus situation is constant; on the basis of the description given by the other individual judgment has been suspended.

Before any further attempt is made to choose among these different vocabularies about physical objects, point-coincidences, pointer readings, tables, goblets, and profiles, one conclusion can be reached. *Stimulus invariance is inferred from response invariance.* Any high degree of observer consistency in response leads to the inference of stimulus constancy. This inference is more likely to be accepted when the responses belong to the language of a science such as physics or biochemistry, and less likely when they fall outside this class. The conclusion that a surface is blue may be inferred from the invariant response to instrument readings which consistently show a pointer setting at 450 millimicrons. The protocol statement about such a pointer setting is invariant, and the invariance from observer to observer is assumed to be empirically demonstrable. Similarly, the protocol statement about a red surface *might* be accepted on the basis of a scientist labeling the surface as red, once again because there is little reason to believe that he has learned the word "red" in a manner different from his fellow scientists and intersubjective invariance could easily be demonstrated. But in all cases the reliance on the description of a physical stimulus depends upon the assumed or demonstrated invariance of the vocabulary of the reporting scientist.[6]

[6] The assertion that all variables, physical or psychological, are constituted on the basis of the scientist's response has also been discussed from various aspects by Bakan (1953) and Jessor (1956).

In discussing the scientist as a learner of environmental discriminations and of labels of objects and events, we assume his competence in respect to both his prior experience and his immediate attention. "Response consistency" is applicable only to those persons who have had the prior learning experience necessary to make acquisition and use of a particular vocabulary possible. Similarly, the psychology of human learning has shown us that the acquisition of labels and discriminations is predicated upon an organism "set" to receive the information.

The classic example of the relationship between response invariance and inferred stimulus invariance occurred at the Greenwich Observatory in 1796. An assistant who consistently produced readings (protocol statements) of stellar transits different from those of his superior demonstrated that an assumed invariant stimulus situation can produce variable response. The consistency of astronomical theory did not permit the consideration of stimulus variability from observation to observation, and the source of the obtained variability had to be located in the observer. Subsequently these observer differences were taken into account by computing the personal equation of each observer, thus eliminating response variability in a rather artificial fashion. What is at work here is the invariance of the astronomical theory that gave rise to the observations of stellar transits. It is an excellent demonstration of the authority and dominance of a well-established theory. To have accepted the possibility of unreliable stellar transits would have required an unthinkable wrench to the established framework. The assumption of invariance of stellar transits was too well entrenched even to consider the possibility of stimulus variability to account for response variability. Thus, it appears that the inference of stimulus invariance may be derived from two sources, either the invariance of observer response, or the postulated invariance of an event within a well-established theory.

The definition of stimulus invariance in terms of response characteristics raises epistemological and ontological questions, but no hard-and-fast position need be taken. The present discussion has been empirical in emphasis; it suggests that statements about environmental characteristics follow psychological laws. The resulting conclusions concerning verbal behavior and statements about events are useful in reconstructing the scientific enterprise. How such a picture of the scientist at work is fitted into a larger picture of the world and man is not our immediate concern.

Two aspects of philosophical importance should, however, be briefly considered. One is the possible conclusion that whenever one starts with the behavior and responses of the human organism, the "existence" or "reality" of the objects and events which are inferred from his responses is somehow artificial. However, the fact that stimulus characteristics are inferred need not lead to the position that there are no objects independent of the responding organism. On the contrary, independent objects are necessary for the kind of learning process that has been formulated above. What *is* inferred from response consistency is the *invariant* occurrence of *specific* objects or events and the applicability of particular attributes. In order to make such a position possible, it has previously been suggested that some posit of reality is necessary. It can be maintained that the world is full of a number of things, but their use and manipulation depend on their identification and perception by way of the organism's responses to them. To say that there is "something" is not enough to permit the accurate description or reaction to "it" which is so necessary to science. Science posits and confirms what there is by its statements and theories. As these events are more finely differentiated, scientists are better able to manipulate and to adjust their behavior to the "realities" of the previously undifferentiated environment.[7]

The second logical question concerns the problem of circularity inherent in the use of response invariance as a source of knowledge about the environment. To determine that a particular situation has invariant characteristics, the invariant response of an observer or a group of observers must be established. However, a statement such as "Three observers reported the occurrence of an orienting response at the first choice point," which establishes the event "orienting response" for a protocol statement, requires the use of invariant terms to describe the behavior of the observers. Any empirical test of the response invariance of a term depends on the use of previously established words. Such a vocabulary must be available in order to make statements about the response invariance of a group of observers. We must start with some terms; some language must be available to describe the process of response invariance. Historically, this problem has been solved by assuming some stimuli, i.e., response invariances, which then form the basis for further statements. Another possibility is to use some class of presumably invariant terms to investigate a second class,

---

[7] For our present purposes it is enough to say that there are "some things out there." A more elaborate discussion of the scientist's posit of reality will be presented in Chapter 9.

which, once established as fulfilling the invariance requirement, can then be used to test the first and other classes of statements.

The assumption of some basic stimulus invariances is similar to the adoption of a basic vocabulary, and actually the common language supplies us with a first approximation of invariant terms. They can be used to develop new terms and the invariance of these will become firmly established both as names of objects or events and as terms within a theoretical framework. Once this new invariance is achieved the now-superfluous terms from the vernacular can be abandoned. In this fashion such terms as "hot" and "red" tend to give way to quantitative terms based on the use of instruments and pointer readings and eventually disappear from the language of physics. In fact, the more advanced a science, the less frequent its use of vernacular invariants.[8]

It might be valuable to note one of these posited classes of objects that is probably the most archaic in the common language—the class of other people. The presence of an observer, an experimenter, or a communicator is such a basic invariant assumption, based on such ingrained learned responses, that the human organism seldom becomes aware of this bit of learned behavior. It forms the basis for the very acceptance of what the communicating individual says or does. If the "existence" of the other communicator were to be questioned, all of the present discussion would be whistling in the dark.

THE ESTABLISHMENT OF RESPONSE INVARIANCE

Response Invariance and the Common Language

Our next concern is the development of terms which show response invariance. What are the conditions under which some terms become more nearly invariant than others? To some extent this will depend on the invariance of the reinforcer's behavior. If the same response is consistently reinforced it will have greater stability than if sometimes one, sometimes another, response is reinforced under the same stimulus conditions. Variability in the behavior of the reinforcer implies that

[8] This phenomenon has given rise to the practice among some contemporary social scientists of creating a new language by fiat. A scientific jargon does not guarantee any correspondence to nonverbal attributes or any invariant correlation with environmental events. There is apparently no short-cut to the laborious step-by-step development which all useful system languages have undergone.

he is saying: "I cannot tell you when the use of this term is applicable and when not." Thus the problem reverts to the invariant behavior of the teacher, whose behavior in turn depends on that of his teachers, and so on in a continuing regress. If one individual is not certain when to use a term such as "empathy," he cannot tell when the application by somebody else should be approved or corrected. And his own uncertainty is probably a function of never having been taught the appropriate use of the term. Such a genetic view of the development of response invariance yields some clues as to the class of terms which are most likely to be invariant. It will include those terms which have the most exact and invariant rules of reinforcement and which do not compete with other responses in identical situations. The better defined the class of responses which the teacher must recognize in himself before he can come up with a thumping reinforcement, the more nearly invariant the response becomes in the language, and the less likely he is to omit a reinforcement or to reinforce a wrong response.

The teacher can identify the appropriate conditions for reinforcement whenever he himself makes the response to be reinforced, or else makes a complex of identifying responses (definition) which remains constant from occasion to occasion. For example, "flag" can be reinforced by the teacher whenever he also makes the response "flag" or when he makes the response "rectangular piece of cloth with seven red and six white bars and with blue field containing forty-nine white stars."

However, the simplest class of invariant terms in the natural language is that which requires only a single response on the part of both reinforcer and learner. It includes such simple adjectives as "hot," "liquid," and "blue," i.e., the now-familiar thing-predicates. It becomes apparent why these have attracted searchers for basic terms. These terms are learned without any mediating identification of the stimulus and show a high degree of invariance. They are archaic terms in the common language with a long history of usage and, except for boundary events such as "viscous" or "purple," they compete with few other responses. In a similar position, though somewhat more ambiguous, are indicator words such as "here" and "now" which are reinforced in particular contexts. A third class of invariant responses are those designating medium-sized physical objects, such as "table" and "pointer." Here extended rules of identification, as in the complex definition of "flag," may become important. In the case of "table" some modern egg-shaped, three-legged, deep-mauve, six-inch-high object may leave the reinforcer in doubt as to the applicability of the term. In such an event additional conditions may need to be specified in extended identification sentences. Reinforcement may be withheld, for example, when the object has fewer than four legs.

We are dealing here with the exact specification of the *equivalence function* mentioned in Chapter 2. It will be recalled that the function of language in specifying the equivalence or nonequivalence of objects or events was considered central to its communication role. This summary function of verbal responses has been subsumed under a variety of labels; it falls under the topic of stimulus generalization and concept formation in psychology textbooks, and it raises problems such as the need for criterial attributes in specifying the universe to which a term applies. The last problem can be briefly discussed here; in the next chapter we shall return to the more general question of the restriction and extension of a verbal response.

The problem of criterial attributes raises the questions whether extended identifications are necessary in all cases of equivalent use, and whether terms are applied only if certain criterial attributes are present. One position implies that the extension of a concept to new instances, e.g., four-legged tables not previously encountered, depends upon the prior identification of the criterial attributes. A different theoretical point of view holds that responses will be made as a function of generalization gradients along physical dimensions such as differential retinal excitation as we go from four to three to two legs. For the present purposes this dispute can be left unresolved. Suffice it to say that criterial attributes are often used in the identification of new instances and that generalization gradients can usually be expressed in terms of criterial attributes. It appears that the specification of criteria is usually necessary in order to insure discreteness of usage. Such specifications permit us to indicate the limiting instances for the term and are used to guard against vague usage. For example, in the sentence "The rat entered cul A," we use the vernacular term "enter." However, for purposes of precision it may be necessary to state that the term "enter" is not to be used unless the animal's forelegs cross a line which marks the beginning of the cul. Such an identification sentence frequently limits the use of vernacular terms which have been taken over into the system language.

It is obvious that for a wide variety of terms, the occasions for reinforcement are spelled out in detail for the reinforcing individual. Concept formation experiments in psychology very often assume just such a state of affairs. When presented with an array of various visual objects, the subject may be told that he is to find out what a "glim" is. For the subject, "glim" is at first just a nonsense syllable, but for the experimenter it represents a short-cut to the identification sentence: "All those, and only those, objects which are circular in shape." Similarly, the subject may be informed of the attributes which make up the universe of instances and his task may be to state the identification sentences which specify a particular concept.

While in general the archaic system leaves little doubt about the occasions for reinforcement for a large number of terms, there is a class of terms for which these occasions are highly variable. These terms have controlling stimuli which are not available to the observer. They include expressions of feelings, emotions, and mental states. Skinner (1945) has discussed the variable conditions of reinforcement under which such terms are learned. In brief, a child may be reinforced for the use of the term "angry" when he exhibits aggressive behavior or when such antecedent events as deprivations or frustrations occur. On future occasions, however, he will be expected to say "I am angry" when certain internal or private events occur. These private stimuli are not under control of the reinforcer and he can only infer their occurrence, however inaccurately. Such variable conditions of reinforcement result in variable, vague uses of terms such as "angry" and "anxious."

While it is reasonable to assume that the source of reinforcements is usually social, particularly in the early acquisition of terms, there is a second class of reinforcing events which may be called self-reinforcing behaviors. It will be seen that they are an important source of response invariance in scientific language.

Up to now the role of the user of a term has been relatively passive. He is reinforced under those conditions which the reinforcing community judges as relevant, and the response is repeated under the appropriate conditions. However, the sophisticated user of words and concepts plays a more active role. An individual faced with the possible use of more than one term may apply several tests (identification sentences) to investigate the applicability of one or the other term. Most terms not only name an object or event, but also appear in other assertions and generalizations. For example, a person presented with an uneven elliptical object several inches in diameter and of a grayish color may hesitate in applying the word "stone" until he has tested several generalizations such as: "Stones are hard." Then, if the object is hard, cool to the touch, and relatively heavy (i.e., evokes these responses), he might conclude that the object is a stone. Such a conclusion would constitute a self-reinforcement in the absence of a reinforcing community.[9] Similarly, one might say that the table of our previous example does not deserve that appellation because it fails to satisfy our notion that tables are symmetrical, have four legs, and are of a comfortable height to serve as eating surfaces. Such an application of identification sentences in which the term is embedded emphasizes that even in the vernacular the use of terms depends on the testing of generalizations and assertions. Given a definition or identification sentence a person may reinforce his own use of a particular term and eventually dispense with the definition.

Before we turn to the specific role of response invariance in the language of science, some of the selective aspects of verbal invariance need to be considered. There are very broad limits within which a verbal response is considered to be invariant. For example, the typographic difference between "THINK" and "think" is not one that distinguishes between two different terms; similarly, variations in spoken words along a pitch continuum are ignored in determining invariance. There are distinctions that are important in language systems other than our own, but the acquisition of English stresses phonemic variations which generally ignore accents, timing, intensity, pitch, and so forth. Similarly, our written language stresses the transcription of certain phonemes. These limits within which verbal behavior operates are among the most ancient parameters of our language; they are acquired unwittingly from infancy on. Furthermore, the broad band of acceptance of verbal invariance is built into the reinforcement procedures. Not only is the proper response to an event reinforced, but the limits of what is acceptable as the "same" response are also set. Terms are reinforced or not corrected whenever they fall within the acceptable spoken or written variations.

Response Invariance and the Language of Science

Much of the previous discussion has been concerned with response invariance in common language. Major stress has been put on the problems of precision and reliability of usage. We have maintained that scientific languages present only special problems, but no major

---

[9] Self-reinforcement is a complex issue in the psychology of learning. Nothing more is implied by the present use of the term than that responses may increase in probability of occurrence in the absence of a reinforcing community.

characteristics different from those of the common language. Nevertheless, the historical self-consciousness of science concerning the precision and invariance of its terms has led to a basic scientific vocabulary which is less variable than even the thing-predicates that were imported from the common language. It can be maintained that science does not need a natural thing-language, and moreover, that it does not in fact use such a basic vocabulary. The development of scientific method aims at successive attempts to increase the precision and reliability of terms which must be adopted in the first instance from the vernacular. It is obvious that such refinements change the character of these terms; a redefined concept becomes a new concept. The variability of thing-predicates as well as of the more complex units of the thing-language has been demonstrated, and actually such terms as "blue" and "hard" have little place in the contemporary vocabulary of physics. It would be a poor chemist who preferred such a vocabulary to describe color variations when he has colorimetric procedures available to him. The scientist prefers pointer readings and space-time coincidences. There is no need at this point to disagree with Brunswik when he suggests that this language of physical measurement represents the basic language. Rather, it is now possible to examine the sources of that language's superiority.

The basic terms of any scientific language depend on two relationships for the development of response invariance. The first is the relation to the occasions for reinforcement when these are external stimulus conditions. It is this relationship which makes for the so-called materialistic or physicalistic appearance of science; its basic vocabulary refers to "things out there." The identification of these external conditions is initially phrased in vernacular expressions which have developed some degree of invariance. But once a term has developed a consistent contingency with stimulus conditions, it becomes independent of the sentences that were initially necessary to define those conditions. A complex definition such as "a massy cloud form with a flat base and rounded outlines piled up like a mountain" gives way to the term "cumulus." Eventually "cumulus" becomes a more-or-less invariant response to the external conditions previously described at length. In other words mediating sentences in the vernacular are short-circuited and the scientist describes his environment in a new vocabulary without going through any elaborate translation procedures. This is particularly the case when the scientific term has a long history of usage. Usage is taught directly to the budding scientist and transmitted by the same process of reinforcement which has been described for vernacular terms.

The second relationship in the development of response invariance is that between a term and other terms and phrases of the scientific language in which it operates. This relationship *also* determines the correct usage for the term. Precision and reliability are independently related to the naming function of a term and to its operation within a language system. The contextual determination of invariance is a function of the stability of the theoretical system within which the term operates. Precision and reliability of usage can therefore be related not only to Skinner's *tacts,* the verbal responses to nonverbal stimuli, but also to *intraverbal* responses, those dependent on other words. The complex set of relationships among words and sentences which form such an important part of scientific activity—the systems we know as *theories*—will be treated at length in Chapter 12. It should be immediately clear, however, that because of their longer linguistic history and resulting precision of the conditions for reinforcement, the older sciences have the advantage of stable terms appearing in stable theories. In physics and chemistry, for example, much less change in vocabulary is taking place than occurs in the newer sciences like physiology and psychology. This stolidity provides all science with a group of invariants which will be used, much as the invariants of the common language are used, in conducting scientific explorations of uncharted areas of study.

We can now answer the question about the relative efficiency of various terms which have been proposed for a basic vocabulary of psychology. For stimulus events this vocabulary has successively been sought in the common thing-language derived from the vernacular, in the language of physics, or in the languages of geography or geometry. The criterion of response invariance and the historical considerations indicated above lead to the conclusion that the vocabulary of the older sciences will frequently provide the psychologist with a basic vocabulary. However, any term from any source may be admitted to this vocabulary as long as it fulfills the basic criterion of reliable inter- and intra-subjective usage. Similarly, response events may be described in protocol statements made up primarily of words from these older vocabularies, or new psychological terms may be introduced and nursed toward invariance.

One of the dangers in psychological vocabulary building is the use of vernacular terms that cannot develop response invariance in the common language. These are the tempting protopsychological concepts referring to emotions, feelings, and images. The conditions under which two sentences such as "x is blue" and "I am angry" are learned are radically different. This does not assert that a term such as "angry" cannot enter into the language of psychology. It will, however, have to be introduced somewhat differently from the terms naming objects or events.

A criterion for scientific terms has now been developed. The major concern with the development of the language of psychology has at times been left aside. We can now turn to the specific aspects of concept formation and development in psychology, particularly to the problem of the origins of a psychological vocabulary.

SUMMARY

The requirement that all science in the long run be a public verbal endeavor and the need for a consistent language for its practitioners have once again brought into focus the question of the final appeal to immediate experience. Traditionally all statements about the world have been considered to be anchored in the link between reality and human speculations about it. We have shown that such an appeal may be cumbersome since immediate experience may vary significantly from observer to observer. On the other hand, we have suggested that the development of a consistent language of science may in turn make these experiences more alike. In either case, the task remained to specify the conditions under which an adequate vocabulary about objects and events could be acquired and used by the science of psychology.

A basic schema for describing the empirical problems of language acquisition was developed. The discussion led to the specification of response invariance as the basic criterion for acceptable verbal responses to environmental events. This specification in turn raised some problems in the psychology of perception. The perceptions of the scientist must usually be dealt with in terms of verbal reports. Constancy in the scientist's environment is inferred from the constancy of his response to posited events.

The establishment of response invariance for any specific term is largely a function of the regularity of reinforcements and the rules which establish their occurrence. Terms that are not direct responses to environmental events but rather operate within language systems—

the intraverbal responses—depend for their invariance on the stability of theoretical and grammatical systems.

In the light of these considerations the superiority of the vocabularies of the older sciences becomes understandable. Nevertheless, we have maintained that psychological terms—whether they are used to describe stimulus or response events—need only fulfill the general criterion of invariance of usage.

chapter four

Sources of psychological terms: I. The common language

THE INSISTENCE ON A RIGOROUS CRITERION FOR *all* scientific terms has led to frequent misunderstandings of the scientific endeavor. These misunderstandings center around the discrepancy between the richness and variety of the world which the scientist seeks to understand and the apparent coldness and restriction of his language. Somehow it is felt that the scientist deliberately overlooks or even denies the possibility of the imaginative insights that abound in art and literature. For obvious reasons, the psychologist in particular is portrayed in this way, devoid of the insights of a Shakespeare, Dostoevski, Melville, or Mann. That psychologists are particularly vulnerable to such an accusation is a natural outcome of the preoccupation of man with his own behavior. However, it is maintained in these pages that science is no less a creative enterprise and calls no less upon the imaginative productions of man than do the arts. What must be kept in mind is that the scientist plays under slightly changed ground rules. He is encouraged to display the same intuitive insights as his poetic brethren, but he must use these achievements in such a way that they are eventually unambiguously available to other scientists and to the community as a whole. Stress here is placed on the qualification "eventually." If we were to insist on the sole use of invariant terms and rigidly discard all statements and sentences which introduce new and less invariant concepts, all psychological generalizations would be restricted to the terminology available at the time. If such a restriction had been introduced in 1910, we would have to do without the concept of "motivation"; if in 1880, without "repression"; if in 1930, without "reactive inhibition" or "habit strength"; if in 1890, without "conditioning"; and so forth. This is not to say that some notions similar to these were not in the air prior to these years, but it took a Woodworth, Freud, Hull, or Pavlov to bring them into the psychological system language.

Imagination and intuitive insight are the necessary steps in the advancement of any scientific system. The application of the special ground rules *follows* the exercise of creation; it does not restrict it. Clarity, precision, and invariance can only be demanded as a goal of a scientific language. Invariance of a term can be developed, but the term or some approximation must be present in the first place. To restrict the scientist to the language available at any point in time would restrict his creativity. But to permit him to continue to use his new language loosely without reference to the scientific community would never bring his insights into the larger body of science. In this sense then, a balance must be found between unrestricted imagination and a necessarily restrictive channeling of its products. In the present and the following chapter we will be primarily concerned with the latter process, the development of invariance for psychological terms.

None of our expositions about experience, learning, cognition, and perception is intended to militate for or against the *content* of particular psychological systems. The scientific restriction that all attributes of the known or knowable world be expressed in verbal (or other communicable) categories does not restrict the range of events or hypothesized events about which that language speaks. Even a system language about phenomenal events is thus possible. The fact that the phenomenal experience plays a useful role as a construct in some psychological theories is not denied by the present arguments. A theory of scientific language and behavior is not necessarily the best theory of nonscientific language and behavior. Surely, the human organism uses attributes other than verbal and communicable ones to order his environment; he also reacts to and behaves in his world in ways which he cannot describe to other people. But those attributes and behaviors are of necessity not part of the public scientific endeavor. Our treatment of scientific language need not concern itself with them.

It can only deal with the verbal behavior of the scientist. This verbal behavior may, of course, name such events as "unconscious inferences," "generic rules," "Gestalten," "the unconscious," and so forth. Such terms may be used by the scientist in describing the behavior of organisms, but they are not necessary in describing his own verbal behavior. These processes may, as we shall see, play an important role in understanding the theoretical and prescientific behavior of the creative investigator.

It was noted earlier that the demand for the publicity of scientific language has for various reasons led to an interpretation of all sciences as being materialistic. The erroneous inference is made that if the simplest scientific terms apply only to observable characteristics which act upon more than one observer at the same time, all such terms must refer therefore only to physical objects and physical characteristics. This interpretation is based on a vernacular and vague appreciation of the term "physical." It appears to derive partly from the notion that the objects of science are necessarily the objects of physics, and partly from the identification of the tangible or observable with the physical. An examination of these two aspects of physicalism and of the general characteristics of events which elicit naming behavior should shed some light on the extent to which psychology may be said to be physicalistic.

PSYCHOLOGY AND PHYSICALISM

It has been shown that there are good historical reasons for the establishment of physical terms as the building stones of all scientific languages. In summary, this superiority can be ascribed to two general states of affairs. In the first place, Western society has since pre-Socratic days envisioned a pyramid of knowledge in which the investigation of matter and its behavior forms the basis of all further developments. It appears that the tangible objects which most easily gave rise to an invariant terminology were the first targets of questions about the nature (*physis*) of the universe. From our analysis of language acquisition it seems not unexpected that the natural language developed and extended archaic notions about the priority of physical objects. This tendency was further abetted by man's early mastery and control of his environment; practical and technical problems demanded a language which spoke unequivocally about sticks and stones. The second, closely related, aspect is the rapid early development of the physical sciences. The scientific tradition started in fact with the development of stable physical language systems. But it is important not to confuse the necessary physicalism of the physicist's language with a more general, pervasive physicalism applied to other sciences and to the common language.

Physicalism, in that general sense, may be interpreted in two ways: First, as the view that all scientific terms must be reducible to terms in the language of physics, and second, as a useful restriction of object-naming to entities in our external environment. The reductionist position has already been seen to be untenable. It is the second basis for a methodological physicalism which will be examined here in detail and which may provide a physicalistic position for the present stage of development of psychological theory. Such a position is advocated in order to avoid the extension of the object terms to inferred, imagined, or postulated entities. Object terms will be restricted to verbal responses which are elicited by discriminable objects of the external world. Physicalism in this sense does not claim that statements in psychology are "nothing but" elaborated statements of physical events. It does assert that once the posited reality which acts on the sense organs of all observers is accepted, the objects and events of that reality in the vernacular sense exhaust the class of events that can be reasonably classed as consistent entities, persisting over time.

The justification for such a position obviously cannot be based on a cavalier stipulation as to what does and what does not belong within the realm of the vernacular "physical" reality. There are two origins of the notion of "physical objects," one as it is developed in the genesis of the common language, the other as it is defined within an elaborate theory, such as that of physics.

In considering the development of the concept of persisting physical objects, we recall our discussion of proper names in Chapter 3. It was noted there that proper names are based on the development of the notion of the preservation and consistency of identity over instances of time. The kinds of objects and events that are subject to this kind of proper naming are also likely to be the physical objects of the vernacular. Can any event, properly identified by an individual, acquire a proper name? Theoretically, this should certainly be possible. In fact, however, proper names are restricted to a relatively narrow range of events. Thus, considerations other than those of sheer presentation and proper reinforcement enter into the selection of events to be given proper names. The argument here will be that one criterion for the physical, persisting object derives from the archaic physicalism which resides in the development of language and perceptual organization.

It appears that visual and tactile impressions, the archaic basis for asserting the "existence" of physical objects, are the preferred modes for accepting persisting identity. In the vernacular, identity is somehow associated with physical existence, and we prefer to make assertions of identity on the basis of these discriminations. The bells of St. Mary's Church are the "same" bells on Easter Sunday and on Christmas Day, but somehow we are not so sure that the sound they make is the "same." Identity decisions usually involve some notion of a tangible physical object which can be pointed at. This is not, of course, a transcendental property of such objects, since it is possible to make identity judgments on the basis of, for example, auditory inputs. Thus, the theme of the first movement of Beethoven's *Fifth Symphony* is the same whether played on the piano, whistled, or sung. But the preferred, primitive notion of identity is reserved for tangible objects, which maintain their identity even though their appearance may change radically over time. Psychologically, it appears that this primacy may be traced to the ontogenetic development of the perception of our world. Piaget, whose arguments in this general area we shall have occasion to examine more fully in Chapter 11, has pointed out that the notion of the identity of the same object is not an a priori notion, but rather develops in the growing child. In discussing the investment of the universe with objects, he notes that

> It is to the extent that the child learns to coordinate two separate schemata—that is to say, two actions until then independent of each other—that he becomes capable of seeking objects which disappeared and of attributing to them a consistency independent of the self. (Piaget, 1953, p. 211.)

It is very likely that the identification of the consistency of visual and tactile presentations is basic to the development of the idea that proper names usually name single "physical" objects.

The notion of the persisting "physical" object based on the initial visual-tactile experiences of the individual finds its counterpart in classical, though not necessarily in modern, physics. Here it is grounded in a vast theoretical network of assumptions and hypotheses about spatio-temporal events and historically in the basic concern with the notion of matter. Our argument then is based on the intuitive function of the notion of physical reality that facilitates now, and probably facilitated historically, the acceptance of a naive physicalism which restricts the use of object and entity names to physical, tangible objects.

This restriction raises a question about such traditionally psychological concepts as "mind," "fear," and "the unconscious." The answer of the scientist who talks about "physical" objects in his protocol statements would be that it is possible to do without such new entities and to speak only of *states* of organisms. It is patently simpler to speak of the state of an organism or of a group of organisms than to introduce new terms and treat them as if they had the same developmental history as the object-naming terms. The term "mind" is not acquired in the same way as the term "table." It arises out of various defining sentences and language habits, most of which are not made explicit. Children are not taught to say "That is a mind," or "This is a fear." Rather, they use the state-language and say, "This man is thinking," or "I am afraid." It appears then to be more parsimonious to speak of states of physical objects until such time as the state-language proves inadequate.

What is here at issue is the tendency to reify, so prevalent in the vernacular. Reification has developed from the identity notion, which is closely tied to physical objects, and from the external conditions of reinforcement that obtain for these objects. The use of nouns to name objects often leads to the generalization that all terms functioning as nouns necessarily refer to something "real." In most cases reified constructs have been introduced within contextual usage and are not controlled by environmental conditions of elicitation. They depend for their precision on their correlation with other words appearing in the language. The present argument does not consider the question whether there are such "things" as fear. The term "fear" names a state of the organism. This state may be ascertained by a variety of different methods, including the statement by the subject: "I am afraid." But it is always possible to describe these states without introducing new entities. We might then be able to dispense with such names and mental entities as "pain," "fear," "anger," "love," by describing states of organisms rather than "things." It is not possible to point to "pains" or "fears." Rather, "a painful leg," "a fearful child" are mentioned. The organism is a necessary part of the description. "Images," "fears," "dreams," and "anxieties" invariably are described as states of the organism. The problem to be avoided is to use them independently of an organism. Such independence leads to the introduction of mental entities which are unnecessary and may be misleading.

The ontogenetic history of the notion of physical objects, as well as the history of acquisition of terms labeling physical objects and entities, suggests a restriction of usage. For purposes of clarity and in order to avoid confusion when talking about mental events, the use of object-names might well be restricted to physical objects in this naive sense. When and if psychology develops the stable theoretical network which will make these terms unambiguous and avoid the suggestion of physical tangibility of "minds" and "intelligences," we may well return to the use of these kinds of names in psychology. However, until a stable theoretical basis tells us what minds are, physicalism in the present sense reminds the psychologist that "minds" and "purple cows" are not parts of his physical environment and that he can neither see nor be one.[1]

ORIGINS OF INVARIANT TERMS FOR PSYCHOLOGY

A cautious physicalism which avoids the proliferation of new entities has been outlined, and some of the processes whereby the major criterion of invariance can be achieved have been described. It now remains to specify the ways in which invariant terms originate. Two major divisions have been suggested by the distinction between names of object-events on the one hand, and intraverbal terms on the other. The former constitute the mainstay of protocol statements such as:

"Rat No. 46 entered cul A."
"0.5 seconds after pressing the bar, the animal was reinforced with a 0.04-gram pellet."
"The S's first response to Card 5 of the Rorschach was, 'It looks like a bat'; his reaction time was 5.5 seconds."

Most of the terms used in these statements can be acquired by differential reinforcement in the presence of the controlling stimuli. We say "*can* be acquired" because they may also be acquired by learning how they function in sentences.

It has already been noted that some terms, e.g., "reinforce," may originally be theoretical terms which quickly enter the protocol language, where they behave like naming or labeling terms, as in the

[1] This discussion owes much to a more general exposition of this point of view by Quine (1953).

statement, "The animal was reinforced." Novel terms appearing first in a theoretical framework may soon, by the use of appropriate identifying sentences, enter into the *description* of behavior. These terms also function in theoretical sentences, as in

> "Vicarious trial and error in the rat and ideation in man are functionally equivalent."

Here VTE (vicarious trial and error) may name an event, but its relation to "ideation" and other processes is just as important for its proper function as is the invariance of its elicitation as a name.

In general then, protocol terms function in intraverbal (theoretical) contexts and theoretical terms may develop protocol characteristics. The following discussion, while addressed mainly to the development and sources of protocol terms, will unavoidably touch upon their function in theoretical contexts.

Invariant terms of both sorts in the psychological system language are introduced from the common language, from other systems and sciences, and finally through identification sentences or definitions. The first two sources will be discussed in the following pages; the problem of definition will be examined in Chapter 5.

THE COMMON LANGUAGE AS A SOURCE OF INVARIANT TERMS

We have repeatedly asserted that the natural language is an inevitable starting point for all scientific excursions. The purgatory of scientific concept formation purifies this language during its subsequent career. There are, however, terms in the common language which land unpurified in the realm of science; they form the basic framework of all but the most esoteric scientific languages.

Obviously, scientists talk to each other mostly in the vernacular. Even when they use scientific terms, they ordinarily use the grammar and rules of their natural language. Not even the most jargon-infested psychologist can really be accused of not talking English, although sentences in jargon may occasionally hide as much empirical ignorance as they pretend to knowledge.

Most psychologists do, in fact, speak their native language. They communicate rather passably with each other when they use such sentences as:

"On the fifth trial the rat first touched the bar."
"Subject A said that the first tone was louder than the second."
"The patient kept his therapist waiting for 2½ hours."
"The experimental room was windowless, and the walls were hung with purple drapes."
"The monkey turned away from the banana."

These sentences demonstrate that many terms and structures in the English language are precise and unambiguous enough to permit their use for scientific communication. All speakers of English use such words as "rat," "louder than," "room," "windowless," and "banana" in more-or-less the same way. They are also likely to read a clock in the same fashion and to respond to the same kind of behavior with the observation, "He turned away." Most vernacular terms, however, retain some flexibility, which has advantages for common parlance. The scientific remodeling process does not enter into the picture until the question arises "What do you mean by that?" It may take the form of the more hostile criticism, "I don't understand what you are talking about," or the somewhat more gentle, "How are you using that term?", or the gallant challenge, "Define your terms."

In all these cases the questioner indicates that the sentence is vague, that he would like some directions as to how to use the terms and when to apply them. Until these questions are raised, we may well be content with the use of the English language as practiced by Webster and by Fowler. Science has a distinct advantage over other fields that are dependent on verbal communication; whenever the going gets rough and terms seem too vague or fail to communicate adequately, it can coin new terms and avoid many purely verbal problems. This method of escape is usually chosen when the natural tendency of vernacular terms to lose precision and to become applicable to many unspecified situations proves too cumbersome. The conditions for reinforcement of a particular vernacular response may vary somewhat from time to time and from user to user. A family of uses may then arise for any single response. Such was the case in the example of the word "table" used earlier. Many different objects are the occasion for the reinforcement of the word "table." Philosophers who attempt to deal with logical and semantic problems within the framework of a common language have often pointed to the emergence of pseudo-problems as a function of such variegated usage. The realization that vagueness may be an empirical problem is not confined to the psychological investigator. Wittgenstein (1953, p. 36[e]) admonishes:

> In such a difficulty always ask yourself: How did we *learn* the meaning of this word ("good" for instance)? From what sort of examples? In what language-games? Then it will be easier for you to see that the word must have a family of meanings.

Science can escape these families of meanings by substituting a new word which is taught according to a specified set of rules. It might be useful for the scientist when faced with a vernacular word to consider the possibility that it does have such a family of meanings, which interfere with invariant usage. In that case he will be following in the footsteps of the Oxford philosophers who have been concerned with just such analyses of terms in both vernacular and scientific usage (see Ryle, 1949). In many cases such an endeavor might illuminate the need for several different terms where previously one term has sufficed. Ryle cites the case of the word "pleasure," which may be used to describe at least two different types of situations: 1. Occasions for enjoying or liking some activity—e.g., a teacher might wholeheartedly enjoy lecturing to a large class; lecturing is his pleasure. 2. Occasions for describing moods such as joy and rapture which are characterized by certain subjective feelings.

This particular kind of semantic analysis cannot, in itself, lead us to the attainment of an invariant vocabulary. It cannot proceed without continuous testing of the refined terms in empirical, intersubjective contexts. While the proponents of common-language analysis do not explicitly claim that their endeavors are designed to develop a scientifically useful vocabulary for psychology (or other fields of knowledge), their general intent parallels ours—to achieve an unambiguous language about psychological events. To limit such a language to the terms presently available in the vernacular is unnecessarily constricting. We may well decide to junk some common terms that are hopelessly vague and ambiguous and to develop new verbal responses which do not exhibit these shortcomings. Similarly, the development of new terms, distinctions, or discriminations must lean heavily on the behavior of both new and old terms in empirical and theoretical contexts. The modern analytic movement does, on the other hand, make important contributions to the development of new terms by pointing out variations in usage and by the refinement of common-language terminology. To the extent that these attempts contribute to the development of a new psychological vocabulary (of both old and new terms), philosophical analysis exhibits precisely the kind of progression from common to scientific language which we have described in these pages. Its heuristic value in arriving at important distinctions in the use of the common vocabulary and in pointing to new anchoring points for empirical investigations is unquestioned. For the psychologist and the philosopher who want to restrict themselves to the common language, such an analysis is inevitable.[2]

A word, carefully avoided until now, was introduced in the quotation from Wittgenstein—the term "meaning." It is so much a part of our vernacular usage that some space must be given to it in this discussion of the common language. It is a commonplace in the vernacular that words and sentences have "meanings." It is these "meanings" which often are debated when using natural terms in scientific discourse. A solution for the avoidance of the term should be apparent, and Wittgenstein may well be allowed to make up for having introduced it to these pages:

> For a *large* class of cases—though not for all—in which we employ the word "meaning" it can be defined thus: the meaning of a word is its use in the language. (1953, p. 20[e].)

The substitution of "use" for "meaning" is not far from the present formulation which asks for the conditions under which a term is or has been used and reinforced. The answer to this question should be sufficient to satisfy most applications of "meaning"; it will specify the variables which control verbal behavior.

The criterion for using terms from the vernacular in the language of psychology might well be the answer to the question, "Will the same verbal response occur whenever the same circumstances recur?" There is no need to debate the definition of "same circumstances." Whenever, in a particular situation, the user vacillates: "That man is angry; or he may be just agitated; or he may well be playing charades," he will do well to consider dismissing any one or all of these descriptions as too vague for communication. Such a test of one's own indecision of usage is usually immediately available, and can be made with profit whether the description is of the behavior of clouds, sunflowers, or people.

Tests for the use of vernacular terms are empirical, and whether or

---

[2] For another point of view in modern philosophy, namely that philosophy may begin with but need not remain tied to the common language, see Quine (1951b, 1957) who is concerned with the problem of how the common language is learned. On the other hand, see Bergmann (1957) for the proposal of artificial languages for philosophy.

not the tests can be immediately applied, a term will stand or fall on the basis of empirical evidence. The evidence may be somewhat slow in arriving, as in the case of abstractions and generic extensions. For example, the child who learns to use the word "red" cannot apply the test indicated above. He cannot ask himself whether he is likely to make the same response under the same circumstances. His only available test is to continue using the word and to be corrected by the reinforcing community whenever he is wrong. This problem has been previously raised in connection with the equivalence function of language and the specification of boundary conditions for particular terms. The generic use of a term may depend on prior specifications of criterial attributes (the boundary conditions) or it may be extended because of particular stimulating conditions which are present in all the instances of various objects or events. The verbal response will occur because of similarities present in the objects. Generic extension will of course take place whether or not the user of the term can specify attributes of these objects other than the term in question, i.e., define the similarity. This is certainly what happens in the use of many abstract or generic terms in the vernacular. A table is a table because the word "table" is appropriate. The child obviously uses many words correctly without being able to specify the relevant attributes.

The disadvantage of generic spread in the scientific language is that it is apt to hinder fine distinctions. When a subject is presented with a "red" surface, we may want to know whether it is bright red, or purple, or pink. A specification in terms of wavelengths of light provides just such a narrowing of the term. It is in these cases where the communicating investigator wants to specify a very narrow band of usage that he will forsake the vernacular and return to the language of measurement and limited spread. In those cases where a variation within the generic breadth of a term is not believed to be important, he will be content with wide and vague usage. It should be noted that "believe to be important" implies a whole host of theoretical and predictive statements, such as:

"The behavior of the rat will not vary with the type of wood used for the floor of the runway; therefore I will only say 'wood.' "

"It doesn't matter whether the patient is tested on the second or third floor of the hospital; his behavior will not be affected by these differences in height."

Generic extensions may be discovered by observing the language behavior of the scientist. The elicitation of a term by a newly discovered or previously ignored object or event suggests further extension of the class of objects subsumed under that term. These objects or events are often manufactured in the laboratory, where extension may be based on simple elicitation, e.g., "There is another kind of grooming response." Extension may also proceed via theoretical, intraverbal specifications, e.g., " 'Mixed dominance' is also to be applied to ambidextrous individuals." On the other hand, generic extension may be limited by the introduction of new terms which restrict previously established classes. All these terms are taught to other scientists either by the use of direct reinforcements, or by the specification of conditions and measurements which accompany these attributes.

Most of this discussion of the vernacular has been concerned with the stimulus or environmental occasions under which behavior is observed. The same argument holds of course for the description of response events. The student in clinical psychology who is taught the term "schizophrenic" may well learn it first by having a variety of schizophrenic patients presented to him. Generic spread, without any specification of boundary conditions, may then permit him to observe a patient some months later and say, "I have a feeling he is schizophrenic." The reinforcement process has done its job; it is now time for the specification of boundary conditions in order to prevent generic spread extending to others, including his supervisor. The very fact that the term may be elicited by the student's supervisor is prima facie evidence for its lack of scientific respectability. Assuming that the supervisor is not in fact psychotic, his provoking of the response "schizophrenic" indicates that he possesses some stimulus characteristics which control the term for that student. The supervisor obviously did not intend this generic spread. The limitation of such extension calls for more exact specification of the conditions of usage. Eventually the student should be able to use the term "schizophrenic" only when certain invariant responses occur regularly, such as those arising out of particular measurement techniques with a minimum of uncontrolled spread (e.g., the patient's pattern score on the Wechsler-Bellevue). Of course the diagnostic term "schizophrenic" also functions in a variety of theoretical systems and sentences which will in turn determine the occasions for its use. In any case, the uses of "schizophrenic" are superior to the vernacular term "insane," which would today be inappropriate within the hospital setting. Once again, there will be behaviors of either patients or rats which are of no particular concern to the observer and which will continue to elicit vernacular terms. Responses dealing with the color of the patient's socks, or his use of his preferred hand to open a door, or the length of the rat's tail will continue to use the vernacular mode.

What is the distinction between the descriptive term that continues to be used as it has in the vernacular and the term that undergoes refinement and restriction by the use of boundary conditions? The difference probably underlies the whole fabric of the scientific enterprise. Some terms, when refined, extend the common-sense knowledge of the environment. Science attempts to make finer and more precise distinctions in the environment and to find lawful relationships among them. When the vernacular is abandoned for better terms, these terms are usually better because they are evoked by different properties of the environment, because they represent new discriminations.

In the development of new discriminations the scientist is not altogether unlike the perceptive and sensitive playwright, artist, healer, or man in the street. He must, however, put his new discriminations into a precise verbal mode. When the term "red" loses its usefulness because distinctions need to be made within the class of all red objects, science switches to wavelengths. There are other new terms which do not require the use of special measuring techniques in order to cut the pie of objects into smaller and more useful pieces; for example, dividing "insane" into "schizophrenic," "manic," or other subcategories. One way for communicating these new terms to other scientific users is by differential reinforcement, as in the case of the clinical psychology student. However, such a method of teaching is not always possible and entails a laborious and time-wasting process of individual instruction with many different instances of the new term. The method of choice is by the specification of criterial attributes which "define" the new concept. But this method seems to involve an infinite regress since the terms used in the definition in turn require specification or individual instruction. Where does the process stop? It must stop with a class of terms that do not call for definitions. This class of terms must have a generic spread which is not discriminably different from user to user. No object or event will elicit one of these terms in one user without eliciting it also in other users who have been properly educated. Conversely, no object or event which fails to elicit such a term from one group of users will elicit it from others. This is the class of invariant terms which forms the basic vocabulary of science.

We now appreciate another reason why the physical thing-language and measurement terms have attracted so much attention. These are the terms individually taught to all members of the scientific and vernacular community by the same differential reinforcement of various instances. The long history of refinement of the occasions for reinforcement for these terms has also assured their lack of generic fuzziness. Few instances, if any, occur where the use of the basic terms is in doubt. We may infer in this case that these terms have been conditioned to single discriminable aspects of the environment. It is quite clear by now that any verbal response that can be taught and maintained in this fashion will be acceptable for the basic vocabulary. Most of these responses are for historical reasons in the measurement and physical-geographical mode. But it is possible for others, including "schizophrenic," to join this class of responses. Such an accretion is a slow process. The term must be taught to the whole community of users of the particular scientific language, and before that can be accomplished the term must prove its utility in the empirical differentiation of the environment.

If, as happens to be the case, the term "schizophrenic" cannot be taught invariantly in the same fashion as terms such as "2 inches long," "450-millimicron wavelength," or "IQ of 115," it will linger in the antechambers of scientific respectability together with other semivernacular terms. It may, however, be of use if its boundary conditions and criterial attributes are invariantly defined. In this fashion the term, with its definition, enters into the scientific language and may eventually be used without its definitional appendix. After a term has long been used to describe differences on the basis of its definitions, the latter may wither away and the term may continue in its own right in the basic vocabulary. The concern with definition, so prevalent in contemporary psychology and to be examined in detail in the next chapters, expresses the search for verbal responses which invariantly correspond to characteristics of the objects and events around us.

In recent years, the increasing concern with oral and written behavior has produced a method for adding new terms to the vocabulary taken over from the physical and older sciences. These terms have been developed in connection with the content analysis of verbal behaviors. The scoring of verbal associations or of TAT protocols has been accomplished by the laborious process of developing reliabilities for categories, scoring criteria, and so forth. This process of individual reinforcement of the correct response, either with or without the use of definitions, may be one way of developing basic vocabularies for psychology which are independent of the older sciences.

Content analysis is concerned with the proper naming and communication of verbal behavior. Verbal behavior is of course one of the major sources of data in psychology. Various examples of protocol statements in the preceding pages have been of the form: "Subject A said, '. . . . . . .' " The most accurate description of the material inside the quotation signs is a repetition of the verbal behavior, which will in most cases be in the common language. For purposes of analysis it may be categorized, broken down into appropriate units, or otherwise translated. The important aspect to be stressed here is that such an analysis involves the scientific study of verbal behavior, and the fact that the language of the subject and of the investigator are highly similar represents one of the problems of a psychological science. The distinction must be made again between the behavior of the organism and the behavior of the scientist:

> [It] must be emphasized that from the point of view of scientific method an expression such as *It's four o'clock* is the name of a response. It is obviously not the response being studied, because that was made by someone else at some other time. It simply resembles the response in point of form. The conditions responsible for the original response may not share anything in common with the conditions responsible for the response on the part of the describing scientist. . . . The field of verbal behavior is distinguished by the fact that the names of the things with which it deals are acoustically similar to the things themselves. As Quine (1940) has said, "A quotation is not a description, but a hieroglyph; it designates its object not by describing it in terms of other objects, but by picturing it." Quine is speaking here of the written report of written verbal behavior. In no other science is this possible, because in no other science do names and the things named have similar structures. (Skinner, 1957, p. 18.)

The naming of the verbal behavior of the subject is one of the simplest sources of invariance. As long as it is kept in mind that the verbal response and its name, or the behavior of the organism and the scientist's label for it, are not the same thing, the names of all utterances in the vernacular can enter into the scientific language of psychology as a highly invariant class of terms. The acceptability of these terms serves to remind us how far we have moved from the physical thing-language. The names of verbal responses cannot, by any stretch of the imagination, be classed as names of "physical things"; but, by our criterion of response invariance, they are at least as respectable as those "basic" terms.

Apart from the names of verbal responses, which are similar to the responses named, verbal behavior may be more accurately described by the use of phonetic symbols, and the achievements of the science of linguistics may be used in its description. For most purposes, however, it is sufficient to name the response by repeating it. The same response may, of course, have more than one name, just as a physical object may have the name "table," "piece of dining room furniture," "rectangular wood panel supported by four legs," and so forth. The response "Der Himmel ist blau" may be named "Der Himmel ist blau," or it may be named "The sky is blue," or it may be described in phonetic symbols.

In the same way as does the language of linguistics, the languages of the older sciences, particularly the physical-geographic ones, offer the psychologist a vast repertory of terms to be used in the description of the organism as well as of the environment surrounding the organism at any particular time.[3] Introduction of terms either from other sciences or from the vernacular does not insure that they will satisfy the criterion of invariance. Terms and sentences from other systems as well as new ones introduced especially for use within the psychological system language often require further examination. The occasions for their use may have to be specified by stating criterial attributes or boundary conditions, shorthand forms for old expressions may be introduced, and vague terms may be refined by continuous reference to their usage both as responses to objects and events and as intraverbal responses. All of these activities fall within the province of definitional procedures to be discussed in the next chapter.

SUMMARY

Some of the necessary restrictions on scientific languages have given them an aura of dryness and otherworldliness. However, the restrictive aspects of language building, with which we are concerned in these early chapters, are subsequent to the exercise of unrestricted

[3] There are three *special* language systems which are essential to a full understanding of the language of psychology—mathematics, logic, and grammar. When we come to a discussion of theory in psychology these intraverbal systems will once more demand attention.

imaginative activity. One of the restrictions which has been responsible for the "materialistic" picture of science has been the stress upon a physicalistic vocabulary for talking about the world of events. While a physicalistic reductionism has been rejected, it is concluded that a cautious physicalism provides the means whereby the proliferation of new entities and the problem of reification can be avoided.

In addition to a vernacular physicalism which provides some general rules for the avoidance of mental entities, the vernacular vocabulary provides science with a variety of terms and rules. The language in which the contemporary scientist talks about most of his activities is his native one. Sometimes, the decision to abandon the common vocabulary and to resort to terms in the system language is related to the need for precision in a particular situation; the common language serves well enough in those instances where no fine distinctions need be made.

In deciding on the use of a particular vernacular word or phrase, we are often faced with the problem of meaning. For present purposes it was decided that questions of meaning may be decided on the basis of word usage. In restricting the meaning or use of a term, generic spread can be limited by the use of definitions or by the specifications of boundary conditions. Those terms which have an invariant generic spread from user to user provide us with the basic vocabulary for talking about the event-world. The decision that the meaning of a term is too vague or that it has too much spread often leads to the development of new discriminations, thus expanding the categories of objects and events that enter the scientist's universe of discourse.

We have indicated that the naming of verbal behavior provides the psychologist with an adequate protocol language about one type of human behavior. In contrast to the naming of other behavioral events, the naming of language behavior has the advantage of resembling the behavior named. Apart from this peculiar advantage for the introduction of invariant descriptions, psychology also uses invariant terms from other sciences in describing the behavior and the environment of its subjects. The specific development of invariance for new terms in psychology or for terms borrowed from the vernacular is partly a problem of definition.

chapter five

Sources of psychological terms: II. Definitions

THE NOTION OF DEFINITIONAL OR IDENTIFYING sentences has cropped up repeatedly in the preceding chapters. In most cases such sentences served to specify the conditions under which a particular term, whether new or old, should or should not be used. Vague terms can be made less vague by providing them with defining sentences which specify in invariant language the conditions or occasions that are "correct" for the use of the term. For the word "schizophrenic" this was found to be necessary because its use may be extended to cases which are not supposed to elicit that particular verbal response. Furthermore it was shown that those terms which do not need definitions or identifying sentences are the invariant terms that constitute the basic vocabulary of science. In a sense, the expression "basic" is misused here because in the ideal system language no term is more "basic" than another; there are only invariant terms, which are used in response to object events, and theoretical terms, which are used primarily in intraverbal contexts. This presumably is the goal toward which the scientific endeavor tends, though whether it is achievable is at least doubtful. In mid-twentieth century few empirical sciences even approach such a state of affairs. Finally, the younger a particular scientific system the less likely it is to have discovered the discriminations of our universe which are the core of its basic vocabulary.

Whenever terms are still vague or ambiguous, as they tend to be in psychology, the role of definitions is important in providing better usage. In this fashion, the term "insane" gave way to Kraepelin's classificatory scheme, and the term "schizophrenic" in its turn is likely to give way to new terms which are invariant. Similarly, a term such as "anxious" may go through a period of being tied to various definitions only to give way to several different terms. In the area of animal behavior, which has consistently attempted to make do with physical-geographic terms, new words such as "VTE," "observing response," and so forth are making tentative appearances. All of these must be supported by definitions, just as the color spectrum would need to be supported by definitional sentences such as "Red is defined as the color No. 7 on the standard chart" if modern colorimetry did not provide for invariant discriminations of wavelengths of light.

Definitions also serve the purpose of introducing vernacular terms into the language of science by specifying their new rules of usage. In this way, as will be seen presently in the case of real definitions, a particular selection of the controlling conditions which elicit a vernacular response can be specified as the *only* conditions relevant for the use of that word. Implicitly all the other stimulus conditions which have haphazardly elicited that response are placed beyond the pale and the response to them is, or should be, eliminated.

In psychology definitions play an important clarifying role. Much of this clarification and explication, however, does not fall into the classical province of definition, which asks for simple equivalences between terms and their defining sentences. Often the question will arise as to the choice among several such sentences. Similarly, we will be increasingly faced with so-called definitions that are in the form of laws or functional relationships. Thus the sentence "$e = mc^2$" is no more just a definition of energy than the sentence "${}_SE_R = f({}_SH_R) \times f(D)$" is just a definition of excitatory potential. These are sentences within theoretical systems. The difference between definitions in the classical sense and such theoretical sentences will presently be more fully explored.

Two general classes of definitions must be distinguished at the outset—*nominal definitions* and *real definitions.* The former class has generally been considered to consist of definitions by convention or stipulation; new terms or words are stipulated to stand for an alternate linguistic expression. Real definitions on the other hand include all those definitional procedures in which a word is defined in terms of some essential characteristic, abstract quality, or "real" constituent of the defined expression.[1]

NOMINAL DEFINITIONS

Generally speaking, nominal definitions are applied for the convenience of the user. Complicated operations or observations which are invariant from instance to instance can be named more efficiently and simply by substituting a single expression or term. A second use of these definitions was indicated earlier; definitions may be used to specify reinforcement occasions for a term. Following extensive use of these specifications, the term *may* develop invariant usage on its own and not show any unwanted generic spread. In that case the definition will slowly be dispensed with and the term will no longer depend on the definitional crutch.

Nominal definitions are generally of the form: *Let the expression* E_1 *be equivalent to, or synonymous with, the expression* E_2. Thus, the concept of hunger might be introduced by the sentence: Let the expression "Intensity of hunger" be equivalent to the expression "Hours of food deprivation." For convenience, the notation "$=_{\text{df}}$" will be used to stipulate the equality or synonymity of the two expressions, e.g., "Intensity of hunger $=_{\text{df}}$ Hours of food deprivation."[2] Other definitions in psychology which illustrate this method of introducing terms are:

"IQ of individual x $=_{\text{df}} 100 \times \dfrac{\text{MA of individual x}}{\text{CA of individual x}}$."

"Operant $=_{\text{df}}$ the property of a response upon which reinforcement is contingent."

"x is extraverted $=_{\text{df}}$ x is an individual with a movement-to-color ratio on the Rorschach which is smaller than unity."

---

[1] Much of the following material is adapted from Hempel's *Fundamentals of Concept Formation in Empirical Science* (1952). For a more extended technical discussion the reader should consult that monograph.

[2] In the course of discussing the definitions of specific psychological terms, we will repeatedly have occasion to include variables which are named by nouns. In Chapter 4, we cautioned against the use of nouns that might be interpreted as object-names or names of entities. It should be clear that the use of the noun form does not entail the postulation of an object. On the contrary, definitional procedures serve to guard against this implication.

The fact that the reader may disagree with any or all of these definitions is not relevant to the use of nominal definitions. They are stipulations, often shorthand substitutions for more cumbersome expressions, and cannot be considered as either correct or incorrect. Arguments over the validity of a definition belong in the realm of *real* definitions—if they are appropriate at all.

The nominal introduction of a new expression for an old one in any *particular* case can be generalized to the more extended introduction of a new name for a *generic* property or class. Thus nominal definitions may do more than simply introduce one expression for another; they may introduce a general term. For example, the definition above which introduces the term "IQ" not only defines the expression "intelligence quotient of individual x" but also may introduce the concept of the intelligence quotient of any individual.

The expression to be defined need not be a single term, but may be a complex sentence, or any compound of units which follows the grammatical rules of the language. So-called *contextual definitions* are a case in point. These definitions introduce a new term by providing definitions for certain expressions which contain the new term, but do not define the term by itself. It has already been seen that many terms in the vernacular and in the scientific languages are introduced and reinforced contextually. For example, if the term "extraverted" is to be confined to occurrences in expressions of the type "x is extraverted," then the contextual, nominal definition given above provides the means for eliminating that term from these particular contexts. Similarly the definition

> "x is more intelligent than y $=_{df}$ the intelligence quotient of x is numerically larger than the intelligence quotient of y"

introduces the relational concept "more intelligent than" for individuals. Thus in contextual definitions the expression to be defined may contain more than just the new term; it will often include logical connectives and other grammatical devices which have acquired invariant usage in other intraverbal situations.

Another use of nominal definitions might be called *event definition*. It does not represent a purely logical process operating entirely within the linguistic structure of scientific language; rather, event definitions facilitate the short-circuiting of cumbersome responses to external conditions. Events "out there" which are well discriminated but which have no "name" may thereby acquire such a name in place of a lengthy description in the basic vocabulary. The use of the term "cumulus" to describe a complex cloud formation is one such example. In psychology the following definitions might be used:

"VTE $=_{df}$ looking-back-and-forth behavior of an animal at a choice point."
"x is depressed $=_{df}$ the rate of speech of x is reduced from his usual rate."
"x dominates y $=_{df}$ x displaces y at the food tray."

It might be noted that in those cases where the definitional sentence eventually drops out, it can still be appealed to in questionable or borderline cases. Such eliminable definitions differ markedly from those procedures which relate a *theoretical construct* to a protocol sentence. A theoretical specification of "drive," for example, relates a term used in many different intraverbal (theoretical) contexts to a sentence which indicates its usage in the world of objects and events. This analysis separates lower-order (protocol) terms, which are elicited by external events, from higher-order (theoretical) terms, which are put into relation to these events by specific definitions.

Nominal definitions play an important role, particularly in the early stages of a science, by providing the means whereby new words can be introduced into the scientific language.

REAL DEFINITIONS

The class of real definitions contains several subclasses which present a variety of different problems in analysis. Hempel (1952, p. 6) has indicated their complex nature:

> A "real" definition, according to traditional logic, is not a stipulation determining the meaning of some expression but a statement of the "essential nature" or the "essential attributes" of some entity. The notion of essential nature, however, is so vague as to render this characterization useless for the purpose of rigorous enquiry. Yet it is often possible to reinterpret the quest for real definition in a manner which requires no reference to "essential nature" or "essential attributes," namely, as a search either for an empirical explanation of some phenomenon or for a meaning analysis.

The characteristics of these two types of real definitions, *empirical analysis* and *meaning analysis,* can be briefly sketched in the following way. An empirical analysis requires empirical evidence and empirical validation for the acceptability of the definitional sentence. A meaning analysis requires a "reflection upon the meanings of its constituent expressions" and no further empirical investigations to determine its applicability. The procedures involved in the two cases can best be demonstrated in the following example.

Hull, in *Principles of Behavior* (1943), defines "state of need" in the following manner:

> . . . when a condition arises for which action on the part of the organism is a prerequisite to optimum probability of survival of either the individual or the species, a state of need is said to exist.

This can be paraphrased to look like a nominal definition.

> "x is in a state of need $=_{df}$ action by x is a prerequisite to optimal probability of survival of either x or the species of which x is a member."

But this definition of need is not offered by Hull as a stipulation concerning the use of the term; rather it is phrased in such a way that it claims to be true. How can the truth or falsity of such a definition be determined?

In the case of a *meaning analysis,* the expression on the right-hand side might be considered to give the usual meaning of the term "state of need." This interpretation implies that the term has some definite use which is, at least intuitively, generally understood. Here the validation or determination of the acceptability of the definition only requires the user to say, "Yes, that is how I would use the term 'need.' " In this case, the expression would convey what Hull believed the use of the term to be. In brief, a meaning analysis describes those conditions, often expressed in the common language, which the user states to be fulfilled when he employs the term. It is most frequently used in the introduction of vague terms from the common language, the vagueness of which is often demonstrated by disagreements over the *proper* definition. The intuitive "meaning" does, of course, vary from user to user to the extent to which the vernacular does not prescribe invariant uses for the term.

An interpretation of Hull's statement in terms of an *empirical analysis* may state that the conditions of the right-hand expression are, as a matter of empirical fact, satisfied only when an organism is in a state of need. Such an interpretation requires empirical evidence that when an organism is in a state of need he will show these characteristics. Prior to such a determination, however, it must be established that the organism is in fact in a state of need. This argument is *not* circular; it only requires some independent identification of a state of need. Such an identification is, of course, empirically established by showing that another definitional sentence applies to the event in question. The empirical analysis, therefore, involves the relationship between two matters of fact, the prior identification of a state of need and the state of affairs indicated by the newly introduced "definition." Such a real definition then will be shown to be true or false to the extent that the relationship between the two empirical assertions can be demonstrated.

In distinguishing between meaning analysis and empirical analysis some cases might be encountered which are not easily put into one or the other of these two categories. In one respect an analysis of the two situations shows a distinct similarity. Both cases assert that the same verbal response is elicited under two different circumstances. In the case of the empirical analysis it is fairly clear that the two occasions are represented by two different sentences or assertions about the world of things and events. The definition implies a relationship between the two occasions which is a function of the theoretical connections among the two sentences and the term in question. Thus, this type of definition belongs to the area of theoretical assertions and predictions, and is empirically testable. In the case of the meaning analysis, it appears that what such a definition asserts is that a term (usually in the vernacular) which is commonly used by various investigators is actually being elicited by the occasions or events which the definition asserts. It attempts to restrict the conditions under which a vague term will be elicited to those stated in the definition, while at the same time trying to obtain agreement that these conditions are at least one such set that have in the past elicited that response. Obviously there will be borderline cases where a particular definition will deal with a term for which there are also available other definitions. In these instances the dividing line between a meaning analysis and an empirical analysis becomes fuzzy. Generally, however, it is possible to distinguish between these two major types of real definitions.[3]

---

[3] The notion of construct validity elucidated by Cronbach and Meehl (1955) is directly related to both types of analysis. It deals with the utility of a term as it is related to the network of statements, theoretical and empirical, in which it occurs. A practical application of this analysis to the concept of anxiety has been published by Jessor and Hammond (1957).

Some of the intricacies of real definitions can be further illustrated by introducing another definition of "need":

> . . . a *need* [is] defined as a regnant tension which is evoked by the perception (conscious or unconscious) of a certain kind of internal or external situation. (Murray, 1936, p. 256.)

Faced with two quite different definitions of need, we may ask to what extent we are dealing with definitions rather than with empirical statements, and what the relation is between two statements, whether they be definitional or empirical, which elicit the same verbal response.

It should be stressed here that by "definition" we refer solely to relationships between expressions within the scientific language, i.e., between words and the labeling of objects and events. Whenever empirical problems enter into the discussion, the resolution moves out of the area of the analysis of the language of science and into the area of the verification of scientific sentences.

The first argument that might be advanced concerning the two definitions of need is that both are intended to be nominal definitions. It could be said that both Hull and Murray introduced a new expression which, by stipulation, is defined by the sentences cited earlier. It is obvious that a scientific investigator may, apart from questions of convenience or of scientific courtesy, use any particular combination of letters and by stipulation make it synonymous with another expression. The argument would then run that the two writers only happened to use the letters NEED, and that they might just as well have used any other word or any other combination of the same letters, such as EDEN. The particular word they used would concern the reader no further. There would be no problem of either empirical or meaning analysis, no concern with relating the defining expressions to a state of paupery or a state of bliss. It will be assumed in this instance that this was not the case, that both Hull and Murray used the term "need" not as a convenient combination of letters but rather because other reasons dictated their choice of that particular word.[4]

Having eliminated the possibility that the two expressions are nom-

---

[4] Hull was particularly careful to introduce new terms which carry little vernacular usage with them. Definitions of $_{S}H_{R}$ and other Hullian constructs carry few vernacular intraverbal connections with them, except to the extent that such words as "habit" elicit old language behaviors from the common language. The responses elicited by "habit" in everyday discourse as well as the many different conditions under which it has been reinforced tend to interfere with the strict interpretation and usage which Hull wanted to assign to the term.

inal definitions, it might well be the case that the two sentences are empirical statements and make empirical assertions. Such sentences do not properly fall into the category of definitions, in the same way that "$f = ma$" is much more than a definition of "force." If they are empirical assertions they indicate necessary or sufficient conditions, or possibly both, for the observation of the "need" phenomenon. In that case they take on the form of general laws and make predictions about needs which presumably have other theoretical connections. Both Hull and Murray might say that if one were to observe or assume the presence of a need, one would also observe the conditions stated in the defining expression, and vice versa. These assertions can then be shown to be true or false, or to use a more acceptable formulation, they are subject to test. Such statements will be more extensively discussed in the section on theory; for the time being it will be assumed that the two statements are not empirical analyses.

Finally, the question of a meaning analysis can be considered. It might be argued that nominal definitions and meaning analyses fulfill analogous functions. The former introduces a "new" expression, while the latter is concerned with the definition of an expression which is already in use. The second condition certainly obtains in the case of the term "need."

To the extent then that both nominal definitions and meaning analyses deal with the synonymity of two verbal expressions (stipulated in one case and assumed in the other), they may be considered to fall into the area of definitional procedures, i.e., procedures *within* the scientific language. The decision as to the "correct" definition of need must be deferred for a while until the import of a meaning analysis has been examined. It will be argued that meaning analyses often represent low-order empirical statements.

Meaning Analysis and Theory

In the first place, expressions from the common language, which are those usually involved in a meaning analysis, fail to be accessible to a completely satisfactory treatment in the language of science. This simply repeats the previous argument that vernacular terms show both intra- and inter-subjective response variability. These disadvantages may accrue both to the term to be analyzed and to the expression defining it. However, there are some terms in the vernacular which show uniform uses. In that case a meaning analysis of a term consists of the characterization of these approximately uniform patterns of usage. It may be possible to take a term from the vernacular and to assert its synonymity with another expression in such a way that few if any other users of the term would argue that the defining expression is incomplete or inadequate. The definition then approaches the same form as a nominal definition, and to the extent that the defining expression is invariant, the definition might be taken into the scientific language as a quasi-stipulation for the use of the term.

Unfortunately, this state of affairs is rarely the case. Terms in the vernacular as in science function in a variety of contexts which elicit the term in question. These contextual relationships to other terms and sentences are rarely explicit in the common languages. Definitions and usage of a term within both the vernacular and the scientific language depend on many interrelationships within a larger framework—the network of theory. The vernacular sentences invoked might be part of a protopsychology, i.e., one concerned with the relationships among quasi-psychological terms. The cultural heritage of a language not only bequeaths word habits to the user, but also includes archaic generalizations and relationships. The terms of the language function within that archaic framework, which represents a basic theory, a grammatical relationship among the terms. It is within this protopsychology that terms from the vernacular, such as "need," function. It follows from this argument that vernacular terms and their definitions will tend to demonstrate the characteristics of weak theoretical relationships which are subject to empirical test. Few definitions of vernacular terms that fulfill the criterion for nominal definitions are likely to be available. Additional definitions for a particular term such as "need" can always be adduced. The adequacy of an analysis of these relationships and of the term analyzed will again rest upon the confirmability of the empirical and observational statements implied. The futility of such an empirical undertaking entirely within the common language has already been indicated.

Explication

Notwithstanding the preceding discussion, terms from the common language are often taken into scientific language systems. The process of rehabilitation of such terms, which is similar to a meaning analysis, has been called *explication.* Explication can proceed in two ways, empirically or logically.

Empirical explication takes place in the successive empirical uses of a vernacular term by the scientist under controlled conditions. The use of the term is refined and made invariant by restricting it to laboratory definitions, by excluding some vernacular intraverbal connections, and by introducing it into experimental procedures which are well defined in invariant basic terms and which restrict the surplus conditions that previously tended to elicit it. Some terms in personality and cognitive theory are presently undergoing this empirical refinement; experimental studies employing concepts such as "anxiety," "motive," "hypothesis," and "thought" attest to this development.

Logical explication, introduced by Carnap, is "concerned with expressions whose meaning in conversational language or even in scientific discourse is more or less vague and aims at giving those expressions a new and precisely determined meaning, so as to render them more suitable for clear and rigorous discourse on the subject matter at hand" (Hempel, 1952, p. 11). Such explication does not use successive empirical approximations, nor does it attempt to specify a commonly accepted vernacular definition for the term. Rather it provides precise, invariant, and often new definitions for a term already in common or scientific use. The particular choice of the defining expression will depend on a variety of factors. It will have nominal aspects in that the explicator wants to fix an invariant use for the term, to be strictly stipulated for future occasions. Empirical analysis is involved to the extent that any explication should fit into known or predicted empirical relationships. Finally, aspects of meaning analysis will enter into the picture whenever the scientist wants to take advantage of established usages of the term.

In practice it is probably explication, both empirical and logical, which best describes the activity of the scientist as he refines terms from the common language. Such activity aims at the elimination of ambiguities and variabilities, as well as strengthening the predictive and theoretical power of the whole system within which the term is to operate.

It is within this general area of endeavor that the two definitions of "need" probably fall. It is likely that both Hull and Murray intended these definitions either to be subject to further empirical refinement or to be conceived as specific stipulated analyses of these vernacular terms, newly incorporated into a general theoretical framework.

First approximations of scientific statements, such as the two uses of "need," are employed until they must be refined. New explications are introduced, new definitions attempted. Kierkegaard and Freud both used the term "anxiety," but it was Freud who saw the need to change his use of the concept. Kierkegaard was content to describe a private phenomenon applicable to all men. Whether or not his formulations may be used as a source for psychological hypotheses, his interest was not in such a starting point for future refinement; he did not try to give first approximations. It is the particular mark of the scientific investigator that his uses of a term, and of a language, are likely to be only stepping stones for future developments. He may passionately believe in the propriety of his approach and his terms, but his defense must be empirical, not verbal.

Two fairly commonly used methods for developing construct precision in psychology—observer judgments and factor analysis—will serve to illustrate the working of explication.

For the judgmental approach we can examine an experimental situation in which it is predicted that a procedure such as failure stress will result in the evocation of anxious behavior in a group of subjects. The definition of anxiety states tends to be rather vague, but for the present purposes it might be said that they include signs of restlessness in the subjects, inappropriate comments, and a variety of other symptoms. The experimenter rates the subjects and finds that, as compared with a control group, they show an increase in these symptoms. However, since the unreliability of these symptoms has been found to be rather high and an observer's report tends to be unreliable when certain response expectations are set up by him in advance, it is decided to have the subjects rated independently by an observer unacquainted with the experimental treatment.

The question arises why independent observers are used in this situation and not when measuring the running speed of a rat, the response latency of a human subject, or the response rate of a pigeon. Two answers can be made: First, in many of these cases graphic records of the subject's responses are available which provide a high degree of invariance for protocol statements, and second, even without graphic records it is not generally expected that observer bias will enter into protocol statements involving such simple operations. While these justifications do admit of exceptions, there is no good reason to believe that there are major sources of error in the response of the observer. For terms such as "restlessness" or "inappropriateness" no such invariance of usage has been established. This is not to say that it could not be established; the training of raters of Thematic Apperception Test stories, who after several weeks of training can show high degrees of intersubjective concordance, attests to this possibility. The difficulty is often one of communication. Much training of raters is carried on at a nonverbalized level and rating manuals are often not too successful. The training of raters often proceeds by reinforcing verbal behaviors without mediating definitions. In the long run, more and more of these rules are verbalized and the communication of rating procedures becomes possible.

Ratings of restlessness and other symptoms proceed on a similar level. The goal of communication is achieved when the rules for the reinforcement or self-reinforcement of certain protocol statements can be transmitted from observer to observer. Given a high degree of agreement between two raters on the basis of oral or written communication, it can be stated that a fairly invariant use of the defining characteristics has been established. In this case the degree of invariance can be described statistically by means of correlational techniques.

The factor-analytic technique can also be helpful in the empirical explication of a construct. While this goal is not often explicitly stated, it is one of the results of many factor-analytic studies. Various behavioral indices of the "same" concept form the initial correlational matrix. The indices may be obtained from theoretical considerations or based on different interpretations of the same term used by various investigators. In the latter case the method relates various explicatory procedures to one another. If the factor analysis of the various measures results in a single factor with high loadings for all the symptoms, such evidence would confirm a theoretical statement which postulated that various behaviors are all related to one central term within the theory. When the tests are derived from various investigators, it indicates a high degree of empirical agreement of usage of the construct, which in turn can be used for predictive purposes. As it happens, the finding of a single factor or simple structure is rare; the contrary finding indicates that the use of a single term for the various behaviors is inappropriate and that some theoretical changes must be made in order to take this empirical discrepancy into account.

In most attempts at factor-analytic explication it is implicitly assumed that the various indices of a particular construct have some theoretical connections, either scientific or vernacular, such that they will show close relationships with one another. In fact, factor-analytic investigators usually tend to name factors with the term most frequently used for the tests which show the highest loading on that factor. Such "naming" often hides higher-order theoretical premises containing the term in question, be it "general intelligence," "emotionality," or "rigidity." [5]

DEFINITIONS IN USE

What is the advantage to the practicing scientist of making various definitional approaches explicit? In the first place it should serve as a demurral against the misguided nominalism of some psychologists. During the past decades much defining and redefining has been attempted in the name of the new methodology. An implicit belief has emerged that terms can easily be purged of imprecision by giving them precise definitions, usually in the form of nominal definitions. While such procedures may avoid some initial misunderstandings, they provide few advantages in the long run. To give a term in use (either in the common or the scientific language) a nominal definition imposes on the definer the stipulative restrictions of such a definition. Either the relations between the term and other terms which have been established prior to the new definition must be abandoned or their empirical relationship to the defining expression must be made explicit. Thus to define the concept of "anxiety" as a score on a questionnaire has been considered "methodologically sound," but it abandons the theoretical surplus—the surplus of uses—which a term such as "anxiety" carries with it. Such an approach of nominal purism would apply with equal force to the use of the term "chocolate soda" in describing scores on the same questionnaire. In both cases, the defense for the use of the particular word would be that the definer simply *decided* to use that word, and he would implicitly deny any relationships to other terms or sentences. A more rational approach might describe why the investigator wanted to call scores on this particular questionnaire anxiety scores, and what the relationship might be, both implicit and explicit, between the items of the particular questionnaire and the concept of anxiety as it operates within a particular theory.

Some reflection on the use of definitions might also provide a more fruitful answer to the challenge flung in so many psychological talkfests: "Define your terms!" The reply might well be: "Define how?" The case of nominal definitions, when a new term is introduced, offers

---

[5] These methods are also related to another approach to the problem of concept formation in a developing science, one which makes use of "indicators" and "references" of constructs (Kaplan, 1946).

no problems, but should be restricted to terms that carry no surplus relationships with them. In other instances the reply may involve a meaning analysis which demonstrates how the term operates within the vernacular system. It might then be possible to say that the term in question is to be used in the context of some communicable common-sense theory, hypothesis, or hunch. Finally, the challenger may have to be offered a complex explication of the relationship between the term and various theoretical sentences on the one hand, and empirical assertions on the other. Attempts at simple definition statable in a word or two run afoul of the fact that we are dealing with the validity of general laws and of generalizations rather than with the cavalier substitutions of words. Frequently, we must be satisfied with partial definitions, reconstructions, and approximations, or use explications which might be unsatisfactory to fellow scientists. Satisfactory answers to a request for definition are not likely to be found easily. This tends to be less the case in the more developed fields of psychology such as animal and human learning, which depend to a large extent on physicalistic variables, and more so in the newer fields of personality investigations, which depend to a large extent on the response to complex human behavior. But the wheels of science and of invariant usage grind slowly and the process of successive approximations appears to be the best that can be expected.

SUMMARY

Definitions play a ubiquitous role in any developing field of knowledge; they are given the major burden of introducing new terms and of purifying the old ones. It may well be the mark of maturity for a science that it can dispense with intricate questions of definition because its terms are invariant in response to events and within laws and theoretical sentences. Until that great time arrives, psychology must concern itself with definitions, redefinitions, and other linguistic crutches.

Nominal definitions provide the easiest and neatest road to the invariant use of terms. They introduce new terms by the stipulation or agreement that a particular verbal response is henceforth to be regarded as synonymous with some defining sentence. This escape route is, however, only rarely available to the working psychologist. He is burdened with terms from vernacular protopsychology and from other more-or-less useful systems. In the context of this inheritance, the question of real definitions, of specifying the correct or essential meaning of a term, must often be dealt with. We have seen that this process of definition, whether it be an empirical analysis or a meaning analysis, leads most frequently to questions of the empirical validity of sentences and sentence systems. In the long run, the definitional labors of most psychologists are concerned with the specific explication, both within the language and in reference to empirical events, of the use of their terms. To define one's terms requires more than verbal facility; it invokes much of our knowledge about the world of words and events.

chapter six

Sources of psychological terms: III. Operations and reductions

DEFINITION HAS PROVED TO BE NOT ONLY A method for specifying the "meaning" of a term but also frequently a way of stating conditions for its acquisition. Scientific languages, however, are not static; they need new words. Such growth properly belongs in the realm of theory construction, which will be considered in Part II. However, two general wellsprings of new scientific terms may be distinguished here. One source lies in the procedures of theory construction, in hunches and hypothesis formation. The second general class of constructs developed within science contains those words which are introduced to name previously undiscriminated events or relationships. They are most often used when a developing science is faced with empirical roadblocks, when new relationships must be introduced in order to provide the scientist with a coherent picture of his event world. The term "cumulus" in meteorology belongs in this category, as do psychological terms such as "operant behavior," "color response on the Rorschach," and so forth. Many of these terms may be elicited directly by events external to the observer, and may achieve a high degree of response invariance. They are usually introduced in order to facilitate verbal generalizations, and to order events into classes, which then enter into more general statements.

A distinction between these two classes of terms, those arising primarily out of theoretical creation and those stemming mainly from empirical problems (i.e., new event discriminations), does not imply a strict bifurcation. Theoretically introduced constructs are often necessitated by empirical problems, while the low-level empirical construct often has its sources in implicit theorizing. The two types differ only in emphasis. The introduction of new terms close to the level of protocol statements in the basic language will be our concern in the following pages.

The invariably messy business of trying to achieve communality of meaning by pulling ourselves up by our bootstraps has led psychologists to seek the panaceas of ready-made solutions and prescriptions for the definition and introduction of new terms. These solutions often are sought in order to bypass the painstaking process of successive approximation, or to rehabilitate old terms which have acquired an aura of unrespectability by meaning all things to all men.

One of these approaches has been graced with the name of a movement in the philosophy of science, that of *operationism*. Another, which grows out of the logical analysis of disposition terms, has led to the development of *reduction sentences*.[1] Curiously enough neither arises out of the body of psychological writing or investigation, but rather from problems in physical theory in one case and from the logical analysis of language in the other. Both approaches may provide the psychologist with guideposts for the development and use of constructs. A blind application of such remedies, however, glosses over specific problems facing a developing field of knowledge. Much more than for the older sciences, the philosophy of science in psychology cannot treat the field as a closed system, but should contribute to its attempt at growth.

OPERATIONAL DEFINITIONS

The purpose of the *operational definition* is to specify the rules which govern the use of particular terms. Many terms in both common and scientific languages are defined or introduced by reference to the particular operations that are associated with their use. For

[1] Reduction sentences represent our second use of the word "reduction." This application of the word should be clearly understood as different from the reduction of science to the thing-language.

example, there is a children's book entitled *A Hole Is to Dig* (Krauss, 1952), the purpose of which is to illustrate words and their uses to the newly verbal child. It presents the word "hole" by pointing out that "hole" is the word to be applied to the result of digging operations. Children tend to define new words in terms of experiences and actions which accompany their occurrence. The budding science may introduce some of its terms in a similar fashion, or it may discover after the fact that this is a good way of looking at its words.

The use of the operational approach by the learning child suggests that there may be archaic reasons for its utility. Operationism is not something brand new but is the specification of an old system of using words. This system represents a major aspect of verbal behavior which has only been touched upon: Verbal behavior may elicit nonverbal behavior. To say to a woman "Your slip is showing" is a surefire method of eliciting a specific behavior sequence which has previously been reinforced. Action will usually follow "You have jam all over your face" and "Go to your room!" A brief reflection upon these and similar instances demonstrates the pervasiveness of this kind of behavior.

The operational definition depends on this type of relationship between verbal and nonverbal behavior. *The use of a term is specified by a set of operations.* To communicate the "meaning" of a term, the scientist need only state these operations, which are usually measurements, in invariant verbal terms; the resulting nonverbal behavior establishes the conditions for the use of the term and insures interscientist reliability.

Needless to say, any verbal behavior which elicits some nonverbal behavior may result in a different state of the physical universe than that obtaining prior to the sequence. To tell somebody "Dig here" usually results in a state of the universe which is called "a hole." Similarly, verbal behavior dealing with jam-all-over-the-face sometimes results in the state of the universe called "a clean face."

In a relatively unimportant sense scientists use names of operational behaviors to describe the general physical, manipulative conditions of an experiment; the scientist does in fact tell his colleague who may wish to repeat a phenomenon: "First do this, then that, and so forth." This use of verbal behavior requires that the descriptions of research procedures serve as adequate instructions for replication. The behavior which preceded the statement "I presented the subject with Rorschach Card No. 1 after giving him the usual instructions" must be the same as the behavior which it elicits in the replicating scientist.

Similar equivalences exist in respect to the handling of animals, presentations of stimuli in a memory drum, and so forth.

The more important function of operational behavior is that it results in changed states of objects, event sequences, or discriminations. It is this type of operationism which will primarily concern us here. The manipulating scientist frequently creates conditions that are not usually found in his environment; they are not "vernacular" events. The specification of an event, or even an object, in terms of the conditions which produce it is a very useful way to achieve invariant usage. Thus, "Give the food-deprived rat a pellet" may define "reinforcement." Nothing need be said about the characteristics of the resulting state so long as the operations which produce it can be elicited in a regular fashion from all members of the scientific community to whom the verbal instructions are addressed. The resulting states may, of course, in turn elicit naming behaviors as in the case of the child's "hole," and it will be expedient to use sometimes one, sometimes the other of these methods (the operational or naming responses) for particular situations. "Table" is more easily named; "length" is more easily operationally defined. Psychological constructs such as "frustration" or "drive" may be defined in terms of appropriate nonverbal behavior elicited by verbal instructions such as "Block the animal's path 10 inches in front of the goal box" or "Deprive the animal of food for 24 hours."

Among scientists, it was Bridgman who first specifically apprised physicists that "a length is to measure," and that "length" is the word to be applied as a result of measuring operations. In addition he made the point that the definition of "length" will vary with the variations in behavior which "to measure" elicits in diverse situations. Bridgman's *The Logic of Modern Physics* (1927) created a stir which found its greatest reverberation in the behavioral sciences, culminating in 1945 in a special issue of the *Psychological Review* devoted to operationism. The speed with which psychologists adopted the operational analysis of their concepts is demonstrated by Skinner's use of the approach in an analysis of the reflex in 1931.

What did Bridgman say that had such a pervasive appeal for psychologists, an appeal so strong that the term "operational definition" has become a household word for psychologists while it has remained of only esoteric interest to the working physicist?

Bridgman's basic thesis is that *a concept is synonymous with the corresponding set of operations.* At first glance this sentence seems to demand that the concept be nominally defined, with the defining expressions containing the set of operations associated with the term. While an operational definition may have the logical status of a nominal definition, the operational approach does not claim to introduce terms by convention or stipulation. An operational analysis asserts that constructs can best be understood in terms of the manipulations and operations of the scientist at work.

Operations which define a term must be a *unique* set of operations. Any change in them changes the definition or the meaning of the term. It is explicitly the experimental situation which specifies the defining operations. In his initial argument for the operational distinction between concepts, Bridgman pointed out that the operations involved in measuring the length of a stationary object differ from those involved in measuring a moving object, which in turn differ from the measurement operations applied to bodies of very high velocities such as cathode particles. Bridgman says that in changing the operations "we have really changed the concept," and the same name continues to be used for different concepts only for "considerations of convenience" (Bridgman, 1927). But "convenience" is surely too weak a term to be applied to the use of the same term in two different situations. These "conveniences" arise out of theoretical considerations which describe the relationships between the two concepts of length.

The extension of the same term to different conditions neither violates the assumption of a *unique* definition of a concept, nor is it just a matter of convenience. Such an extension indicates a communality between $length_1$ and $length_2$ at a higher level, i.e., in theoretical contexts. The operational extension of a theoretical term is similar to the partial definition to be discussed shortly. In psychological usage, it might indicate that a construct such as "drive," behaving more or less invariantly in theoretical contexts, may be defined in several ways, e.g.:

$Drive_1$: Hours of deprivation.
$Drive_2$: Blood sugar level.
$Drive_3$: Amount of consummatory behavior.

The operations involved in these different ways of defining "drive" are radically different, and therefore require the different subscripts. They *all* define "drive" because of theoretical notions about the way in which drive functions and what conditions may elicit or measure it.

The very concept of length, which Bridgman used to illustrate the operational approach, indicates the highly developed nature of the terms to which an operational analysis may be applied. "Length" is no common-sense term, no vague borderline notion in need of refinement. Developments in the theory of relativity showed that the concept of length has at least two defining operations, and the position of these defining operations within the theory—the conditions under which the two lengths operate—indicated that a unitary construct no longer sufficed. Compare this situation with some of the terms in psychology for which operational analysis has been prescribed. It becomes obvious that we are dealing with words which differ markedly in their *preoperational* status. For example, the term "intelligence" has repeatedly been "cleaned up" or made rigorous for scientific discourse. Psychologists started with a word that had a long and highly variable vernacular history; it enters into few theoretical generalizations in psychology and has few agreed-upon observational referents. Yet the great operational intervention has attempted to make it scientific by saying, too often nonfacetiously, that "intelligence is what the intelligence tests measure." Such a definition purges the term of most scientific utility. No directions are given about the relationship between it and other terms, and even operational definitions of the term "intelligence tests" are lacking. Such an operational analysis of a vague, prescientific concept provides psychology with little more than self-satisfied smugness. When it is applied to well-elaborated and empirically well-developed constructs, an operational analysis may provide useful guides to communication and invariance.

Another instance of the way in which operational definitions introduce theoretical issues has emerged from the literature on child development. The question that is posed concerns the relationship between child-rearing practices such as weaning and toilet training and personality characteristics at a later age. The operations required for such a study seem to be obvious; observe the child-rearing practices to which a group of individuals are exposed and several years later measure the predicted personality characteristics. However, in order to reduce the length of such a research project some investigators have used a short-cut which is simple and time saving. Both kinds of data are collected at the same point in time, the child-rearing data from the parent, the personality data from the children. Leaving aside the theoretical issues involved in accepting parental report of events long past, this is a situation where Bridgman's dicta might well have been heeded. There are two ways of obtaining information about child-rearing practices, two distinct sets of operations—one based on observation, the other based on parental report or, child rearing$_1$ and child rearing$_2$. Until the relationship between the two constructs has been theoretically and empirically explicated they must be kept distinct.

In contrast the two concepts of length (length$_1$ and length$_2$) are exhaustively linked in physical theory where "the transformation formulas of relativity give the precise connection between the two lengths" (Bridgman, 1927). The psychological operationist is far removed from such formulas. To overlook this requirement may result in the assertion that *any* operational definition of child-rearing or any other term is all right as long as it is operational. The problem is similar to the facile use of nominal definitions discussed in the last chapter. When a term appears in a system of theoretical sentences, they *must* be taken into account when it is defined, nominally *or* operationally.

Unfortunately, it is neither particularly scientific nor useful to adopt a word and to define it in terms of some set of operations. This *alone* is obviously possible in the most tender-minded investigation; it is a trivial bow in the direction of scientific respectability and satisfies only the most primitive notions of scientific communication.[2] However, the use of a term which is *already* functioning in a scientific framework imposes certain limitations on the investigator, and this imposition tends to be a function of the historical and theoretical use of the term. When a new set of operations is employed for a particular term, its definition is extended. At this point an operational analysis will be helpful in specifying new areas of application and new grammatical relationships. The relationship between the two uses of the term can and must be empirically described, if the scientist still wishes the two terms to be considered within a general class of "lengths" or "child-rearings."

The problem of different operations used for the same construct, a procedure which in the operational approach creates different members of the same class of terms, can also be raised for that class of instances where no different operations are intended. Because of the impossibility of exact replication of any event or set of operations it might be argued that a strict application of operational principles breeds particularism, an endless multiplication of terms. Stevens has adequately answered this criticism in pointing out that "the process

[2] Bergmann (1944, p. 143) has pointed out that "a person's weight multiplied by the number of his hairs and divided by the third power of his blood count is a correctly defined empirical construct, and still one can safely predict that it will never receive any attention in science."

of generalization proceeds on the basis of the notion of classes" (Stevens, 1939). The question whether different operations define the same term or introduce new ones can be decided by examining the collection of operations which are supposed to define the term. The question of class membership can be settled either by enumeration or by any of the previously discussed methods of generic extension. Many different motor behaviors may all elicit the response "measuring distance with a ruler," but the fact that they all have a common result establishes them as members of a single class of operations. Similarly the "deprivation" class contains all instances of "not allowing an animal to eat or drink or copulate for a specified period of time."

Stevens argues that class membership is dependent upon the "fundamental operation" of discrimination. When "crucial" differences can be discriminated between an instance A and other already determined instances which are designated as members of class X, then A can be rejected as not belonging to class X. Larger classes can be formed by the combination of two or more sets of previously discrete operations.[3] Of course, the determination of "crucial" differences and the formation of new classes must perforce be made by the investigator, and therefore demand the ingenuity and inventiveness which form part of the theoretical endeavor of the scientist. Crucial operations or suggestions for new and larger classes of defining operations are not fortuitously found. The history of science, strewn with the remains of useless discriminations and worthless classes, attests to the intricacy of this particular task.

OPERATIONS AND RESPONSE INVARIANCE

The communication of measuring operations in terms which are already invariant—and usually physicalistic—is an extremely efficient way of achieving intersubjective invariance. The language of "operations" provides another set of terms for a basic vocabulary of science. This does not detract from the operational credo; rather it puts it into perspective with other approaches to the problem of fundamental languages. Simple instructions, directions as to "what to do," are usually phrased either in highly invariant terms of the older sciences,

---

[3] Discrimination in Stevens' sense can, of course, be translated into the framework of response elicitation. The "crucial" differences would refer to the presence or absence of specific responses.

in physical or geometric language, or introduce vernacular terms which are also invariant, such as "First do A, then do B" or "Say to the subject."

Classification of the operational vocabulary as a set of basic terms affords an insight into a problem which has plagued operationists, namely the distinction between physical and mental operations. Many terms are introduced and used quite legitimately by way of operations involving "paper and pencil" procedures. The latter are usually preceded by mental "operations," by the cogitations, generalizations, images, and computations of the scientist. The question arose whether the latter should be admitted into the arsenal of the operationist, thus including both physical and mental operations. The fascination with operationism seduced psychologists into making everything "operational." Eventually "at the one extreme, the scientist's perceptions were decked out to be a species of operations; at the other, his verbal and computational activities were as so-called symbolic operations herded into the same corral" (Bergmann, 1954).

But what are "mental" operations? How can they be described and put into language? Is the number 4 to be defined in terms of the "mental" operation: "$2 + 2$"? Is adding really just a mental operation? It should be obvious by now that private events, mental operations or not, cannot be adequately named in the language of science. Our discussion of phenomenology is directly relevant to this point. To define a term operationally by stating the private conditions for its use is just as impossible as the admission of any term which is controlled by events not publicly available. However, if "private" events have public corollaries such as the operations of mathematics, they are implicitly admissible through the acceptability of the public events. Thus, if need be, "adding" is publicly available—it is certainly taught under conditions of external control of stimuli and reinforcements. Similarly, other private operations may be accepted by analogy if public events determine the usage and elicitation of imaginal, computational, or symbolic processes. In the long run it might even be possible to teach a person invariant usage to events which are now private. Private operations may be made public by a future psychology; the internal stimulus events may be externalized and then responses to autonomic and possibly even cortical events might be taught efficiently. Such an achievement belongs to the province of the psychology of language. Once it has been accomplished it might be very useful to the language of psychology.

Bridgman attempted to resolve the question of mental operations by saying that it was desirable for the scientists' paper-and-pencil operations to make eventual contact, possibly indirectly, with instrumental operations. He amplifies "indirect contact" by appealing to links through theoretical generalizations (such as "the equations of elasticity theory") which would eventually bring theoretical paper-and-pencil terms and operations into contact with the operations of the laboratory. Such an amended operationism states that a concept which does not have direct operational criteria may attain these through theoretical relationships with instrumental (observation) terms. In that case the operational meaning of a term is conceived as residing in these low-level operations. This is a restatement of the reductionist position discussed in Chapter 1. Complex higher-order terms should be reducible to more primitive, basic operations. This version must be rejected on grounds similar to those used against the earlier position, primarily because theoretical terms depend on many complex relations for their usage and cannot be exhaustively reduced to observables.

One last word regarding the operational analysis. That it is not a complete system in the philosophy of science has been frequently shown in the philosophical literature. It is neither the only road to scientific purity nor the specific nostrum for an undeveloped science such as psychology. It is one useful method for the clarification of low-level constructs and must share its role with other contributions to the basic vocabulary of invariant terms in science. It is particularly helpful when terminological differences can be demonstrated to reside in differences in manipulations or operations. In some cases the operational method may be preferable to an analysis in terms of the thing-language; in other cases the order of preference might be reversed, or a third approach might prove to be more useful. *Any* attempt to increase precision of usage contributes to the analysis and the development of the scientific vocabulary.

REDUCTION SENTENCES

Definition in terms of operations can be extended to the general case: the definition of a term by the conditions which elicit it. These can generally be classed into two groups; namely, *antecedent* conditions which specify experimental conditions, and *consequent* conditions which occur subsequent to the introduction of an experimental variable, or which specify the behavior of the organism. An analysis in terms of antecedent and consequent conditions results in the so-called *reduction sentence* (Carnap, 1936, 1937).

Hempel describes the reduction sentence, and its relation to the operational approach, as follows:

> . . . an operational definition of the simplest kind stipulates that the concept it introduces, say *C*, is to apply to those and only those cases which, under specified test conditions *S*, show a certain characteristic response *R*. In Carnap's treatment . . . : If a case *x* satisfies the condition *S*, then *x* is an instance of *C* if and only if *x* shows the response *R*. [This formula] . . . is not a full definition; . . . it specifies the meaning of [*C*] not for all cases, but only for those that satisfy the condition *S*. (Hempel, 1954, pp. 217–218.)

The case of disposition terms fits neatly into this formulation. These terms describe the disposition of an object or organism to display a certain characteristic or response under certain given conditions of stimulation. In psychology they include such terms as "aggressive," "hungry," "anxious," and so forth. The general verbal form of such a reduction sentence might run like this for *one* definition of the term "hungry":

> "If x is presented with food then x is hungry if and only if x eats the food." [4]

This sentence specifies the use of the term "hungry" only for those cases where the antecedent conditions of food presentation apply. Whenever they do not apply the sentence is meaningless or not applicable. Similarly, the sentence is false, i.e., the term cannot be used, when the consequent eating conditions are not present.

One of the immediate advantages of reduction sentences is that each one provides only one of many possible definitions for the concept *C*. The same term can be introduced for any other combination of *S* and *R* terms or sentences. Take the following additional definition of the term "hungry":

---

[4] The logical notation of a reduction sentence is "$S \supset (C \equiv R)$." Whenever *S* is true of all cases it reduces to a simple nominal definition "$C \equiv R$." It is false only in those cases where *S* is true and *R* false, which is the exact case where we would want to note the absence of a disposition. The reduction sentence also avoids the problem of material implication when the definition is put in the form "$C =_{df} S \supset R$." In that form *C* would apply even if *S* is false. See Hempel (1952) for a detailed discussion of this problem.

"If x has a low blood sugar level, then x is hungry if and only if x shows an increased activity level." [5]

The only restriction for the use of the same term in more than one reduction sentence is an *empirical* one. Thus it must not be the case that the two response terms (call them R_1 and R_2) are incompatible. The two sentences imply that R_1 and R_2 covary—that whenever an animal eats, his activity level will also be increased. Obviously, the particular series, or chain, of reduction sentences which is introduced depends on the investigator's hypotheses or hunches. Furthermore, these sentences are far removed from a linguistic convention; they are related to empirical matters of fact. In the example used, the two reduction sentences combine to form the following empirical statement, which does not use the term "hungry" at all:

"Whenever x is presented with food and has a low blood sugar level, x will eat the food if and only if his activity level increases." [6]

What are the specific advantages of reduction sentences? First, they avoid the logical problems introduced by other forms (see footnote, p. 115). Second, they provide a formalization of the operational requirements. The operations to be performed and measurements to be obtained are presented in the particular basic language which happens to be chosen. By using several reduction sentences, the same term may be introduced for different operations. This method specifies the class of operations or observations for which the term holds. Third, the use of reduction sentences does not restrict further expansion of the concept; it is not restricted to one particular nominal definition. Correlated features can be viewed as symptoms of one and the same abstract, nonobservable construct. This openness of definition gives a sounder account of the function of terms in science than an exhaustive definition, such as would be found in strict nominalism or operationism. Finally, the form of the reduction sentence illustrates rather nicely the use of the invariant parts of the protocol language, which are specifically introduced as conditions under which a new or more complex term is to be used.

The partial definition of terms is of special utility for a developing

---

[5] In none of the examples given are we concerned with the empirical validity or usefulness of the definitions.

[6] In symbolic notation:

$$\text{“}S_1 \cdot S_2 \supset (R_1 \equiv R_2).\text{”}$$

science. A new term can be introduced by one reduction sentence. Its scope can be extended by adding more such sentences, and conversely, these can be dropped if found to be empirically useless. Such multiple definition procedures are particularly suited for complex theoretical notions. Terms in the basic vocabulary do not display this multiple relationship to a variety of different operations or conditions. The disposition term "anxious" is a good example of a construct which can be elucidated by reduction sentences. Incidentally, we are here specifically dealing with the permissible interindividual use of this term and not with a name for private events, though an attempt can be made to bring the latter into the purview of science.

The expression "x is anxious" may be introduced by several different reduction sentences. Some of these, among many others, are:

"If x is told that he will be given an electric shock, then x is anxious if and only if his skin resistance drops 1,000 ohms or more."
"If x is given an anxiety questionnaire, then x is anxious if and only if his score falls in the upper 20 per cent of the distribution."
"If x is told he will be given an electric shock, then x is anxious if and only if he says 'I am anxious.' "
"If x is told by his therapist that he really hated his mother, then x is anxious if and only if the content of his associations changes."

These examples are deliberately oversimplified to indicate some of the crude ways by which various behaviors may be brought to bear on the same problem. In actual usage, the reduction sentences (particularly for the last two examples) will be much more complex.

These sentences should fulfill the empirical requirement which has been stated for chains of reduction sentences, i.e., the compatibility of the consequent conditions. Given the appropriate stimulus conditions, the following should be true:

x's skin resistance drops if and only if x says "I am anxious," and
x's associations change if and only if his score on the anxiety scale is high,
and so forth.

To the extent that these assertions are not the case, we may conclude that all is not well in the world of anxiety. However, there is no need for panic. What has happened is that the same term, derived from both vernacular and theoretical statements, is used differently by different investigators. The empirical implications of their various reduction sentences often help to illuminate this situation. Once again, however, we note that the *use* of the same word does not insure its empirical or theoretical applicability in diverse situations. In the present case the term "anxious" is variously used to describe transient or permanent states of the organism, as well as physiological or verbal responses.

Some writers have counseled against the analysis of constructs in terms of reduction sentences. The first reservation stems from the desire to bring all problems of meaningfulness and testability within the province of logical analysis. Philosophers of science have traditionally attempted to analyze and explicate problems in the language of science as problems in logic. Such an analysis stipulates basic terms, such as those of the thing-language, and conducts all further enquiry entirely within the framework of the rules and uses of symbolic logic. A purely logical analysis is not feasible for reduction sentences. This particular method for the introduction of terms and sentences not only involves logical operations, but also appeals to questions of empirical fact. Whenever a particular covariance of response factors, or an antecedent-consequent relationship, does not hold, such evidence is relevant to the use of the term within the language. Logical analysis alone will not cover these exigencies. Similarly, the argument for the use of reduction sentences rests partly on the partial and incomplete nature of the constructs introduced. Such a process is of advantage to the growing edge of knowledge, and it avoids the static nature of nominal definitions. But this state of affairs is not conducive to a logical analysis, which requires stable terms, usually introduced nominally. The shifting sands of reduction sentences may vitiate a rigorously logical analysis of the scientific language. However, to the extent that nominal definitions also change in the course of time, the same disability is encountered in their use.

Bergmann (1954) has argued that whatever the advantage of partial definitions, they must be rejected because they preclude a purely *logical* analysis of scientific procedures; the problem of the growth of knowledge is the task of the behavioral scientist not of the logician. This viewpoint appears to make an unnecessarily rigid distinction between logical and psychological problems in theory construction and concept formation. Granted that the *process* whereby knowledge is increased is an empirical psychological problem and that the analysis of the status of a concept is primarily a logical task, it still need not be the case that a logical analysis must be limited to an interest in what has already been achieved. The logical analysis might well concern itself with the status of terms which do in fact continually change in meaning and definition. Two questions should be distinguished; one is how a change is brought about, and the other concerns the conditions under which a definition makes it possible to enlarge the meaning of a term. Reduction sentences provide the latter possibility; they say nothing about the process of scientific discovery or growth.

A second argument of Bergmann's is that the definitional aspect and the theoretical significance of a concept should be kept separate, that "the significance of a concept . . . reflects itself, not in its definition, but in the laws in which it occurs" (Bergmann, 1954). While agreeing with the latter point, we have questioned the possibility of ever completely separating the definitional from the theoretical functions of a term. It must be emphasized that a reduction sentence is not only a partial *definition* to the extent that some indicators or conditions are specified, but that it is also a theoretical sentence and functions within the larger body of language.[7]

Finally, the use of reduction sentences differs from the notions introduced in connection with operational or physicalistic languages in that they suggest one way of expanding the language of science without

---

[7] The usefulness of reduction sentences in the early stages of scientific enquiry has also been pointed out indirectly by Marx (1951). Without reference to reduction sentences per se, Marx suggests that a so-called E/C intervening variable might be useful in the "exploratory phases of scientific theory construction." He suggests that these constructs be defined in terms of differences in stimulus and response observation between an experimental (E) and a control (C) group. Such an approach, which defines constructs in terms of the antecedent and consequent conditions of the experiment, allows the experimenter "to draw upon the suggestions of a theoretical model and yet remain on a strictly operational level of discourse." This method might specify stimulus conditions S_1 which are identical for the two groups, as well as other stimulus conditions such as S_e and S_c (or $\sim S_e$) which differ for the two groups and introduce the manipulated variables. Two sets of response conditions, R_e and R_c (or $\sim R_e$), are expected to indicate response differences between the two groups under the respective stimulus conditions. In logical form these two sets of conditions can be represented in a so-called reduction pair:

Experimental condition: $S_e \cdot S_1 \supset (R_e \supset C)$

Control condition: $S_c \cdot S_1 \supset (R_c \supset \sim C)$

In other words, given the experimental stimulus condition, then the term C is considered applicable if the response R_e is made. In the control condition the term is *not* applicable if any other response (such as R_c) occurs. Similar applications of this paradigm demonstrate that the practicing investigator does, in fact, use some implicit logical notions in order to determine the applicability or non-applicability of a particular construct.

making any commitment as to the basic terms to be used in that language. What vocabulary is to be used in the description of the antecedent and consequent conditions of a reduction sentence or a chain of reduction sentences is entirely up to the particular investigator making use of this way of introducing a term.

SUMMARY

The previous chapter dealt with the definition of terms which name psychological events. The present chapter has been largely concerned with the introduction of terms into psychological science by the specification of the operations and conditions for their use. We noted that the communication function of language is often expressed in the elicitation of nonverbal operations. The invariant naming of nonverbal behavior was seen to be one of the attractions of operational definitions. While operationism is not an ultimate panacea for the ills of scientific usage, it is an important contribution to the rules of the basic vocabulary. It is most useful in the specification of alternative definitions of a theoretically stable term—a condition rarely found in psychology. In addition, it frequently provides a more appropriate way of term specification than the simple naming procedure.

In the more general case of the specification of conditions—the reduction sentences—questions of validity of empirical or theoretical assertions intrude even more frequently than in the use of operational definitions. In this connection we stressed the utility of partial reduction sentences in a fluid field of knowledge where few stable laws or relationships have been developed and where constructs must continuously undergo readjustments.

chapter seven

The vocabulary of psychology: Review and summary

IN PROCEEDING FROM OUR ORIGINAL DISTINCTION between the vocabulary and the grammar of a language, it has become increasingly difficult to avoid grammatical and theoretical problems. Particularly in the last chapters repeated reference has been made to "empirical" statements and to sentences in theory, i.e., to statements and sentences which make predictions about the world of events and objects. The grammar of science, the business of putting words together in sentences which make statements about the world possible will be developed in the following chapters on theory. The point has been made that neither terms nor theories can function independently of each other. However, as in infant speech or in any other language acquisition, the vocabulary had to be developed before the grammar could be considered. Not even the most astute student of the French language can arrive at that acme of early language learning "La plume de ma tante est sur la table" without first acquiring a vocabulary about pens, aunts, and tables. How much of a vocabulary have we achieved at this point? If we are ready to form sentences, what are the things that we can now talk about?

In the first place we have suggested a criterion for all scientific terms. Whether they belong to the simplest level of describing the world around us or whether they occur only in intricate theoretical laws, scientific words must conform to the requirement of intra- and inter-subjective reliability. All scientific terms must show some degree, and preferably a high degree, of response invariance. It has been shown that invariant usage can often be traced to the way in which a term is acquired. As a corollary, response invariance can be achieved by controlling language acquisition. The process of continuous approximations to invariant usage was seen to be an important aspect of any developing science. Scientific like any other respectability must be acquired at some cost to the individual aspiring to it and the slow achievement of invariance requires proper conduct. Finally, it has been argued that no particular class of words or terms, such as those of physics, has any prior claim to such respectability, although our criterion has been shown to be more often satisfied by the terms of the older sciences. Any term may aspire to invariant usage; its success will depend on its utility in the general business of science. The utility of a term depends on its empirical fruitfulness, as well as on its linguistic characteristics.

With a criterion for the vocabulary of psychology established, various ways were examined by which terms have been introduced or refined. Table 1 presents a simplified summary of both the common and the scientific language. The stress here is on the *simplified* aspects of the table. In actual use the relationships tend to be much more complex than the labels and arrows of the table indicate.

We can differentiate three levels of complexity of scientific terms. The lowest level contains those terms which constitute the basic vocabulary of a scientific language. It has been shown that these terms are acquired as responses to the events and objects of the world which the scientist investigates and classifies. The learning of these responses requires little more than the presence of a reinforcing community which properly reinforces an appropriate occurrence of the response. Many of these terms are elicited by the common physical objects of our environment, and this phenomenon has given rise to the proposal of a physical thing-language as *the* basic vocabulary of science. Other terms which were seen to be part of this lowest level are elicited by, or elicit, commonly performed operations and actions. One of the closest contacts between the scientific and the common language was observed in this low-level vocabulary, largely because of the language-learning experiences of all the members of a language community. It was agreed that some terms of the language of common experience do in fact function as invariant terms and may therefore be useful in

Table 1

	COMMON LANGUAGE		SCIENTIFIC LANGUAGE
Theoretical terms	Terms used in vernacular generalizations	Adoption of → prototheory	Terms appearing in laws and hypotheses
	↕		↑ Empirical analysis ↓
Low-level terms	Terms used in descriptions and low-order generalizations	Meaning analysis → Explication	Terms used in low-order generalizations
	↕		↑ Reduction sentences Operational definitions Explication Nominal definitions ↓
Basic vocabulary	*Common experience* Names and labels Phenomenological vocabulary Common thing-language ↑	Nominal definitions → Meaning analysis	*Protocol statements* Invariant labels Operations Carnap's thing-language ↑
		Objects and Events	

scientific discourse. Other terms may be adopted from the common language by nominal definitions, which specify the conditions for usage of a term. Attempts may also be made to specify the vernacular usage more exactly by way of a meaning analysis.

The terms of the basic vocabulary enter into the simplest sentences in science—the protocol statements. In science these statements play the role of the communications of "common experience." They state invariantly what does or does not take place. In this connection we posited a "reality" independent of language. This posit of reality states that there *are* events and objects to which the scientist responds. In connection with the discussion of theory, it will be seen that such a posit has to be extended somewhat to the specific objects and events which the language of common experience and the protocol statements of science name or label.

Finally it was shown that the phenomenological vocabulary of private experience does not fulfill our criterion of response invariance and is therefore not part of the basic vocabulary of science.

The second level of terms contains all those words which are introduced by definitions or reduction sentences. These terms may be elicited by environmental events, but in most cases they are not. Even though they may label complex events, their usage depends on their definitional relationship with sentences which are phrased in the basic vocabulary. They are only one step removed from the basic terms; that step consists of a specification of the conditions and operations involved in their use. In psychology this class includes such terms as "reinforcement," "anxious," "VTE," and so forth. It is this class of terms which often shows different usage from one investigator to the next and which most often elicits the demand for a definition. These terms may also, by the process of meaning analysis or explication, be taken over from the vernacular.

The last level of terms embraces those that function primarily in intraverbal contexts, the theoretical terms. These terms are normally introduced *within* the language and the initial occasions for their usage are frequently not external events but other verbal units. In a theoretical language they are related to the event world by links to lower-order terms. This process of achieving empirical import for higher-order theoretical sentences will be seen to be an important part of theories and their interpretation. Theoretical terms of this order in psychology may include "drive," "demand," "libido," "unconscious," "personality," "habit strength," and many others. These words may at times be taken over from the common, often archaic, prototheory of everyday discourse.

Much of the previous discussion has rested on an empirical analysis of vocabulary acquisition and maintenance. Such an analysis was of particular importance in determining the basic vocabulary of psychology, the words which are elicited by the event-world. Having described this vocabulary and the conditions for its emergence, we have established a link between the language of science and the common experience of the human scientist. This link consists of the protocol statements, which may be considered to take the place of the vague immediate experience, the direct observation, or the elusive phenomenal givens with which science is expected to make contact. In moving on to more complex terms and relationships, we will have less need for an analysis which speaks of eliciting conditions, responses, and reinforcers. However, we will continue to stress science as human behavior, and new empirical statements will be introduced in order to understand the theoretical behavior of the scientist.

Using his native grammar, our psychologist is now able to talk very simply about the events in his environment. He has developed a vocabulary about the behavior of his subjects and about the environment in which organisms behave. He now needs to put these simple words and protocol statements together into larger systems, to relate them to each other, and to achieve prediction of behavior. For these achievements he must be introduced to the world of scientific theory.

part II

Theory in psychology

chapter eight

Introduction to theory

THE THESIS HAS BEEN DEVELOPED IN EARLIER chapters that the building of a scientific vocabulary can be related to general principles of learning and to the use of words in the everyday common language. An argument of similar force can be presented to tie scientific theorizing to what we know of human behavior. In going about such an analysis we will again be concerned with some of the traditional problems in the philosophy and history of science. These problems are not neatly separable into those relevant to the vocabulary of psychology and those relevant to its grammar. It should be no surprise therefore if a number of the issues adumbrated in earlier chapters make a reappearance in slightly variant form. Science is all of a piece and principles applicable to the scientist's use of words will be seen to be applicable as well to his use of more complex language units. We will take the risk of repetition to avoid the sins of omission; whereof one can speak, thereof one should speak often.

Talking about the scientist as an ordinary human being meets with some cultural resistance; the scientist of Hollywood and the comic books is likely to be considered a species apart, concerned with nuclear destruction, hypnosis, or space travel, and with these in ways which are not available to the general public. For the scientist, life may become "a flight from science–science a game" (Koffka, 1935), and there is little doubt that the enormous amount of special training required for competence in today's disciplines has tended to make the construction of theories seem an esoteric puzzle. Perhaps this alienation of the work of the theorist from the day-to-day activities of plain people is promoted by the use of elegant and well-developed theories as prototypical examples of what the scientist usually produces. In the face of Hilbert's axiomatization of geometry, or Einstein's formulas in physics, or the statement of astronomical postulates, the intelligent commuter or college student is hard put to understand how such formulations are related to what he knows about measurement, billiards, and the Big Dipper. Even scientific disciplines with less history and fewer data are not free of their own peculiarities in the statement of theory. In illustration, consider these examples from psychology.

> Experience shows us that this path leading through the preconscious to consciousness is barred to the dream-thoughts during the daytime by the censorship imposed by resistance. During the night they are able to obtain access to consciousness; but the question arises as to how they do so and thanks to what modification. If what enabled the dream-thoughts to achieve this were the fact that at night there is a lowering of the resistance which guards the frontier between the unconscious and the preconscious, we should have dreams which were in the nature of ideas and which were without the hallucinatory quality in which we are at the moment interested. (Freud, 1900 [1954, p. 542].)

or

> In case an animal is taught an act through a given reinforcement and then is given a gradually increasing series of non-reinforced massed response evocations always followed at once by primary reinforcement, the r_G will become attached to the traces of these non-reinforcements in such a way as to reinforce them, largely neutralizing the I_R accumulating and thus permitting very long primarily unreinforced behavior series to occur. (Hull, 1952, p. 135.)

Quotations like these, frankly out of context, are not meant to demonstrate that Freud or Hull should speak in a lingua franca that all may understand. Quite the contrary. These excerpts from important theories illustrate the complexity necessary in the formal statement of scientific assumptions. But, by their complexity and first-glance incomprehensibility, these paragraphs pose in a dramatic form the problems of this and the following chapters. What is a theory? More specifically, what is a theory in psychology? How are theoretical statements related to the commonplace behavior of people and objects? What is the relation between theoretical words and the basic vocabulary developed thus far? Where do theories come from?

The attack on this set of questions must be offered tentatively and piecemeal. In search of a common ground from which to proceed, several quite general characteristics of a theory can be laid out, with a promise that they will be properly annotated and refined later on.

THE EMPIRICAL BASIS OF THEORIES

Scientific theories, particularly as they grow more abstract and take on a specialized vocabulary, seem remote from everyday events like baseball and arguments between husbands and wives. But no matter how recondite a theory may be, it must always have some way of getting down to "brute facts" or "raw data." Theory construction may profitably be considered as a kind of game with words, in which the theorist fits and patches his constructions to make the final product neat. But if theory-making is a game, it is one with rules, and no rule is more important for the scientist than the one which states that a *theory must be interpretable.* The connections may be elaborate and tricky, but at some point a theory which claims place in the scientific canon must demonstrate its relation to objects and events. Freud's discussion of the censorship of resistance aims, among other things, at an understanding of the way people dream; Hull's discussion of massed response evocations aims, among other things, at an understanding of why people gamble. A more striking but cognate illustration of this point is the evolution from atomic physical theory to the bomb at Hiroshima. The popular distinction between theories and facts, expressed usually in a derogation of theory, is a distinction which will claim our attention later, but it can be said at once that if a set of statements cannot provide a bridge to something "out there" in the world, it is not a scientific theory at all.

To say that a theory is about something is, in a sense, to say that theories are directive, that they imply some injunction to action or some instructions about action. If one is concerned with eating problems in a two-year-old, a theory of eating problems should indicate what other behaviors of the child to observe, or what aspects of the environment to note, or what changes in parental behavior should be introduced. This injunction to action may be no more than a prescription to observe, as in the case where you want to know about the next eclipse, but in general, a scientific theory always states "Go do this" or "Go look at that." [1] A partial history of the development of science could be written around the demand for empirical reference. Legendary is the story of the student of scholastics who dared to interrupt a learned discourse on the number of teeth a horse has to look in a horse's mouth. Zilsel has described the early stages of modern science quite vividly.

> The seats of medieval civilization were not towns, which in the early centuries were rare, but monasteries and castles in the country. The castles and the cultural accomplishments of the knights have little bearing on theoretical thinking. The monasteries, being the centers of medieval scholarship, are more important. . . . Monks, by the conditions of their lives, are not much disposed to look at the world with open eyes. Inclosed within walls, intrusted with the task of transmitting established doctrines to successors by scholastic instruction, they were compelled to indulge in abstract reasoning and to develop their sagacity. This attitude of mind was later taken over by the universities of the late medieval cities. Up to the thirteenth century the method of investigating that appears to be the most natural one to modern science was practically unknown. When medieval theorists, or theologians, intended to solve a problem, they looked first for relevant passages in the Holy Scripture, the patristic writings, and certain works of Aristotle. Then they compared affirmative and negative statements of colleagues and predecessors and, finally, drew conclusions by means of logical deduction from the premisses collected. . . .
>
> By the end of the Middle Ages, however, a few scholars, among them Roger Bacon in England and Albertus Magnus in Germany, had begun to understand the importance of experience. . . .
>
> . . . With the inventions of the fifteenth and sixteenth centuries the technology of the Middle Ages was completely revolutionized. Similar effects were produced by the great geographical discoveries. On new shores animals, plants, and things never seen

[1] As will be seen, the directive injunction of an entire theory is somewhat more complex than the analogous injunction to perform certain defining operations.

before were found, which even the most acute monk would not have been able to deduce from his authorities. Authorities and syllogisms had been beaten by experience; a new empirically minded type of man went out to conquer the world. (Zilsel, 1941, pp. 53–55.)

Somewhat surprisingly, the battle for statements which can be checked against what happens has been a continuing one. The recent entrance to prominence of the logical positivists was through the door of a search for verifiability, for the empirical support of speculative statements. Within the social sciences, as we have seen, a question which invariably claims the attention of the scientist is: "What is your operational definition?"

Clearly, this requirement on theories that they be interpretable, or empirical, or directive, underlies much of the earlier discussion of definition; the place of definition in the making of science is precisely that it permits the reference of the theory, however elegant, complex, and distant from here and now, to the basic scientific vocabulary and, through that vocabulary, to the common experience of men. As a first approximation, the automobile road map is a good illustration of this aspect of theory-building. The road map is an artificial, symbolic, and reduced representation (a theory) of the terrain, and the schooled reader of the map may act in a reasonable way (behave factually) over that terrain with the help of the map. The rules for interpretation of the map correspond in a rough way to definition in theory construction.

THEORIES AS ANTICIPATION SYSTEMS

If one understands a road map and its rules for interpretation, it would produce a shock of surprise to wind up in Boston when aiming for Philadelphia. The practical use of the map demands that those events occur which we expect to occur. Something like this seems to be the case for scientific theories as well, and this tendency of theories to set up certain expectations can be called the *anticipation function of theories.* This notion was implicit in the discussion of the directive character of theory; just as the set of assumptions instructs us to perform particular acts, it also establishes a readiness to observe particular consequences of these acts. In the case of the child with a feeding problem, the mother's compliance with her pediatrician's instructions to ignore the child's refusal to eat would lead her to expect some change (hopefully, for the better) in the baby's behavior. If no change occurred, there would doubtless be some reservations entered about the adequacy of the "ignore him" theory. How closely this homely analogy fits the model of formal scientific theory cannot be decided immediately, but it presents some suggestive leads which warrant further examination.

The anticipatory function of theory has been treated at length under another label—*prediction*. When a researcher tests the hypothesis that high levels of motivation produce fast learning, he may, for example, make predictions or forecasts about the specific behavior of rats in a maze. This prediction expresses an expectation, an anticipation, on the part of the researcher that hungry animals will make fewer errors than well-fed animals. Again, it would produce some surprise if this turned out to be a wrong anticipation, an incorrect prediction. Before we go further along, it should be noted that we do not propose to substitute vague expectation feelings of the researcher for the important concept of prediction. Rather, in blocking out the wide area of what theories do, it helps to set our task if the two ideas are put in apposition.

Complex scientific theories are hard to use in illustrating this relation, but much simpler forms are available to us which can be analyzed in detail. For instance, from navigation comes this archaic formulation:

> Red sky at night, sailor's delight;
> Red sky in the morning, sailor's warning.

First off, do these statements fit the earlier requirement for theories that they be about something? In part at least, they do. Without laboring the problems of color perception, skies can be judged to be more-or-less red. The other part of the "theory" poses more difficulties, and some interpretation or definition would certainly be necessary for "delight" and "warning." It seems, however, that this nautical law can be put fairly easily in touch with observations. Is it also an anticipation system in the way we have talked about it? Again, yes. Insofar as the statement is believed in or insofar as the law is highly confirmed, the observation of red skies in the morning will set up expectations of storm and, in all likelihood, produce changes in the behavior of captain and crew. This prototheory of weather can be taken quite seriously as a reduced model of more impressive and far-reaching theories. If it is openly recognized that we are handling

Table 2

THREE PARTIAL THEORIES

Theory	Observations	Anticipation
Sky color and weather	Particular color of morning sky	Storm
Orbits of rotation of celestial bodies	Particular relation of earth, sun, and moon on January 11	Eclipse on November 14
Social learning of aggression	Particular attitude toward parents	Prejudice

only a small part of the intricacies of theory-building by drawing this parallel, it will help in outlining a more detailed treatment to consider the comparisons of Table 2.

In each of the cited instances, there is an instruction in the theory, that is, a specification of conditions under which a prediction or anticipation can be made. To some extent, too, the failure of the predicted events to occur would occasion surprise in every case. To understand the importance of this reaction of surprise, let's return for a last time to the road-map analogy. When the Philadelphia-bound tourist arrived in Boston, he would as a reasonable man suspect that either the map was improperly drawn, or he did not know how to read (interpret) the map correctly, or the terrain had shifted since the publication of the map. Quite analogous interpretations could be made by the more sophisticated theorist; if an eclipse does not occur as scheduled, the astronomer may doubt his basic theory, or wonder whether he has adequately applied the definitions which relate the theory to the basic vocabulary of astronomy, or even ask whether the celestial bodies have changed their operating procedures. This last possibility appears ludicrous when stated for highly developed sciences;[2] it is not nearly so amusing when applied to observation systems where there is relatively rapid change, e.g., animal behavior.

In a simple way, the further question of theory revision is set by

[2] The Greenwich error in estimation of stellar transits, for example, was not resolved by assigning variation to the stars (see Chapter 3); well-elaborated sciences do not easily abandon their basic expectations.

these examples. A formulation, whether it concerns everyday behavior ("Never draw to an inside straight," "Redheads are fighters") or complex scientific endeavor ("$e = mc^2$," "${}_{S}H_{R} = f(N)$"), sets up, through a more-or-less involved set of interpretations, an anticipation about what is going to happen. If the expected event fails to occur, some revision must be made in the theory or in the interpretation rules or else it must be decided that the formulation does not apply to this particular situation.

Throughout this discussion of the anticipation character of theories, even the most ordinary examples have shared with elegant theories one important characteristic—statement in words. All of the assertions are phrased in the language symbols of English. Formulation in symbols of one sort or another is an invariable characteristic of scientific theories, but for completeness' sake, it should be noted that not all anticipation systems have this symbolic expression. When one reaches for a coffee cup at breakfast, one certainly expects to wind up on the cup handle and not in the middle of scrambled eggs. There is no verbal statement of this expectation, no rehearsing of "If I relax the biceps so that only a force of 14 dynes is applied against the shoulder joint . . . ," yet a prediction is being made about events in the environment, and genuine surprise would result if the prediction were not confirmed. Most of the ordinary behavior of men can be seen as having this motor-predictive character; there is no explicit theory of climbing stairs, but the human body is set to receive "confirmations" from the environment at each stage of the maneuver.

For a number of reasons, such a description of human action is not so trivial for an understanding of theory-making as it might appear at first glance. We are able to do many things for which we have no explicit formal theory. Farmers grow corn without degrees in botany, sailors find their way by star signs without courses in astronomy, and people who have never heard of Freud raise their children. Thus, for many of the phenomena which the scientist tries to encompass with his theory, there exist *action-theories* in the public domain. There are, as has been noted earlier, protosciences built into human beings by their species characteristics and their history, and these protosciences may show little similarity to formal theories. Eddington illustrated this variation in "theory" in his discussion of the two tables.

> One of them has been familiar to me from earliest years. It is a commonplace object of that environment which I call the world. How shall I describe it? It has extension; it is comparatively per-

> manent, it is colored; above all it is *substantial.* By substantial I do not merely mean that it does not collapse when I lean upon it; I mean that it is constituted of "substance" and by that word I am trying to convey to you some conception of its intrinsic nature. It is a *thing.* . . .
>
> Table No. 2 is my scientific table. It is a more recent acquaintance and I do not feel so familiar with it. It does not belong to the world previously mentioned—that world which spontaneously appears around me when I open my eyes. . . . It is part of a world which in more devious ways has forced itself on my attention. My scientific table is mostly emptiness. Sparsely scattered in that emptiness are numerous electric charges rushing about with great speed; but their combined bulk amounts to less than a billionth of the bulk of the table itself. (Eddington, 1928, pp. xi–xii.)

In the light of the present treatment, there should be added to Eddington's classificatory scheme "Table No. 0," to which we respond quite adequately, but never talk about at all. For so simple an object as a table, there can be stated a number of "theories," in the sense that there are different anticipation systems concerned with this object. The carpenter's action-theory of the table and Eddington-the-physicist's formal explicit theory of the table are different in a number of ways, and it is in the detailed examination of such differences that the place of scientific-theory construction will be made clear. For the moment, it is enough to note that they are both attempts to anticipate events "out there," however much they may vary in explicitness, reliability, and degree of confirmation.

Protoscientific formulations are characteristic not only of laymen, and in our attempt to understand the scientist as theorist, it is important to remember that the best-trained researcher or thinker brings to his work the archaic theories which reflect his dealings with the run-of-the-mill world of people and things. If the premise of science as human behavior is taken seriously, one of the implications of this commitment to prototheories is clear—changes in widely held assumptions will be slow indeed, whether demanded of professional scientists or of laymen. The response of his colleagues to Galileo's description of the moons of Jupiter or the vilification that met Freud's postulation of infantile sexuality underline in bold strokes the pressures that protoscientific, quite frequently unverbalized, assumptions exert against changes in established anticipation systems, whether vernacular or scientific.

The phenomena which have been considered under the heading of action-theories are doubtlessly important in human behavior and include a much wider range of man's activity than is dealt with in formal scientific theories. An objective and somewhat unkind critic of psychology might say, for example, that if we behaved only on the basis of what we knew to be justified by explicit theory and adequate empirical test, we would hardly be able to get out of bed in the morning. But even granting the failure of formal theories to account for the intricacies of what goes on in the world compared with the success of ordinary behavior, are we justified in considering the unverbalized anticipation systems of people to be theories? Because some men are skillful poker players but cannot communicate their techniques, is it useful to think of their operating with a poker-playing theory? More to the point of our present concern with psychology, is it useful to consider as theoretical the sometimes superior predictions of the insightful psychotherapist, who cannot communicate or teach his "system"? A firm answer to these questions is necessarily somewhat arbitrary, but if our treatment of theory is to be in line with the customary usage of scientists and philosophers, these action-theories, however successful they may be, must be ruled out of court. One of the most important demands we have introduced for the creation of a basic vocabulary and which applies as well to theory construction is the demand for *publicity,* i.e., statement in an explicit and communicable form.

THEORIES AS WAYS OF COMMUNICATION

At any stage in the development of an empirical discipline, techniques are chosen and observations selected on the basis of prior work, so that each generation of scientists stands on the shoulders of earlier researchers. Conant (1947) has made this point in speaking of the "accumulative knowledge" of science, with its dependence on the history of theories and research, as against the nonaccumulative knowledge derived from poetry or metaphysics. If science depends on its history in this way, then the requirement of communicability of scientific theories is inescapable. Only if a theory is available for interpretation and test by other researchers, only if it can be compared with other attempts to anticipate the same events, can a theory be admitted to the canons of science.

Obedience to this limitation shuts out of our consideration a great deal of what we know to be true from our experience as ordinary citizens, and leads on occasion to attacks on scientific theories as arid, sterile, lacking in the richness of immediate experience, trivial for the conduct of one's life. Insofar as these attacks reflect something like "I am aware as a human being of many things—the beauty of flowers, the holiness of some men, the force of moral obligations—for which scientific theories have no place," they must be accepted as legitimate. The supposed aridity of science is in part ascribable to the fact that some of the more involved and complicated aspects of experience have not been subjected to systematic examination. Leaving this practical consideration aside, it will always be possible, indeed necessary, for reasonable men to behave in ways which no formal theoretical system anticipates. The restriction of theories to public and explicit forms necessarily leaves behind the individual detail of personal experience.[3]

Our preliminary outline of the use of the notion of *theory* has brought us this far: A theory, through a set of definitions or rules for interpretation, must be about something (it has empirical reference); a theory is a more-or-less complex anticipation system (it permits prediction); a theory must be stated in a way that is communicable (it is public).

THE LANGUAGE OF THEORY

The most general requirement for the language of theory is that it be understandable by other people. There is not available any rigorous specification of how many "others" are required or what special qualifications they should have; a loose but useful description of "competent auditors" would be the community of the theorist's colleagues, the men who are concerned with the same kind of empirical events. It would be much too stricturing to demand that the theorist's formulations be understood by everyone, or even by holders of college degrees and winners of quiz programs. Like it or not, scientific theorizing is a specialized business, and the undemocratic implications of this fact may account in part for the tendency toward alienation of the work of the theorist from the daily exchange of citizens.

This removal of the language of theory from ordinary discourse is a relatively recent event, however, and one still largely confined to the

[3] The relevance of this limitation to the basic vocabulary was discussed in Chapter 1, and will come up once more in treating of "clinical insight" in Chapter 14.

highly developed sciences. Just as the basic vocabulary borrows words from the common language, one of the closest contacts of theory-building with other behaviors of men is its frequent use of the vernacular. The scientific theories of Americans are written in English, just as poetry, sermons, and newspaper columns are. A glance back to the chapters on the learning of language will show how essential this link is. The theorist, no matter how far he may have gone in his thinking beyond the talk of the market place, must, if his work is to continue, tell others, particularly his students, what he is talking about. Such uninformed auditors come to the theorist with a special set of language skills—American English, for example—in terms of which the theorist must lead the way to the novelties of his formulation. For this reason, there are many theoretical words which have a place both in common language and in the language of formal theories. "Force," "inertia," "work," "momentum" have been dried so thoroughly in the theoretical kiln that little confusion results between their vernacular and their scientific usage. Not so with "drive," "habit," "instinct," "culture," and a host of other constructs of the social sciences; the possibilities for infiltration of use between the vernacular and the formal languages are almost limitless. It is an intricate process, but the development of scientific theories like the development of basic vocabularies can often be described as the denaturalization of common words. Scientific theories grow out of common language, just as scientific techniques grow out of everyday activities, and often the theories carry with them some of the evocative power (e.g., "force," "power," "drive," "energy") encased in the natural history of their vocabulary. The study of a scientific theory demands, therefore, careful and repeated analysis of its language in order to determine the relation of the theory to "things out there" and to the common language.

Thus far, our detailed treatment of the language of the science of psychology has been limited to an analysis of its vocabulary and the rules for the introduction of constructs. Essential as this task is, it provides an incomplete picture of the language of psychology. The terms of a science always appear in sentences or statements, and an understanding of these sentences is necessary to an understanding or use of the theory. We have seen that there is merit in the injunction to "define your terms," but an unadorned collection of words would not constitute a theory, even if each word were accompanied by a properly formulated definition. A dictionary of psychology represents a scientific system of behavior no more than a dictionary of English represents a system of social communication. For example, a definitional psychology would be limited to such series as:

Drive   Cue   Response   Reward

or:

Id   Ego   Superego

Even these apparently trivial examples carry an implicit assumption of grouping, an assumption that our dictionary has chapters entitled "Learning Theory" or "Psychoanalysis." The study of theoretical language cannot be confined to the study of words alone, but must include an analysis of *rules of statement construction,* i.e., of the ways in which the vocabulary of a science is sewn together to provide the collection of sentences called a theory.

It has been repeatedly emphasized that words in formal theories often carry with them the marks of their origin in a common language. So too the rules of statement construction. At least in the preliminary stages of theory-building, the grammar of the vernacular is as freely borrowed as its vocabulary is, a consideration which poses another analytic task for the student of theories. Perhaps more than any other contemporary, the biologist Woodger has been concerned with the necessity of freeing formal theories from the limitations of natural languages, and he justifies a detailed and difficult statement of a relatively simple set of cellular phenomena in the following way:

> Because we learn [common languages] during the most impressionable period of our lives, they become to such an extent part of ourselves that we come to use them without ever being aware of their conventional and arbitrary character, and thus of certain of their properties which are least admirable from the point of view of science. Conventions which are so deeply imbedded in our nature have the force of moral and religious principles. They are extremely difficult to face and criticize frankly, and departures from custom in such matters are likely to arouse antagonism. (Woodger, 1939, p. 2.)

Thus, the theorist is put in a remarkable dilemma; in order to communicate his theory, he must start from the natural language of his culture, and yet be constantly aware that the vernacular vocabulary and grammar may infiltrate his formal system and damage its usefulness. The resolution of this dilemma is another of the themes which is repeatedly heard in the history of science, and one of the easiest criteria to apply in judging the developmental age of a discipline is the measure of the degree to which it has freed itself of the overtones of popular speech.

SUMMARY

Human beings, in their everyday behavior with things and other people, make predictions about what is going to happen next. Most of these predictions, or anticipations, are not given an explicit statement. The skilled driver of an automobile does not set down the premises of a gear-shifting theory and draw a proper deduction relevant to traffic signals—he acts. But the presence of an anticipation or expectation is best detected when the prediction fails—if unaccountably the car moves in reverse, the driver is surprised. These ordinary anticipation-systems or *action-theories* bear some resemblances to more formal and elegant scientific formulations of theory. Both the popular and the formal systems depend for their usefulness on being related in some way to events, to what goes on in the world. They both attempt to anticipate or predict what some unknown events will be. The chief difference between the theory of the driver and the theory of the gear-box designer is that the latter is *explicit, public,* and *communicable.* Scientific theories are stated in ways that permit them to be tested against events in a systematic way, whereas the action-theories are usually hidden from public view, and are "tested" in a less formal fashion.

Popular theories are sometimes expressed in a public way, however. Theories on the order of "Red sky at night," share with more refined systems another characteristic—their common relation to the common language—and in this case, the distinction between the formal and the informal theory becomes much harder to make. Not only are they both empirical and predictive, but they both are stated in more-or-less interrelated sentences. It will be one of the goals of the succeeding chapters to ask how popular protopsychological theories and formal scientific psychological theories may be distinguished.

Our first outline of the nature of theory can now be stated in a compressed form: *Theories are sets of statements, understandable to others, which make predictions about empirical events.*

chapter nine

The nature of psychological theories

THE ASSERTION THAT THEORIES ARE SOMEHOW concerned with "empirical events" is deceptively simple. One of the continuing problems of philosophers turns on the specification of the nature of reality, a subject which is surely of interest to the scientific theorist who bases his work on factual confirmation. Whatever other disagreements may separate scientists, the hard core of shared principle is a commitment to testing a theory against what really goes on in the world. But what are the facts, the data, the descriptive bases of science?

To set the issues in focus, imagine that there is a prize fight in progress and that, at a certain moment, a call is made for its description. Among the sentences which might result, these appear:

1. A short dark man hits a large pale man on the chin.
2. The champion knocks the challenger down.
3. An object A with such-and-such properties comes into contact with an object B with such-and-such properties at time *t*.
4. Two high anthropoids illustrate the instinctual character of play.

No great ingenuity is required to elaborate from this example a long list of statements which can make some claim to be factual or descriptive. The list is not made very much shorter even if we confine ourselves to an experimental setting, e.g., watching a rat pressing a lever. A zoologist, a physiologist, a behavior theorist, or a layman would in all likelihood come up with quite different versions of the rat's activity. But, what is "really" going on?

One of the implications of this question concerns the nature of reality, and we may ask at once whether the notion of reality is a useful or necessary one. Perhaps the sensible procedure would be to abandon the distinction between facts and non-facts as an arbitrary and purely conventional separation. No attempted justification will be complete but, without entering into the intricacies of a subject that has plagued philosophers for centuries, there seem to be some primitive grounds from which to defend the utility of "reality."

THE NATURE OF REALITY

In the first place, and commanding most serious attention, there are occasions where the evaluation "That is so" can be made with a very high level of confidence. Chairs, rats, other people, colors, displacements in space—all are reacted to reliably and without hesitation, regardless of the speculations of psychologists and metaphysicians. It is this irreducible not-thought-about behavior which is the central justification for the continued use of the idea of factual reference. Animals and men were able to move "reasonably" through their environments long before any suspicion was thrown on the utility of the discrimination between real and not-real.

It is important to note, too, that the sports writer at the prize fight and the psychologist at the lever box can communicate to their audiences without serious consideration of questions about reality. Scientists, as a matter of fact, are notorious for their rather cavalier refusal to be upset by the subtleties of ontological or epistemological argument; they go on as if they were working with some hard stuff, with adequate representations of a genuine reality. The wisdom of this attitude can be determined only by a systematic examination of the history of science; germane to the present discussion is the observation that human beings, plumbers or physicists, accept more-or-less uncritically the presented environment of people and things as real. Empirical science is rooted in this conviction, and the basic operations of test and confirmation are unthinkable without it. This is not the same thing as saying that scientific theories are *about* common objects; the example of Eddington's tables refutes neatly any serious consideration of science as "organized common sense," but science begins with, and its theories must be related to, the objects and the changes in objects to which men react. For convenience in comparing it with more sophisticated aspects of theory-building, this primitive view of the nature of the world, shared by scientist and layman, can be considered an extension of the *posit of reality* advanced in Chapter 3.

This posited reality, the world of common objects, is the arena of day-to-day living, and can be most easily understood as representing the shared action-system of human beings. The characteristics of the human organism for perceiving and responding, together with historical contingencies of reinforcement for certain ways of acting, have led to response patterns which are relatively invariant from one person to another at least in a particular culture at a particular time. In the earlier chapters on the learning of language, one set of these invariances—naming responses—was treated in detail, and the discussion there can be taken as a model for the more general point: There are important clusters of responses reliably elicited by objects and events which can usefully be considered as representing the starting point of theory-building, whether popular or formal. These are the behaviors that Skinner (1957) has called "tacts."

There are dangers to communication in the application of the term "reality," as Cohen notes in his passionate defense of reason.

> If terms that have no genuine negatives are to be condemned as devoid of significance, the word *reality* should head the list. I am not unmindful of the many attempts to define the unreal. But the question is: What corresponds to these definitions? The Hindu mystic is deeply irritated when the wise Chinaman suggests that the realm of Maya or illusion does not really exist, or that it is not worth while worrying about it. . . . The difficulty here is classic. What I am more especially concerned about, however, is to call attention to the fact that the word *reality* maintains itself as a term of praise rather than of description. To be "in touch with reality" is our way of expressing what our less sophisticated brothers and sisters do by the phrase "in tune with the infinite." It is an expression which carries an agreeable afflatus without dependence on any definite meaning. (Cohen, 1931 [1953, p. 455 f.].)

With this warning in view, it is worth our while to state carefully the range of meaning the term "posit of reality" will have here. There are two interpretations which it is *not* meant to have.

1. *Traditional metaphysical views of reality.* In their essays at finding the root character of knowledge, philosophers have presented a number of ingenious "solutions." Among the most persistingly discussed are the derivatives of Aristotelian realism and Platonic idealism, with libraries of books the result. It is difficult for the practicing scientist to be patient with many of the distinctions made in classical metaphysics; they seem oddly irrelevant to lining up a nuclear bombardment or studying the distribution of suicide in Chicago. This position of studied ignorance on the part of the researcher does not damage his effectiveness; one would be hard put to find any evidence that the metaphysical posture of the scientist has much to do with the conduct of his research. To put it in a way which will probably offend the metaphysician, there is no obvious correlation between a man's steeping in controversies about ontology and his ability to design and execute empirical studies. However relevant metaphysical speculation may be to "the complete man," it is possible at least to bypass the issues raised by such speculation if we remain concentrated on the task of understanding theories as explicit systems of prediction. The posit of reality, then, does not entail any specific position as to the transcendental nature of being or knowledge.

2. *The reality of phenomenal experience.* Phenomenal experience is a more alluring possibility for a starting point of theories, particularly in the present concern with psychology. For that very reason, the notion has to be handled rather gingerly. We have already noted that if by "phenomenal" or "immediate" experience there is designated an inferred state of the organism the assumption of which makes it easier to predict behavior, then "immediate experience" is part of the theoretical content of psychology, but hardly the initial position of science which is being sought. If, on the other hand, by "phenomenal experience" there is meant the ineffable and private presentation of the world to an individual, then "immediate experience" is not only unutterable, but uninteresting in discussing the language of science.

Having excluded these two proposals for the use of the term "posit of reality," it is possible to continue with an outline of the use to which it will be put in the present formulation. The important accent in the phrase should be placed on "posit," because the intention of the term is much like the child's game of "Let's pretend." Human beings show certain regularities in their behavior which make it possible to carry on such important shared activities as building bridges, making love, and gossiping. These regularities of behavior, particularly the regularities in the use of common languages, suggest that we assume or postulate for our investigation of theory an initial "matrix of enquiry." This matrix will comprise those inferred events toward which people act or speak with reliability and without hesitation. In any adult population, the names of these events will provide a beginning vocabulary for science. As more and more checks against anticipation are made, within science or in less specialized forms, it may turn out that part of the initial language (using the word "language" here to include all reliable responding) is dispensable or in error. In such a case, the language will be changed, and a new game of "Let's pretend" will start. There is nothing in this formulation which requires that the reality thus posited be immutable or transcendental—the chief claim of such a rough-edged and ordinary postulate is that it permits the making of a temporary housing for human knowledge which can be modified with changes in the efficiency of human action. Quine has indicated the tentative character of all scientific presuppositions in these words:

> The totality of our so-called knowledge or beliefs, from the most casual matters of geography and history to the profoundest laws of atomic physics or even of pure mathematics and logic, is a man-made fabric which impinges on experience only along the edges. . . . A conflict with experience at the periphery occasions readjustments in the interior of the field. . . . the total field is so underdetermined by its boundary conditions, experience, that there is much latitude of choice as to what statements to reevaluate in the light of any single contrary experience. (Quine, 1951b, pp. 39–40.)

The answer to the question about the nature of reality which was posed at the opening of this chapter can now be briefly stated. Systematic study requires the assumption of a set of working principles. The world of common objects and their movement in space, because it is familiar to us and has a wide range of application, can be *taken as real;* that is, we will posit the reality of events that are reliably reacted to and spoken about as a tentative postulate in our attempt to make correct predictions.[1]

---

[1] This view of reality underlies the cautious physicalism outlined in Chapter 4.

THE RANGE OF INTENT

The posit of reality just proposed determines scientific discourse somewhat, but still leaves an extremely wide range of choice available to the theorist. What, from the overwhelming number of empirical events, will be selected for study? It does not advance our critique of theory-building to say that the goal of science is the prediction of *all* events; even if this were so, and some weighty arguments can be entered against the position, the present status of human knowledge is far from adequate to the task. All scientific theories are limited in scope, taking into consideration a relatively small fraction of the reality available for study, and treating that fraction in rather specialized ways. Much the same thing is true of ordinary discourse; even the most intellectual of cocktail-party conversationalists is hardly expected to be competent on subjects as diverse as agriculture, philately, hockey, Chinese social structure, and the nature of God. Nor can this limitation be ascribed to defects in our educational system. There are an almost limitless number of events which can be responded to by human beings, and literally a limitless number of statements that can be made about them in the common language.

This manifoldness of reality can be given a simple demonstration by reflection on the number of factual statements that can be made about the immediate environment at any time, statements which would meet all reasonable requirements of intersubjective reliability. Standing on a city corner and collecting "raw facts" for a while could produce a list of great length and of remarkable variety. For instance:

1. From here, the Chrysler Building looks taller than the Empire State Building.
2. More women than men go into Sara Lee's Dress Shop.
3. All of the motion-picture theaters in view are advertising films with "The" in the title.
4. Seventeen people jaywalked in less than ten minutes.
5. There is a Mercedes-Benz SL-160.
6. Nobody has smiled since I got here.

Trivial as this listing appears, it is by no means at the lowest level of descriptive elaboration. There are represented such important characterizations as "more than" and "all." Our observer might have been set the hypothetical task of applying the predicates "moves" or "is red" to every appropriate discriminable object he detected, and he could have even on this basis come up with a rather impressively long recital of facts. The same recognition of the variety and number of possible factual statements can be achieved by glancing through an encyclopedia or almanac. Even if the range of fundamental empirical statements is limited, as was proposed earlier, to the reliably discriminable stimulus properties of common objects, an immeasurable number of these statements can be made.

The consideration of this infinite variety permits us to note one of the chief functions of theories—their specification of *a range of intent.* No human discourse, popular or scientific, aims to include in its predictive or anticipatory domain all possible empirical events. To some degree in every theoretical formulation, there is a restriction of focus to a relatively small set of facts. In informal human communication, limitations are put on the range of discussion in socially determined, though not always explicit ways; the debate, the panel discussion, professional kinship ("Doctor P. is in gynecology, too"), and conversational directives ("Did you read the new O'Hara book?") limit the extent of discussion. Each of these techniques, in a more-or-less rigid way, sets boundaries on what facts or observations will be admitted to the discourse; they restrict the number of appropriate verbal responses. In scientific treatments the limitation of intent is usually made more explicitly, but it has a function analogous to the boundaries of ordinary conversation; the statement of range of intent tells the reader of the theory what it is about, what selection of empirical events is under consideration. The day is long past when a scientific writer, as Comenius did in the seventeenth century, would dare speak "of all language and science."

Theory and the "Pure Empiricist"

The limitation in range of intent which is necessary to any scientific endeavor has a number of implications for an understanding of theory construction. Throughout the history of modern science there has been a running debate between two groups of researchers on the issue of the utility of theories. On one side have appeared the defenders of abstraction and speculation, the people who, like James (1892) calling for a "Lavoisier or Galileo of psychology," see theory as an essential step in the scientific process. For them, the mere recitation of accumulated "facts" would never constitute a system of knowledge, but rather they seek the great theoretical insight that will reveal the secrets of nature. Counter to this devotion to generalized statement is the attitude of the research workers who are usually called "pure empiricists." From Newton's (1713) celebrated and probably misunderstood *"Hypotheses non fingo"* to Skinner's (1950) "Are learning theories necessary?" there has been a steady line of defense drawn for the position that what matters in science is the patient collection of data, to which end worrying about heady abstractions will be more of a diversion and waste of time than a help to prediction and control.

As will be seen when there is occasion to talk about this difference in strategy for psychology, the operating distance between the two stands has often been exaggerated, with little gain for science in the disputation. In relation to the statement of range of intent at any rate, the positions differ in no important way. Whether the search is for an overreaching system for the prediction of empirical events, or a highly concentrated collection of facts, in both cases only a small part of the possible range of data is included in the researcher's treatment. If this precondition of scientific activity—the designation of a limited area of relevant observation—is considered to be a "theoretical" maneuver, then all of science is "theoretical." It should be added, of course, that there is enormous variation from theory to theory in the width of the specified range; it is possible to study the verbal production of Miss A. in psychoanalytic therapy or the distribution of mollusks in Lake Como, or more generally, the psychosexual development of adolescents or the evolution of metazoic forms in the Jurassic. But in every case, some decision is made by the scientist about what he will study.

Scientific Omniscience

The restriction of coverage of scientific theories has had another consequence of more general moment. Because so much can be seen in everyday life and so many things said in the common language, and because systematic study has surveyed only a relatively small part of this variety, there have arisen some misconceptions about the role of the scientist in society.[2] When he is concentrating on his local spe-

[2] Limited as the range of systematic study may be when compared with the multiplicity of events, the corpus of printed scientific communications is staggeringly large. A mathematician has computed that, in order to keep up with the current periodicals in his field, he would have to read eight hours a day! So far as breadth of interest is concerned, one has only to reflect on such phenomena as the thirty-seven volumes of the Proceedings of the New Jersey Mosquito Extermination Association to realize that systematic study can be quite various too.

cialty, he is likely to be viewed as too distant from "real life," too isolated in his ivory tower. When the scientist moves to broader study, however, he may find himself accused of demonstrating the obvious or else of trespassing in areas which are not his concern. It is apparent that physicists are not necessarily better mechanics than the men at the corner garage, and that the children of child psychologists are not necessarily freer of neurosis than the children of dentists, but there persists in our culture the theme that there should be a theoretical exposition for everything that can be seen or, even worse, everything that can be said. The mythical scientist is supposed to have an answer for just about everything. In a recent gibe at science, Standen said of psychology:

> What sort of things do we really want to know about a man? We might want to know if he is good company. A completely unscientific question—cut it out. Is he honest and reliable? Is he selfish? Is he materialistic? Is he given to old-womanish gossip? . . . You will get little help from a psychologist in answering these questions. You will get even less help if you want to know anything about really important human qualities, such as goodness or holiness. A psychologist would be horrified at the thought of having to say anything about holiness (except on Sundays, which don't count). . . . It is amazing, but true, that it is possible to go clear through a course in psychology without ever hearing what the various virtues are, and which are intellectual and which moral. (Standen, 1950, pp. 134–135.)

Although there are probably psychologists who would be willing to discuss holiness even on Tuesday, Standen's basic thesis is beyond argument: There are questions which can be asked in the common language about which no formal or systematic theory treats. There are perfectly reliable observations which are not predicted by a science. That this is so may be bitter to those who look to scientific method to provide an Up-to-Date Ethic or Modern Approach to Life, but the researcher struggling to make sense of the narrowly defined area in which he works can only agree with the objection and go on about his business. The expectations of omniscience implicit in some valuations of scientific theorizing are rather like saying of Beethoven: His work is all right as far as it goes, but his handling of comic opera is pitifully inadequate.

The Range of Intent and the Unity of Science

In the first half of the twentieth century, with the prodigious advances of scientific research and with the development of specialized interest in the philosophy of science, there has been an increasing emphasis on the unity of all scientific endeavor. But, if every theoretical formulation requires the drastic limitation in scope which is under discussion here, what does it mean to say that science is unitary?

First of all, if we accept the world of common objects as the starting point of systematic study, the unity of science is not a unity of subject matter. Botanists study plants, geneticists study morphological changes in fruit flies, psychologists study the behavior of animals. Each academic discipline has carved out its special domain among the possibilities for study, and although there exist marginal areas in which similar sets of data are relevant, it would take a severe twist of meaning or a retreat to speculations about "sense-data" in order to maintain that the content of all science is the same. Science is not united by subject matter.

Another plausible interpretation of the unity of science which must also be abandoned is the view that the goal of scientific activity is the building of a single superscience. This ambitious position often goes under the label of *reductionism,* with a tenet that one of the aims of science is the translation of more "complex" disciplines such as political science and psychology to more "basic" disciplines such as physiology and anatomy; these latter, in turn, will in the reductionist dream be translated to chemistry and physics.[3] Because of its peculiar position between the biological and the social sciences, psychology has been a cockpit for argument on the reductionist thesis, and we will return to a systematic examination of the problem in Chapter 14. For the moment, it is sufficient to note that there does not exist even a program for the superscience alluded to here; each discipline functions within the limits of its range of intent and within the restrictions of its language. The hope for a unified system of laws applicable to phenomena of every sort is a tempting one, but for the science of our time, we must be content with a less grandiose version of scientific unity.

---

[3] This is the third use of the word "reduction" to occur in our exposition. It is related to Carnap's early thesis about the unifying principle of science—reduction of all scientific language to a basic vocabulary of thing-predicates (see Chapter 1). It is not related to the definitional device of reduction sentences (see Chapter 6).

The fundamental assumptions or posits that bind the scientific community together are few in number and, when stated in simple words and baldly, seem hardly remarkable. One of these posits has already been discussed at length. The scientist is committed to confirmation operations involving the real world, or the world of common objects. He may create fanciful theories and spin subtle speculations almost *ad libitum,* but his task as scientist is only fulfilled when he has stated a test operation that will permit checking his creation against observations which can in fact be made. As a corollary to this requirement, science is public and communicable; as has been pointed out earlier, the private (or even published) musings of the poet may be pregnant with meaning in some wider sense, but unless their import can be reliably shared with other men, they are free of scientific pretension. Finally, scientists are bound together by their rejection of capriciousness in the world. The search of the systematic investigator is the search for regularities, for general statements which in the ideal form at least allow of no exceptions. These several criteria are the distillate of centuries of scientific history, and they serve to distinguish fairly precisely the areas of human study which are considered scientific in the ordinary sense. A stricter drawing of the lines of separation might include emphasis on the use of logic and mathematics or on the practice of manipulative experimentation, but the practical unity of science does not depend on techniques, content, or language, but rather on commitments to make reliable invariant statements about the world and to develop testable predictions.

THE CONTENT OF PSYCHOLOGICAL THEORIES

Perhaps one of the most commanding pressures on the scientist to see himself as united in some way to workers in other disciplines is the remarkable proliferation of specialties which has occurred over the past several generations. During the millennium which preceded the Humanist revisions in European universities during the sixteenth century, academic study was rigidly stabilized in the Trivium (grammar, rhetoric, and logic) and Quadrivium (arithmetic, geometry, astronomy, and music) of late Roman origin. With the renaissance of interest in classical study and the beginnings of empirical science in England and on the Continent, the first changes of curriculum began to appear. But even with the introduction of languages other than Latin, and sciences other than astronomy, the selection of studies available to the university scholar remained narrowly limited until the end of the nineteenth century. At that time, the age of specialization in academic study and in scientific work started its runaway growth to its present level. A casual but illuminating index of this change is afforded by a comparison of the curriculum of Yale University in 1884 and in 1957. In the former year, 60 courses were open to students throughout their four-year stay, while in the more recent catalog, there are almost as many departments, offering more than 700 courses. Of especial interest to the immediate goal of outlining the content of psychological theories is the observation that the nineteenth century's single course has been succeeded by 26 undergraduate and 52 graduate courses in psychology.

The message of these numbers, which could be repeated for any Western university, is clear. Academic specialization in the study of behavior, and with it the staking out of areas of specialized research, has increased to an unparalleled extent over the past fifty years. Whatever the social antecedents of this proliferation, it presents an almost unmanageable obstacle to the precise and formal definition of psychology. For a number of reasons, present-day psychologists will not have their discipline described as "the study of mind," and the more acceptable "science of behavior" hardly differentiates psychology from zoology or economics, to name but two. It remains for the social historian to chart the historical accidents which have resulted in the establishment of separated academic disciplines and distinct professional groups; no attempt will be made here to erect definitional boundaries between psychology and allied fields of study. A procedure better justified by our interest in the language of psychology is to accept the division of disciplines as given, however artificial it may seem, and proceed with the more accessible question: What do psychologists talk about?

Even this limited question cannot be answered short of an encyclopedic history of the science,[4] but the general cast of psychological thought can be shown in less ambitious ways. Consider the titles listed in Table 3. These are the titles of the first ten articles from the *Psychological Review* of 1894 and the first ten articles from the same

[4] Brett's *History of Psychology* (1912–21) or Peters' (1953) abridgement of it provides a thorough treatment of psychology before the twentieth century. Boring (1929) has written of the more recent history of psychology with care and great skill.

Table 3

A Sample Survey of American Psychological Theory

The Titles Listed Are Drawn from the *Psychological Review* for the Years 1894, 1904, 1914, 1924, 1934, 1944, and 1954

1894		1904	
The Case of John Bunyan	J. Royce	The Participation of the Eye Movements in the Visual Perception of Motion	R. Dodge
Arithmetic by Smell	F. Galton	An Inquiry Into the Nature of Hallucination	B. Sidis
The Psychology of Infant Language	J. Dewey	The Limits of Pragmatism	J. M. Baldwin
The Psychological Standpoint	G. S. Fullerton	Theory and Practice	W. L. Bryan
Community and Association of Ideas: A Statistical Study	J. Jastrow	On the Attributes of the Sensations	M. Meyer
Reaction-Times and the Velocity of the Nervous Impulse	C. S. Dolley and J. McK. Cattell	The Law of Attraction in Relation to Some Visual and Tactual Illusions	H. J. Pearce
Freedom and Psycho-Genesis	A. T. Ormond	The Relation between the Vaso-Motor Waves and Reaction-Times	W. R. Wright
A Study of Fear as a Primitive Emotion	H. M. Stanley	On the Horopter	G. T. Stevens
Experiments in Space Perception	J. H. Hyslop	An Experimental Study of the Physiological Accompaniments of Feeling	L. P. Boggs
Personality-Suggestion	J. M. Baldwin	The Psychology of Aesthetic Reaction to Rectangular Forms	T. H. Haines and A. E. Davies

1914		1924	
Individual Differences before, during and after Practice	H. L. Hollingworth	The Problem of Consciousness	W. S. Hunter
A Time Experiment in Psychophysics	D. L. Lyon and H. L. Eno	Behaviorism and Behavior	A. P. Weiss
The Effect on Foveal Vision of Bright Surroundings	P. W. Cobb	The Structure of Thought	O. L. Reiser
The Expression of the Emotions	A. M. Feleky	Introverts and Extroverts	M. Freyd
A Slit Mechanism for Selecting Three Measurable Monochromatic Bands	H. M. Johnson	The Mental Test as a Psychological Method	L. M. Terman
Psychology as a Science of Behavior	B. H. Bode	Principles of Selection in 'Trial and Error' Learning	W. R. Wilson
The Self and the Ego	K. Dunlap	A Psychological Description of Intelligence	R. H. Wheeler
The Phenomena of Indirect Color Vision	J. W. Baird	Symposium: Contributions of Freudism to Psychology	L. L. Thurstone, J. H. Leuba, K. S. Lashley, J. Jastrow
The Mental and the Physical	H. C. Warren	The Measurement of Intelligence: The Present Status	E. L. Thorndike
The Theory of Two Factors	C. Spearman	Four Varieties of Behaviorism	R. S. Woodworth

Table 3 (Continued)

A SAMPLE SURVEY OF AMERICAN PSYCHOLOGICAL THEORY (Continued)

1934	
The Vectors of Mind	L. L. Thurstone
The Concept of the Habit-Family Hierarchy and Maze Learning	C. L. Hull
The Physiological Basis of Linguistic Development and of the Ontogeny of Meaning	I. Latif
Tonal Fusion	C. C. Pratt
Constructive Reactionism: Knowledge of Reality from a Psychophysiological Viewpoint	R. Dodge
The Conceptual Framework of Tolman's Purposive Behaviorism	S. C. Pepper
Frequency, Duration and Recency *vs.* Double Stimulation	M. F. Meyer
Emotion: An Example of the Need for Reorientation in Psychology	E. Duffy
Recent Trends in Science and the Development of Modern Typology	H. Shuey
A Consideration of Interacting Pattern Theories of Feeling and Emotion	R. M. Bellows and R. G. Whisler

1944	
The Logic of Psychophysical Measurement	G. Bergmann and K. W. Spence
Repetition and Learning	T. W. Cook
The Screen Test in Military Selection	W. A. Hunt C. L. Wittson H. I. Harris
The Nature of Theory Construction in Contemporary Psychology	K. W. Spence
If-Then Relations in Paralogics	H. M. Johnson
Brightness Enhancement in Flickering Light	T. L. Jahn
Violence between Nations; Deeper Sources; The Way of Liberation	G. M. Stratton
The Analysis of Verbal Behavior	J. B. Carroll
The Realism of Expectations	F. W. Irwin
Social Interaction and Collective Behavior	M. Smith

1954	
The Physiology of Motivation	E. Stellar
The S-R Reinforcement Theory of Extinction	H. Gleitman J. Nachmias U. Neisser
Punishment: I. The Avoidance Hypothesis	J. A. Dinsmoor
The Measurement of Values	L. L. Thurstone
A Neural Model for Sign-Gestalt Theory	J. Olds
The Place of Physiological Constructs in a Genetic Explanatory System	G. Smith
A Note on Stimulus-Intensity Dynamism (V)	F. A. Logan
Three Dimensions of Emotion	H. Schlosberg
A Mathematical and an Electronic Model for Learning	L. B. Wyckoff, Jr.
A Statistical Theory of the Phenomenon of Subception	D. Howes

journal during several following decades. This hasty survey, biased as it is by selection from a single source and limited by its small scope, serves as illustration for some general points that can be made about the development of psychology.

Several persistent themes run through the titles over six decades—an interest in the biological determinants of behavior and a dedication to method are the most obvious—but the variety in which they are imbedded is manifold. Psychology is somehow concerned with human and other animal behavior, but the specific character of the field will depend at any given moment on considerations which are not yet fully understood. A new technique, such as barpressing or psychoanalysis, will set off a long line of speculation and empirical research which could not readily have been anticipated before the technique was announced. A new conceptualization, such as Lewin's formulation of conflict or Piaget's view of thinking, may divert enormous energies into a reevaluation of previous positions and start a new group of theoretical arguments. Here again, what is the case with less esoteric approaches to reality is true of systematic study—the acquisition of information and the definition of an area of study do not proceed with easily predicted regularity; just as the use of the hit-and-run stratagem in baseball requires a new alignment of the game, so some "breakthrough" in science may require a revision of the interests of a discipline.

Psychology, over the historical haul, has been peculiarly disposed to such restatement, having been variously the science of soul, of mind, of mental acts, of glandular secretions and muscle twitches, of human behavior, of instincts and their modification. In the face of this disorder, it is unwise to attempt a new general definition. Rather, at any moment, the content of psychology can be specified by two criteria—the aspects of reality to which the psychologist attends and the theories he invents about those aspects. The first limitation asks: What is the psychologist studying? What parts of the socially shared environment does he want to predict or control? On this count, some limited definition of psychology is possible; most of the phenomena that have been subjected to examination by psychologists fall into the categories *movements of animals* or *movements and speech of human beings*. Though this is hardly a rigorous setting of boundaries, it is perilous to be more exact. On the second criterion, i.e., the theory the psychologist uses to order his descriptions and to make predictions, not even a loose statement can be made defining psychology. Almost all kinds of words have been used at one time or another to categorize and explain the movements and speech of people. Only after we have surveyed some of the alternatives available at mid-twentieth century can we return to a consideration of what properties they share. For the present, no restriction will be suggested for the content of psychological theories.

TWO FALLACIES IN THE DEFINITION OF PSYCHOLOGY

It has often been said that, whatever other characteristics psychology may have, the study of human behavior is unique in one sense—its *immediate* relation to experience. In Chapters 2 and 3, the appeal to immediate experience for a language of science was seen to be untenable. Even psychologists, when talking *about* experience, need to use a non-phenomenological language. A related aspect of this problem can be seen in considering the thesis that a science of psychology is fundamental or propaedeutic to all other sciences. According to this thesis psychology is fundamentally unlike the natural sciences, which deal with derivatives of experience, with phenomena like rocks and stars and chemical compounds that are *mediated* by human perception. Psychology on the contrary is concerned with the raw stuff of which other sciences are made, the immediate relation of man with things. The so-called propaedeutic character of psychology has received its most elegant and convincing statement from a non-phenomenological point of view by Stevens, who writes in part:

> A word or statement means something in psychology, as in physics, only if the criteria of its applicability or truth consist of concrete operations which may be performed. . . . Complex operations are always reducible to more simple discriminatory acts, and all 'explanations' consist of detailing a complex set of operations in terms of simpler ones. . . . *The elementary discriminatory reaction on the part of human beings, then, is the fundamental operation of all science;* and by discrimination is meant the concrete, 'physical' reactions of the organism to either internal or external environmental conditions. (Stevens, 1936, p. 94 f., italics ours.)

We will argue later with this conception of "explanation," but to the point at hand, it is important to note that Stevens rules out explicitly the suggestion that psychology is prior or propaedeutic to other sciences in any *historical* sense:

> Indeed the historical perspective renders somewhat ridiculous the picture of a German professor [Wundt] implying late in the nineteenth century that his newly founded science investigates the phenomena which determine what physics can or cannot be.

But, if psychology is not historically prior, and if the grounding in raw unique experience is abandoned, in what remaining sense is the study of human behavior *fundamental?* One answer is obvious—only human beings make science—but the advocates of propaedeusis seem to mean more than this. Stevens maintains that the hypothesis of propaedeusis is necessary to take account of the epistemological infinite regress.

> Psychology studies the nature of the organism which determines in part the nature of science. But, it will be objected, this is equivalent to saying that psychology studies the organism which determines the nature of psychology—an obvious circle. . . . Nevertheless we must start somewhere, so we plunge *in medias res,* and, although we then face the problem of an infinite regress, we try to understand rather than to worry about it.

It has been the burden of an earlier discussion here that systematic study must start somewhere, that we must "plunge *in medias res.*" One may disagree with Stevens, however, in holding that such a plunge *necessarily* lands you in the arms of psychology. There is an essential distinction to be made: Although science may in fact start with discriminatory reactions of human beings, this is not equivalent to saying that *a science of discriminatory reactions* is fundamental to science making. Human behavior is propaedeutic to science, but psychology as a systematic discipline is not. This point is closely related to the subject-scientist distinction discussed in Chapter 2. The investigation of the behavior of the scientist grows out of the science of psychology, but the science is not prerequisite to the behavior. Failure to understand or to predict the scientific behavior of human beings places no limitations on their behavior. In analogy, you don't have to know about the let-down reflex to milk a cow.

However, there is an important point contained in Stevens' argument which deserves underscoring: ". . . whether we like it or not, we are dealing with a universe of continuities with no ends to grasp," and throughout the scientific process we must make posits about a number of issues on which we cannot adduce satisfactory evidence. It is the insistence on *particular* posits to which an objection is entered. In some future "Let's pretend" of science, a strict treatment of human discriminatory reactions may be an essential part; it may even be that an early investigation of them is good general strategy, but the procedures of scientific investigation are not so rigidly set that we can safely insist on a formal hierarchy of disciplines. The task of psychology is to predict behavior, including that of the scientist, but it seems unlikely that even complete knowledge of human modes of perception will change the utility of Maxwellian equations or the virtues of Euclidean geometry in surveying terrestrial areas, regardless of their innocence of psychological sophistication.

If a sharp focus is kept on the central goals of precision and prediction, then the relation of one area of study to another can be restricted to the requirements of those goals; if variation in astronomical observations sets a problem that only the study of the astronomer-as-human-observer can resolve, then a call is made for psychological information; if the apparatus for recording heart rate is being crowded by interfering "noise," then a textbook on electronics becomes relevant. Both the game of making psychology dependent on physics, and the defense-by-reversal of making physics dependent on psychology suffer from a failure to recognize that science is a shifting collection of reliable information, leaps of faith, and more-or-less good guesses. The geometrical analogy of human knowledge as a pyramid with physics (or psychology) as its base is probably inferior to a symbol which emphasizes the interrelations among disciplines and, even more to the point, the provisional character of all scientific knowledge.

The second fallacy in the definition of psychology concerns not the central place of psychology but rather its hopelessness. According to this *dogma of ineffability,* the regress which Stevens has noted makes it impossible to carry on a systematic study of human behavior; Jones looks at Smith's behavior, but his conclusions will be contaminated by the determinants of his own behavior, which include the observation of Smith, and so on. This objection to scientific psychology has two aspects. The first concerns the technical problem of reducing the "interference" which may exist between observer and observed, and it is to this important procedural and conceptual point that the earlier treatment of the subject-scientist distinction was addressed (see Chapter 2). The second aspect of the ineffability position is that there is some logically necessary difficulty in the study of human behavior which demands that we abandon on a priori grounds the search for regularities. Certainly it is true that questions of human choice and the complex psychological issues invoked by a discussion of free will preclude a glib statement of simple determinants of human behavior, but once more this objection can only be met on the pragmatic ground of whether or not the prediction of behavior becomes more efficient in spite of these complexities. The "decontamination" of the psychologist will continue to be a technical hurdle to an effective science of human behavior, but the attempt cannot be ruled out of court on nonempirical briefs; the history of science is too well laced with accomplished "impossibilities" for the researcher to accept seriously metaphysical or theological injunctions to stop work.

SUMMARY

In order to proceed with the construction of theory, i.e., the anticipation of empirical events, it is necessary to establish some elementary posits or primitive postulates about which no argument is relevant and for which only inadequate justification can be given. The usual starting point of systematic study is the everyday world of common words and unhesitating action. These reliable and shared behaviors of ordinary living are the basis of what is called the *posit of reality*. This notion, together with others about the lack of capriciousness of events and the stability of certain phenomena, permit the scientist to go ahead with the slow accumulation of observations and testing of guesses which result in explicit theories. Such theories are necessarily limited in extent, and take into account only a relatively small fraction of the posited reality. Beyond this limitation, the entire theoretical structure, from primitive posit to detailed hypothesis, is subject to revision when measured against the adequacy of its predictions. Thus, any scientific theory is a rather limited and temporary specification of rules and of data, subject to change at all levels.

In the history of empirical research, different disciplines have separated themselves from the parent study of philosophy, becoming more highly specialized in technique and theory, yet retaining a relationship to other systematic study which makes the precise definition of a particular science hazardous. Psychology, although its definition has been changed several times in its brief independent existence, seems at present to be concerned largely with animal movement and human speech, treating of these aspects of ordinary reality in widely variant language systems. Because psychology is about human behavior and because science is a human activity, psychology has sometimes been seen as the propaedeutic or fundamental science. Moreover, because the human study of human behavior invariably raises questions about choice and free will, the impossibility of a systematic psychology has on occasion been maintained. Considering the tentative character of scientific endeavor and its justification by successful anticipation, neither of these positions appears to be justified.

chapter ten

The protocol language of psychology

THE DICTUM THAT THE LANGUAGE OF PSYchology has something to do with animal movement and speech requires only that, at some point in the process of theory construction and test, reference be made to events of this sort. It should be recognized at once that this requirement does not narrow the range of admissible language systems a great deal; it does not, for example, permit an immediate choice between

"The Ego presents itself to the Superego as a love object"

and

"${}_{S}H_{R} = f(N)$"

on grounds of theoretical usefulness. So long as these general statements lead somehow to protocol statements in the basic vocabulary of psychology, the dictum is respected.

What other restrictions operate on the language of psychological theory? On what grounds can we choose one formulation over another? The latter question introduces the problem in its most general form by emphasizing that, among the sentences which make up the language of psychology, there is a wide range in *degree of acceptability*. Some sentences ("That is a rat," "Subject 16 is premenarchal," "He called Card 5 a butterfly") are almost never argued about; other sentences ("Learning is dependent on reduction of stimulus intensity," "Color shock is an index of impulse breakthrough," "Men desire, but fear, incest") are accepted by relatively small numbers of people, and argued over by professional psychologists. Sentences of the first sort contain a now familiar vocabulary—the invariant terms of psychology which name objects and events. It may appear that use of the basic vocabulary alone determines acceptability, but reflection on the following sentences in the basic vocabulary emphasizes that acceptability depends on more complex considerations than appropriate labeling:

"Rats solve anagrams faster than people."
"Hunger given to activity increases the dog."

Conversely, sentences not in the basic vocabulary may be highly acceptable. For example:

"Reinforcement increases the probability of response emission."

To put it another way, variation in the acceptability of statements relates to the degree of choice a reasonable man has in evaluating them. Few of us would insist that rats cannot learn mazes, but our sanity would not be at issue if we disagreed with, say, a learning-theory analysis of schizophrenic symptoms. *Acceptability* is elusive to precise description, and doubtlessly can be best represented as a continuum of change from the obvious to the absurd. Yet, even if a justifiable line between the acceptable and the unacceptable cannot be drawn clearly, it is important in understanding psychological theory to examine those statements which fall at the extremes of this dimension.

Moreover, acceptability varies in at least two major aspects—the reasonableness of a statement or its testability on one hand, and the degree of confirmation a statement has met with in actual test. For the present, no hard-and-fast separation will be made between these two sources of acceptability. In the present chapter, some words and sentences in the language of psychology which are highly acceptable will be under discussion; in the chapters which follow, words and statements about which honest contention is possible will be treated.

THE BASIC VOCABULARY AND PROTOCOL STATEMENTS

Among the most highly acceptable words in a scientific language are those of the basic vocabulary. It will be recalled that many common-language terms find their way into technical-language systems with little modification: Designations of organisms such as "rat" or "child," designations of space such as "up" or "in front of," designations of time such as "before" or "while," and many other words of everyday usage are gathered up into systematic language almost without notice.[1] Such words function in both the common language of the street and the sometimes artificial language of the scientist precisely because they can be used reliably and with little chance of errors in action directed by them. These words are part of the basic language —the *protocol statements*—of any science.

Another group of words operates in the same way that the invariant terms drawn from common usage do; these are the words specially introduced into the scientific language by some definitional device (see Chapters 5 and 6). These constructs may seem farfetched and strange to the layman, but they share with much of common language the essential characteristic of having highly invariant usage. On this criterion, the technical observation words of the scientist are also part of the vocabulary of protocol statements.

Protocol statements are the sentences which are usually found in the Method and Results sections of journal articles, detailing information like:

> *Procedure.*—The *S* was placed in the starting box of the alley, with the starting-box door closed and the goal-box door open. When the starting-box door was raised, the shock and the timer were turned on, and *S* could run to the end of the alley. When *S* crossed beneath a white line on the Plexiglas of the end box, *E* threw a toggle switch which stopped the timer, and simultaneously the door of the goal box was lowered.

or

---

[1] Even such indicator words as "up" and "before" can be freed of the disabilities discussed in Chapter 1 when they function in sets of sentences.

> Latency scores (total time spent in the high-shock alley) were transformed into speed scores by multiplying the reciprocal of the time score by 100. For each *S* the median speed of the last five trials was calculated, and for each group the mean speed was determined from these median speeds. (Campbell and Kraeling, 1953, p. 98.)

The difference between these protocol statements and what will later be called theoretical sentences can be illustrated by jumping ahead in the same article (p. 100) to the Discussion section:

> These findings tend to negate any theory of learning which is based on absolute amounts of stimulus change, and make it necessary to consider the drive level before and after the drive reduction. However, these results were not intended to give a precise Weber-Fechner fraction for reinforcement. They merely indicate that a given amount of reinforcement is more effective at low levels of drive than at high levels of drive.

Juxtaposed in this somewhat unnatural way, the shift from a language which may be technical in spots but is always comprehensible and acceptable to psychologists over to a language of interpretation and commentary outlines a central problem in constructing a language of psychology: What do you say about what you observed?

Drawn as it is from one of American psychology's most elegant and well-worked areas—animal learning—the foregoing example does not represent an extreme in the leap from "description" to "interpretation." In many attempts to understand and predict human behavior, conclusions of a highly argumentative character follow (at least typographically) from rather limited and commonplace observations. Freud's (1910) treatment of da Vinci may stand here as representative of *le grand jeté* in psychological analysis.[2]

However complex theories may be, they all rest on statements of evidence, on the protocol sentences of a science. This is so homely and obvious that several important implications of the special nature of protocol statements may be missed. The central theme of earlier chapters has been that human communication, and most especially scientific communication, depends on the existence of a shared language about which there is relatively little argument, a foothold in

---

[2] This is not to assert that Freud's analysis is necessarily wrong, or that animal research is necessarily more fruitful for psychology; what is under examination here is the range of acceptability of statements in psychology.

ignorance which will permit us to start any investigation. Just as the common language of a cultural group serves communication among members of the group, so the protocol language of a science is the shared reference point for systematic research. It is not putting it too strongly to maintain that protocol language, the statement of relations among terms in the basic vocabulary, is the irreducible minimum of empirical science—irreducible in at least two senses. First of all, protocol statements represent the end point of intersubjective agreement—whatever arguments may exist on more abstract levels of scientific language, there must be no argument about protocol statements or else a science cannot exist. A researcher may think his colleague unwise to spend his effort on the investigation of learning in Acoela, but he cannot doubt the assertion that "S moved closer to the glass rod within 0.5 seconds of the rod's immersion." Statements in the protocol language represent what are more usually known as facts or data, and the only responses which can be made against their acceptance is "You lie" or "You made an error of observation." It is a posit of great importance in scientific research that assigns truth value to protocol statements—they are the last parts of a language system to be tampered with in rebuilding a theoretical model.

As well as representing a terminus in the attempt of scientists to understand one another, protocol statements are the irreducible minimum of empirical science in another sense. Systematic language is not made up of sentences about individual events; scarcely anyone would be interested in a recitation of the doings of Rat A, then Rat B, then Rat C, and so on, no matter how solidly acceptable the language of the recitation may be. Scientific statements are made about "rats," not about "Rat A," about "people," not about "Miss A," usually with reference to the behavior of groups of organisms, or of deviations from some value, or of comparisons among groups. Unlike the raw protocol statements about individual events, which are accepted or not on the extrascientific grounds of the researcher's competence and honesty, these summary statements can be said to be *more or less probable* according to certain arithmetic and statistical rules. For example, a research report may state that a group of animals deprived of food for four hours ran an alley more slowly than a group deprived for thirty hours, or that those subjects who had high scores on a questionnaire containing questions about indigestion, palpitation, and sweating also had long latencies to Card 9 of the Rorschach. The research may be based on an elaborate theory about physiological mechanisms in hunger or derive from Freud's speculations about the function of anxiety, and may moreover lead the researcher to write at length about the implications of his findings for other behavior in animals and people.[3] But the probability values that are printed in his journal article pertain to sentences based on the specific behavior of organisms treated and observed in quite specific ways. The significant statistical test justifies an assertion of the likelihood that a similar handling of similar animals will produce the same result; there is no such mathematical apparatus for giving a confirmation value to the theory from which the research develops, or even to a more limited hypothesis which is not stated in the protocol language.[4] We do not confirm, by the usual statistical techniques, the presence of pathological trends in children deprived of adequate nurturance—we rather express the probability that someone else following our directions will find a similar relationship between certain observable conditions and certain observable behaviors. The precise statement of how the relevant observations were obtained and what relationship resulted is properly made in terms of the protocol language. The justification for this requirement rests on the resolution of the notion of *similarity* in the assertion: If the conditions of the observation are similar, the results will be more-or-less duplicated.

The best assurance that the similarity criterion is met comes from the use of a language system which is minimally vague and ambiguous, which has the widest range of understanding and the least possibility of error in application. Unless we have a basic language which permits the inference of class membership (i.e., that Condition A is like Condition A′), the application of statistical methods becomes impossible. Thus, it is not only on grounds of ease of communication among scientists, but also in order to meet a precondition of statistical generalization, that protocol statements form an irreducible minimum for empirical science. Scientific language cannot be less than this, or it fails to meet the fundamental requirements of repeatability; that scientific language can be more than a collection of protocol statements will be the theme of later chapters.

Although the development of a vocabulary and grammar adequate to the task of describing research techniques and results is clearly an essential element in the scientific process, we have seen that the basic vocabulary is not easily come by. This "best" language of reality forms

---

[3] Quite properly on occasion, but not by a process of statistical induction (see Chapters 11 and 12).

[4] The convoluted issue of theory confirmation will be discussed in Chapter 13.

slowly in any empirical science; a researcher may believe his communication to be utterly unambiguous, only to find that someone else either cannot follow his directions or else disagrees with his statement of findings. In either case, at least one of the workers is not using the "best" or protocol language, and a change must be entered.[5] However, in all but the most hoary sciences, it is misleading to speak of *the* protocol language; in the face of a single event, it may suit the purposes of different observers to use different verbal responses and the only continuing restraint is that the language chosen be highly acceptable to a cadre of experts in that it permits them to act in accord with the language with little chance of error. Over a period of time, as observations are accumulated, as techniques develop, as misunderstandings are resolved, a core of statement forms comes to be widely used and rarely questioned. Dull on occasion, the refinement of the protocol language—the language of what you "see"—is requisite to the nobler language of theory—the language of what you think about what you "see."

PROTOCOL STATEMENTS IN PSYCHOLOGY

Under the general *caveat lector* that the notion of protocol language is not an absolute one by any means, that today's theoretical hunch may be classed as obviously unambiguous tomorrow, just as today's easily accepted description may turn out to be highly complex and obscuring, we can attempt a rough classification of the kinds of protocol statements which appear with relative frequency in the language of psychology.[6]

Statements of Recognition

In this first category of protocol statements are the indications by the scientist of what he is going to talk about, the pointing out of the

[5] The second worker may obtain different results without forcing a change in the protocol language; there may be after all a lack of confirmation of a prediction. What is referred to here is a disagreement in the *statement* of obtained results, in the structure of the language of "raw data."

[6] Even the least ambitious classificatory schemes tend to become rigid and prescriptive. Like the man who was somewhat ashamed of his flat feet until he learned that he had *pes planus,* the classifier sometimes promotes the obvious without adding much information. The classification proposed here is meant to serve as a way of speaking, descriptive at best.

empirical events under his consideration. This is oftentimes so obvious that no explicit statement is made, but if it aimed at completeness, a protocol language would contain sentences like:

"This is a rat."
"This light is the conditioned stimulus."
"When the lever goes down 2 centimeters, it is a bar-press."
"A description of a man is scored '*H*'."

These sentences are event definitions, combining the terms which are acquired in ways treated of earlier (see Part I, *passim*); most of the considerations which determine the admissibility of the basic vocabulary into the language of psychology apply as well to the sanction of statements of recognition. Nothing is added beyond the indication of class inclusion so that everyone concerned is sure about what events are relevant to observation.

Narrative Statements

Narrative statements are given even less conscious heed than the primitive statements of recognition. These ordinary parts of the language of psychology carry the burden of communicating the researcher's methods and often his results. The first two quotations on pages 165–166 are largely in the narrative style of protocol language, and contain what the writer thinks is important for his reader to know about the experiment. In general, the narration of procedure is put in the common language, using the vocabulary and grammatical forms of English, although specialized reporting systems such as IBM punched cards might also serve as "narrative statements." In the historical development of a science and with the growth of editorial power, the narrative protocol language tends to become more and more stylized and rigid, with an accompanying increase in jargon words—words new to the common language or having a somewhat different use from their normal one. In the examples which follow, one from an early volume of the *Journal of Experimental Psychology*, and one from a more recent issue, note can be made of changes in the character of English style. In 1924:

> *Preliminary training.* In a series of preliminary experiments in which the electric shock was used to produce the opposing stimulus, it was found that on the first trial the rat walked with little hesitation on to the brass plates, and when he had received

> the first shock he continued across the plates about as often as he turned back. However, in his subsequent experiences with the plates his behavior was quite different. As a rule, unless given some very strong stimulus which would make him do otherwise, he tended to keep clear of all contact with the plates. When given the necessary stimulus to make him approach the plates, he would go up to them very slowly and would cautiously reach out his foot to touch them. In most instances the foot was jerked back before it had even touched the plates. After crossing the plates and receiving the shock a second time, this avoiding behavior was more pronounced. I see no better way of explaining this change in the animal's behavior than to say that from his first two experiences with the plates he had "learned" to avoid them. From these experiments and from many other observations, I am convinced that with the lower animals as well as with the human, a single experience is very often sufficient to cause a marked change in the animal's future behavior. . . . Just as in the case of the man who having gone thru certain experiences is 'never the same again,' so this rat, having once received the shock, would never willingly come in contact with the plates again. (Moss, 1924, p. 166.)

And, in 1954:

> The *S*s were 96 experimentally naive, male albino rats of the Wistar strain. The ages of the *S*s ranged from 50 to 75 days at the beginning of the experiment.
>
> The apparatus was two single-unit T-mazes, identical except that one was painted white and the other black. The roof of each maze was covered with .25-in. mesh hardware cloth. Cloth curtains, the same color as the maze, were placed in front of the doors to the goal boxes. Guillotine doors of light sheet metal were operated by *E*. The floor and sides of the left goal box of each maze were covered with .25-in. mesh hardware cloth; the right goal boxes remained unlined. The use of these different cues was intended to accelerate learning by decreasing stimulus generalization from one side of the maze to the other. (Moltz, 1954, p. 419.)

Although the latter method of reporting may fail to make use of the possibilities of English expression, the increase in comprehensibility and the reduction of "noise" consequent on the establishment of a standard narrative style well outweighs the loss.

Narrative statements in the protocol language, therefore, serve to communicate (usually in the terms of the common language of the writer) in as unambiguous a way as possible a report of the researcher's behavior and of the behavior of his subjects. Except for specialized or jargon words and phrases, the narrative language will normally be comprehensible to the intelligent layman.

Instrument Statements and Auxiliary Hypotheses

In the sections of research reports which most readily fit the description "protocol language," there often appear sentences having to do with mechanical, electronic, or other instruments. Counters are used to record bar-presses; optical systems of great complexity are required in some psychophysical research; the lowly stop watch measures running times, latency of response to projective material, and duration of task-performance by industrial workers; timers, stimulating equipment, a very flood of apparatus is used in present-day psychological research. Yet, when these complicated devices are referred to in the description of a study, their mention is almost casual—the scientist who will be careful to insist that his animals are not from the Bar Harbor strains but were developed locally will toss off the statement that his data were obtained from a 16-channel Grass electroencephalograph. This is certainly not a protocol statement in the sense that it represents the closest reasonable approach to the language of common reality; the construction and working of a stop watch or a Hunter timer are often mysteries to the people using them, to say nothing of the complexity of the theoretical systems which underlie the functioning of even simple physical devices. It is probably not uncommon for the theory of the apparatus to be more abstract than the psychological hypothesis under test. Still, rarely does a psychologist feel called upon to publish the circuits of his apparatus in detail, much less to discourse on the implications of quantum theory for his research. To understand how even tough-minded empirical researchers can so easily accept the theories of other disciplines in the presentation of their own "raw" data, we must digress for a little to discuss the notion of *auxiliary hypothesis.*

When a psychologist sets out to study certain behaviors, say the effect of fatigue on reaction time, he sets up his hypothesis in a certain way, and carefully specifies the observations he will make, together with a description of his procedures. Whatever results he obtains are presumably relevant to the hypothesis under test. But the interpretation of the results depends on the confirmation of quite a few hypotheses which are not being tested in the experiment—among them, that his clocks will operate in the same way when he is running Group I as they do when he is running Group II, that the cumulative recorder will not click twice for right-handed subjects and only once for left-handed subjects, that the relays will not vary in their performance as a function of the experimenter's mood. All of these assumptions serve as auxiliary hypotheses which are taken as confirmed in interpreting the results of the study; the experimenter, in addition to all the other assumptions he must make about reality, makes a posit of instrument stability, and does not anticipate that casual variation in his clocks, or vacuum tubes, or mechanical systems will play an important part in determining his results.[7] Fortunately for the psychologist who has a fondness for gadgetry, hypotheses about the determinants of instrument function and the physical theories which pertain to optical and mechanical systems are so highly confirmed and stable that there is usually no need for him to test for curious variation. Thus, to the protocol language based on common reality, there can be added quasi-protocol statements about phenomena which have been thoroughly investigated and which have had the reliability of their occurrence highly confirmed in other disciplines, a condition which makes the protocol languages of psychology a blend of street talk and the elegancies of physics.

The auxiliary hypotheses implicit in a sentence like "Subject 4B ran the alley in 14.3 seconds, as measured by a Springfield timer" do not in themselves warrant further discussion; auxiliary hypotheses are of critical importance in a scientific language, however, when they are *not* highly confirmed outside the research in which they function. Statements about paper-and-pencil "instruments" in psychology are pertinent illustrations of the operation of the posit of instrument stability (auxiliary hypothesis) where we are much less sure that the values obtained do not vary, say, as a function of the researcher's mood.

The phrase "very compulsive by Rorschach test" is not admissible to the protocol language of psychology, not because it fails to have the ring of physics, but rather because its acceptance requires the confirmation of a number of auxiliary hypotheses which have not yet been put to adequate test. The auxiliary hypotheses relevant to the Rorschach

[7] Quite incidentally, one of the best *formal* arguments against the easy acceptance of parapsychological hypotheses is that the operation of such notions as psychokinesis would substantially weaken, if not preclude, the posit of instrument stability.

example would include statements about the stability of human behavior, the relationship between personality and perception, and so on. There is probably nothing *necessary* in the superiority of statements about physical gadgets over statements about psychological gadgets, but it is a compelling matter of fact that sentences about timers, oscillators, and relays are highly acceptable; many of those about testing "instruments," diagnostic hunches, and psychological "observations" are not.

Statements about Numerals

There is a group of auxiliary hypotheses which figure in the protocol language of psychology even more frequently and on occasion with lower confirmation value than do auxiliary hypotheses about instruments. These are the assumptions which underlie the use of numerals.

Each empirical science, as it piles research on research in the development of techniques and principles, becomes increasingly dependent on arithmetic or other general mathematical statements of its results and conclusions. Quantification has become the brand of "true" science and Number is called the Language of Science with little objection from anyone. This plausible exaggeration depends for its acceptance chiefly on two considerations—the central importance of measurement in the empirical sciences and the unique communication characteristics of the mathematical way of speaking. The use of numbers has so infiltrated our lives, both everyday and scientific, that we can scarcely conceive the importance of this curious and ancient language of mathematics. Imagine trying to build a house, or buy a suit, or describe one's fiancée—to say nothing of the more complex tasks of a technical civilization—without the communication tools of numbers. Here is a unique language, so general and abstract that it functions across people, common languages, and time with a remarkably low loss in intelligibility. Because of the invariance of intraverbal connections in mathematics and the implied precision of communication, science would be inconceivable without an arithmetic of some kind.[8] As

[8] "Training in science, logic, and mathematics consists in part in establishing strong restricted intraverbal responses. . . . The trained logician differs from other people precisely because he possesses strong and effective intraverbal responses in the field of logical thinking. One of the chief purposes of a reduction to symbols is to avoid interference from the chaotic intraverbal reinforcements of everyday discourse." (Skinner, 1948, p. 48.)

Dantzig writes:

> The mathematician may be compared to a designer of garments, who is utterly oblivious of the creatures whom his garments may fit. To be sure, his art originated in the necessity for clothing such creatures, but this was long ago; to this day a shape will occasionally appear which will fit into the garment as if the garment had been made for it. Then there is no end of surprise and of delight! (Dantzig, 1954, p. 231 f.)

Not only is *some* mathematical statement necessary to science, but the particular kind available has much to do with the definition of what the scientific discipline can accomplish. The intimate relation between Newtonian physics and the invention of the calculus, or the changes in social science research with recent developments in statistical theory serve to emphasize the interlacing of mathematical tools and empirical science. Even notational techniques prejudice the course of systematic study, as some reflection on the difficulties of simple multiplication in Roman numerals, or the problems of computation before the introduction of 0 will illustrate. The junior sciences like psychology are heirs to a mathematical apparatus of notable precision and generality, and a glance through professional publications in the social sciences will indicate a strong bent to use as much of this apparatus as possible.[9]

Yet for all its virtues as a language for science, mathematics has certain peculiarities that must be recognized by physicist and psychologist alike. Unlike ordinary communication systems which are useful and meaningful to the extent that they are about something, the operations of mathematics can be performed without this reference.[10] It is possible to add without adding anything, to develop intricate mathematical proofs without proving anything about events, even to invent whole new systems of mathematics without anticipating their relevance

---

[9] One of the difficulties in making guesses about the future success of scientific attempts in psychology stems from the impossibility of predicting what kinds of mathematics will be found useful over the next years. With some impressive exceptions, psychologists have not had "their own" mathematics, but rather have depended on the legacy of the older sciences. See von Neumann (1947) for a discussion of the invention of mathematical techniques to meet empirical requirements.

[10] Except in the trivial sense that the mathematician works with paper and pencil or blackboard and chalk. In Skinner's terminology, contemporary mathematics is entirely intraverbal, and contains in its language no tacts. We shall see that the counting response is not part of mathematics in the present sense.

to anything that goes on in the world. Mathematics is the game with rules par excellence, and the use of numbers, unlike most games, can proceed without reference to time, work, or income.

This relative freedom from the constrictions of common reality no longer holds when numerals—the words like "one" or "thirty," the symbols like "½" or "62"—are *used* in the procedures of empirical science. For then the pure mathematical system is interpreted, and some use is assigned the terms which the mathematician has been treating emptily. In figuring up the monthly grocery bill or in stating the results of an experiment, the mathematical abstractions have been put into some relation with the occurrences of the day, usually by a set of translation statements which indicate what "3" or "+" or "Σ" means in the common or protocol language. For convenience, we can call the numbers of the pure mathematical theorist "numbers" and the interpreted numbers of the empirical scientist "numerals." The first group has the characteristics and rules for use which are developed for it within the language of mathematics; the latter set has to do with events and observations in the world of the researcher, and does not necessarily function in the same way that the mathematician's well-behaved numbers do. Therefore, when numerals appear in the reports of empirical scientists and they are treated as though they were numbers, some rather heady auxiliary assumptions are being made about the fit between the empty mathematical premises and the interpreted system of the researcher. Because this goodness of fit is often not explicitly tested in a particular study, interpretations and conclusions drawn from the study must take into account the presence of a potential discrepancy—that the mathematics may be inappropriate to the task at hand. Many factors will influence whether or not this discrepancy occurs, but almost all reports of empirical research carry explicit or implicit assumptions about the use of numerals.

Understanding the scientific function of numerals is further complicated when we consider that there is no single interpretation scheme which hard work or ingenuity will uncover; numerals may be used in science in several quite different ways. In the paragraphs to follow, some of the possible interpretations of numerals in the protocol language of psychology will be dealt with.

NOMINAL (INDEX) NUMERALS. The most limited function of numerals is in naming a class of events or indicating class membership. One group of animals in an experiment may be called Group I, with no assumptions that this numeral serves any purpose but to provide author and readers with a convenient name. Certainly, there is no suggestion that Group I is one-half of Group II in any sense, and a non-numerical reference (Experimental Group and Control Group, for example) would have done the nominal job as well. The only requirement on the use of index numerals is that they be employed in a stable way throughout the discourse, Group I always meaning the same collection of animals, and so on. Numerals sometimes occur in everyday settings without even this limitation; the numeral "88" on the back of a football player's uniform may permit you to anticipate that he's more likely to be an end than a quarterback, but the player in question may be unthinking enough to change his dirty "88" for a clean "84" at half time. Such liberties are not normal in the protocol language of psychology, but there is little more needed for a numeral to qualify as nominal. The information provided by the use of this numerical mode is, briefly:

1. A class named by the numeral "x" is different in some way from classes otherwise named.
2. The members of the class named by the numeral "x" have some characteristic in common, i.e., they are responded to as equivalent.

Because ordinary words often do as well for these purposes, index numerals are not of great interest in science. Their chief advantage is that they provide labels which bring little surplus meaning with them.

ORDINAL (COMPARATIVE) NUMERALS. A step of great importance to empirical science is taken when numerals are used to indicate sequence, succession, or order. Not only do the numerals name class membership; they also carry an implication that one class has more of something than another, or is larger than another, or differs in an orderly way from another on some discriminable basis. Numerals in ordinal use share with the numbers of the mathematician the premise that 1 is somehow more than 0, that 2 is somehow more than 1; stated generally, that $n + 1$ is greater than n. Unlike the case of nominal numerals, ordinary words rarely fulfill the purpose of ordering as well as the classical mathematical notation, as the Case of the Olives will demonstrate.

Ripe olives (the stuffed and cocktail varieties are on a different scale) are sold under the labels "large," "extra large," "mammoth," "colossal," and "supercolossal." Besides the wonderland quality of the smallest commercial olive having the name "large," there may be some confusion for the unwary housewife in deciding whether "mammoth" is bigger than "colossal" or the other way round. There might be poetic loss but there would be certain communication gain if the grading system were numerical. In that case, we could know from a can labeled "#4 Olives" that there are smaller sizes available and that #5 Olives are larger than these. The improvement in unambiguous communication which follows the use of numerals to structure an ordered series is impressive, but it is only a part of the value to empirical research of working with ordinal numerals. When a group of events or observations is laid out in an ordered way, so that the number series "1, 2, 3, 4, . . . , *n*" can be properly applied to the elements in the group, then the numerals are fit for mathematical manipulation of a fairly high order. The algebra of inequalities and the rapidly proliferating statistics of ranks become tools for the researcher in his attempt to understand and communicate his findings. But there must intervene between the purely mathematical regulations and their use in a particular empirical case the statement of translation rules, the *interpretation* of whatever mathematics is involved. These rules are essential in order to make mathematical systems empirically useful.

For ordered series, the formal sentences which must be given some "real" import have to do with *coincidence* and *precedence;* to use the mathematics of ordered series in his research, the scientist must specify empirical operations which serve to interpret the expressions "equals" and "is greater than." [11] The success of these *empirical* operations determines the propriety of using the mathematics of ordered series in the treatment of data. For well-established measurement systems this demand poses little difficulty—two dollars will buy more apples than one dollar, people six feet tall can see over the heads of people five-and-a-half feet tall, a car traveling sixty miles an hour into a telephone pole will be more severely bruised than one traveling at fifteen miles an hour. For numerical applications like these, the scientist can go beyond ordinal mathematics to more powerful measurement tools, but psychological research cannot always call on such powerful measurement schemes and may even have difficulty on occasion in using effectively the more limited comparative or ordinal scales. Consider the following example.

---

[11] This is an elliptical statement of an important problem in the logic of concept formation. See Hempel (1952) for a lucid account of comparative (and other) concepts. The defining sentence for an ordered series is: "Two relations, *C* [coincidence] and *P* [precedence], determine a *comparative concept,* or a *quasi-series,* for the elements of a class *D* if, within *D, C* is transitive, symmetric, and reflexive, and *P* is transitive, *C*-irreflexive, and *C*-connected" (Hempel, 1952, p. 60).

A group of adolescents is presented with a story about a social rebuff ("Tom is told to leave the party even though he didn't start the ruckus") and they are asked to complete the story in their own words. The researcher sets out to order a series of responses so elicited along the dimension of "defensiveness." The appropriate procedure would presumably be to set up empirical operations for the expressions "Defensiveness A equals Defensiveness B" and "Defensiveness C is greater than Defensiveness D." How can this be done?

1. The researcher may order the stories himself. In this case, the interpretative statement for "is more defensive than" becomes "I believe this story to contain more defensive elements than" and "equals" becomes "I could not make a differentiating decision." On the grounds discussed earlier, this is a perfectly proper procedure; the basic requirements for setting up a quasi-series have been met. The questions which any competent reader would ask—Would someone else make the same ranking? Would the same adolescents given another (or even the same) story have their responses ranked in the same order?—cannot be answered by an appeal to formal scaling procedures; they are questions of fact which only an examination of the observations can illuminate. At the very best, the numerals will be interpreted only for a single user of the procedure and, for a publicly communicable scale, this is insufficient evidence that an invariant ordinal scale has been constructed.

2. The researcher may call on judges to order the stories. Then, the translation rule for the ordering terms would be something like "Response A is more defensive than B if, under a certain set of instructions and after a certain amount of practice, the judges say that it is more defensive." This step is almost always taken in research on complex human behavior; it complicates the set of auxiliary assumptions by adding some about similarity of training among judges, about the precise kind of communication (e.g., contamination) that goes on between researcher and judges, about the status of combinatory rules when judgments are "pooled," and so on. If the formal characteristics of an ordinal scale have been achieved, then the skeptic must shift his attack to the associated empirical questions of stability of the judgment, theoretical import of the scale, or efficiency of the particular procedure employed. The advantage of this technique over the first, or single-judge, method is that it provides some information on the generality of the rules for ordering. This latter point was discussed

earlier in connection with judgmental procedures as examples of empirical explication (Chapter 5).

3. The researcher may set up an "objective" index of defensiveness in the stories; in an extreme case, the length of story in number of words might be used. The problem of ordering then becomes trivial; no great expertness is necessary to count words. But once again, the critical reader may ask a number of questions about the scientific utility of this translation of the expressions "more defensive" and "equally defensive," regardless of their precision.[12]

In each of these skeletal examples, we must return to the heart of the matter of using ordered numerals in psychological research—what have you got *after* you have stated your interpretation rules? It should be clear from what has gone before that no general answer is possible; *the utility of a particular ordering procedure depends on the theoretical context in which it is used.* It will not do to say that defensiveness is what defensiveness tests test; this answer is either cutely evasive or too elliptical to be of much use.[13] The researcher has in fact presented his subjects with a complex stimulus and recorded their complex responses; it may be of assistance to understanding or communication to arrange these responses along some quasi-dimension, but this procedure never of itself permits the researcher to say more than "The ordering can be done." In order to say anything more important, it is necessary to relate the responses which have been seriated to (*a*) other responses, (*b*) specified stimulus events, or (*c*) theoretical statements. This is the case no matter how elegant or numberlike the ordering procedure is. So much effort has been expended by the philosophers of science and the scaling brand of psychologists in the discussion of

---

[12] Although they are shorn of many subtleties, the three examples may stand as outlines of common procedures in psychological measurement. Case 1 is represented by the "raw clinical hunch," the intuitive assessment of a behavior or behavior protocol; Case 2 is the more-or-less standard procedure in the exploratory study of human personality—in a sense, the researcher says "I can put some order into these responses; let's see if anyone else can"; Case 3 represents an extreme instance of "objective" testing, such as intelligence testing, rote scoring of projective devices, "anxiety scales," "guilt scales," and so on.

[13] This unhappy formulation is not only inadequate as a definitional procedure (Chapters 5 and 6) but also is evasive when it is used to dress up exploratory research as studies in the scaling of anxiety, or aggression, or child-rearing attitudes; it is elliptical when it stands for the much more involved expression: On the basis of extensive empirical work and careful thought to theoretical issues, it is useful to take results from this instrument (e.g., the Stanford-Binet) as the best representation of a reconstruction of what has been known in common language as "intelligence."

"measurement" that Bergmann and Spence (1944) are justified in their indictment of investigators who substitute a search for "true or valid measurement" in the place of a proper search for empirical laws. As is true for all language construction (see Chapter 7), the usefulness of ordered series in psychology depends on the accessory information available to assess their place in a larger system.

Against this background of reservations about the employment of ordinal numerals in psychology, we can go on to a discussion of what can and cannot be done with ordered series. The usual technique has been to compare two or more sets of ranked data, as in the following paradigm:

Rank on Variable or Dimension	
A	*B*
1	5
2	4
3	3
4	2
5	1
6	10
7	9
8	8
9	7
10	6

Then, with whatever statistic seems appropriate, a further statement is made about the relationship and its likelihood of recurrence. Perhaps too often this method is thought uniquely characteristic of correlational studies of human personality. For better or worse, experimentation even with animals is of the same general model; dimension *A* may be hours of deprivation, amount of prefeeding, number of reinforced trials, and so on; the *B* dimension may be strength of pull, number of bar-presses, speed of running, and so on; a statistic of difference may be used rather than a correlation coefficient—but insofar as the variables are treated as in an ordered series, the problems for the rat runner and the personality researcher are analogous. The advantage to the researcher in such well-worked areas as animal learning is that he may not *have* to treat his data as though they were on a merely comparative scale; some of the dimensions which are of interest to him (distance, time, speed) have measures with well-established advantages in mathematical operation and ease of communication.

A difficulty arises almost at once when the only numeral assigned to the response of a research subject is his rank in the sample. The psychologist investigating adolescent defensiveness may make highly reliable seriations of groups of story-completions, but what if he wants to compare two stories on amount of defensiveness elicited, or defensiveness of children in New York with that of children in Los Angeles? The most tempting answer would be to combine the two groups of story-completions and make a new ranking, assessing the outcome with one of the available nonparametric statistical tests. Even granting that the groups are comparable on other counts, this procedure would soon become extremely cumbersome if one were required to rank hundreds of responses. Moreover, it would be difficult for another investigator to duplicate any findings about the behavior of "highly defensive" adolescents if the only information available was that "highly defensive" is a term applied to the top ten ranks of the particular local sample studied. These problems have promoted a search for some more general form of expression, an ordinal procedure which permits communication of relative standing beyond the limitations of a single study or a single sample.

The most common technique, and apparently the most successful as measured by the amount of research generated, is to order a given set of responses according to some easily communicated (i.e., objective) instruction (Case 3, p. 180). In this case, the interpretation of the operations "greater than" and "equal" are made in an explicit and highly invariant form. For all the complex mathematical operations that may be involved, this is the procedure in intelligence scaling. To a standard set of questions (subscales, age-appropriate items) subjects give a distribution of correct answers; the ones who give more correct answers are given the high ranks, those who give fewer correct answers get lower ranks. Similarly, although the point is so obvious that it is rarely explicitly made, the experimenter of the stricter variety orders his subjects in terms of number of lever-depressions, or percentage of "Yes" responses in a psychophysical study, or number of trials to criterion in a rote-learning experiment–interpretation statements which are homologous to those that put a Wechsler-Bellevue score of 148 above one of 68.

This technique of ordering by a standard "instrument" is important because it aims at including further information by the assignment of the numerals. Instead of labeling a group of subjects

1 2 3 4 5 6 7 8 9 10

on the basis of how many questions on an intelligence test they answered correctly, they are ordered

151 138 122 110 108 105 97 82 78 65

on the basis of scoring procedures found meritorious in the history of the particular test given. What has been added? Nothing, so far as permissible mathematical operations are concerned; the value of a rank difference of 1 is as indeterminate as the value of an IQ difference of 13; one cannot add, subtract, multiply, or divide one set of numerals with better warrant than the other—so long as the requisite translation statements have been made, the two ordering procedures are formally equivalent.

The point deserves special emphasis. In our everyday use of numerals, we have built up a protoarithmetic which leads us to expect, among other things, that the difference between 2 and 1 represents something systematically different from the difference between 138 and 151. Much of this archaic theory of numeration is based on the most common interpretation rule for arithmetic—counting; the useful fact that a pile of stones containing 138 members is enormously larger than a pile containing only 2 is the model for our expectation that numerals applied to other ordered series will behave in a similarly "sensible" way. Unfortunately, numerals do not behave in an intrinsically lawful fashion; one has to know the rules for use of numerals in any system before they can be understood and interpreted. Until these rules are added, no systematic distinction can be made between the numeral "2" and the numeral "138".

What *has* been added in the case of IQ scores is an *abbreviated statement of empirical findings.* The numeral indicating an IQ is used in empirical studies of the relationship between test-performance and other indices of human behavior; as a result of thousands of such studies, the IQ numeral now reminds the reader of the network of empirical generalizations which have been proposed for "intelligence." The designation "IQ of 138" has the edge over "Intelligence Rank 2" in reminding the experienced reader of results from research with people of a high IQ. The single phrase "IQ of 138" summarizes a great deal of empirical research and justifies inferences like:

"Most people in a randomly drawn sample will make lower scores than this."

"If this person is tested again with the same instrument, it is highly probable that his re-score will fall between 120 and 150."

"It is highly probable that, if he has a high school education, this person can enter and continue through college."
"It is highly improbable that, if this person is an American adult, he is an unskilled laborer."

None of these sentences can be said of a simple *rank* numeral index of intelligence, which may after all be assigned in a group of defectives or of college professors. It bears repeating that the superiority of the intelligence-test score derives not from the intrinsic virtues of scales with arbitrary means of 100 and specified standard deviations nor from any necessary advantage of information subtests over story-completions—the superiority is a matter of fact, resting on a sizable corpus of data about the relationships of the IQ numerals to one another and to other indices of human behavior.[14]

Another attempt to reach beyond the limitations of sample-determined rankings depends on auxiliary assumptions about the distribution of certain events in independently sampled groups. Responses can be segregated on a criterion of degree of *extremeness,* as indicated by some statistical computation like standard score. The weighty assumption underlying this procedure is that, within limits, extreme scores (e.g., standard scores higher than 2.50) on the same "instrument" are likely to be similar even though the distribution of raw scores may show marked dissimilarities between two groups. Of the same order of inference is the experimentalist's comparison of results from different apparatus or of those based on somewhat different methods—high score values have some similarity even if, absolutely, they may be markedly different. Once more, the suitability of this procedure is determined not by the merits of the ordering rules themselves, but by the relationships among the results of their application and other empirical laws.

One last problem in the use of ordinal numerals in psychology will focus again on the central problem under treatment—the status of auxiliary hypotheses in empirical research. Assume that the investi-

---

[14] One of the ironies of present-day psychology is that researchers in animal learning, with rigorously stated theory and the support of powerful measurement techniques, cannot provide as general a statement of behavior variation as can the intelligence testers. Ask, for example, what numeral representing speed should be assigned a "fast rat" which would be useful from apparatus to apparatus, experimenter to experimenter, and university to university. Melton's plea (1936) for standardization of experimental procedures among researchers remains unanswered in 1959.

gator of defensiveness decides that he wants additional indices of this characteristic of his subjects and to this end has them complete three stories instead of one. He and his judges rank each of the story-completion sets and get a "pooled" estimate of defensiveness by taking each subject's mean rank on the three story-completions as his score. Remembering that in ordinal scales, only the expressions "equals" and "is greater than" have been interpreted, with no provision for the mathematical operations "+" or "÷", there is clearly no warrant for adding and dividing within the rules for setting up the scale. On what basis can a subject with ranks 1, 1, and 28 be said to be "equal in defensiveness" to one with ranks 10, 10, and 10? To say "they are equal by definition" is to evade the issue, and to mask what is an important assumption in the research. It should be emphasized at this point, and strongly, that no one can legislate against the application of whatever mathematical operations the researcher wants to use on his data. It would be antithetical to the overall theme of this book if psychologists were warned off any procedure simply because it lacked the imprimatur of the philosopher of science. But there is a difference between the auxiliary assumption that 1 minute, 1 minute, and 28 minutes add to the same duration of time that 10 minutes, 10 minutes, and 10 minutes do and the auxiliary assumption implicit in the example given from the study of defensiveness. In the first case, the empirical success and theoretical strengths of physics have resulted in a powerful measurement system. It is this kind of measurement, e.g., of length or electrical resistance, that the philosophers of science have used as models in their discussion of "fundamental" measurement. In the case of the measurement of defensiveness, we are without strong support from theory or from an extensive set of empirical findings to bolster the fruitful interpretation of "+" or "÷".

Summarily, there are grounds for adding lengths and times; there are no such grounds for adding defensiveness. The key for the psychologist is that the application of a measurement system does not so much depend on reference to some a priori "axioms of measurement," but rather depends on the relationship of his assumptions about measurement to theoretical premises and predictive success. If the empirical researcher finds that the cube root of the total score on a questionnaire he thought up while shaving is reliably related to some other measures of human behavior, or has some value in sharpening a theoretical issue, he need not abandon his idea because of this or other disquisitions on "measurement"; if he is not so fortunate, however, it may not be because, say, defensiveness is in fact unrelated to creativity in adolescents, but because his auxiliary hypotheses about the use of numerals were badly chosen or lacked confirmation.

FUNDAMENTAL MEASUREMENT. When, to the interpretation statements about coincidence and precedence, physical theorists added empirical translations for such mathematical operations as addition, multiplication, and so on, a much more powerful numerical tool became available to them. There is nothing mystical in this; the history of science is such that length, time, electrical resistance, and a few other variables, by virtue of their theoretical status and the support of research, could be profitably treated as behaving in the way that the mathematics demanded. We know about the measurement of mass, for example, that (40 grams – 39 grams) is equal to (2 grams – 1 gram) and that 6 grams are equal to three 2-gram measures. If one substitutes in the preceding sentence "hours of food deprivation" for "grams," the inapplicability of the mathematics of "fundamental" or physical measurement to such psychological variables is made obvious. The word "fundamental," in addition to labeling a group of measurement techniques in physics, unfortunately also carries with it an implication that all science must somehow use these techniques in order to apply powerful mathematics. Other sciences, including psychology, may be dealing with phenomena which defy the fruitful application of operations such as "plus" or "minus". If this turns out to be the case, sciences other than physics will have to develop their own theories of "fundamental" measurement.[15] Fundamental measurements in physics are powerful precisely because the auxiliary hypotheses involving their use are of extremely high confirmation. This does not mean, of course, that the use of the classical centimeter-gram-second schedule makes for better psychology—there are psychologists who will maintain something like the opposite—but it does focus our attention on the essential requirement for fundamental measurement in the wider sense—that it be relevant to theoretical and empirical considerations and not merely adopted from physics.

In summary of the use of numerals in the protocol language of psychology, it is essential to remember that the wondrous complexities of formal mathematical systems cannot be made a part of psychology by fiat. The researcher usually faces an alternative: Either he confines his mathematical operations to those which are proper to the

---

[15] For a discussion of measurement in physics, particularly interesting in its history and the logical relations underpinning it, see Hempel (1952) or Campbell (1920).

empirical translation rules he has established between his data and the mathematics of measurement, or else he goes beyond these limitations under cover of a set of auxiliary hypotheses, the confirmation of which is relevant to his conclusions.

Statistical Statements

The behavioral sciences have drawn heavily on the specialized branch of mathematics called statistics, to the point that a psychology without the support of probability theory is almost inconceivable. Reputable research workers are expected to state, when they present their findings, some index of likelihood of the recurrence of the events described, oftentimes with quite a bit of sophistication. The apparatus of confirmation has become largely statistical, and the psychologist must become a part-time statistician or else have "a friend who . . . ." The points which were made at length in the preceding discussion of the use of numerals in psychology can be applied *mutatis mutandis* to the use of statistics. Statistical theories, like the theories of measurement, have certain axioms which determine the appropriateness of application of tests of covariation or difference to empirical data. Because the central theme of the present treatment—that attention must be given to auxiliary hypotheses in the protocol language of psychology—has already been stated, and because there are excellent works on the assumptions relevant to various statistical techniques [e.g., Cramér (1946) or Feller (1957)] only a cursory and largely illustrative discussion will be attempted here. This neglect should not be taken to imply that the auxiliary assumptions of statistics are less worthy of attention than those involving the use of numerals in measurement; statistical assumptions are almost certainly abused as frequently in psychology as are measurement assumptions.

It will be trite to anyone who has explored several different ways of putting his data under statistical analysis that the method chosen is not irrelevant to the values obtained—statistical operations are not simple mirrors of the researcher's results. Take, for example, the double array of ranks on page 181. There are a number of techniques available to assess the relationship between the two sets of hypothetical orderings, among them the common Greek trio, phi, rho, and tau, yet conventional computation of these indices of correlation reveals a rather remarkable discrepancy. Phi is +1.00, as substantial a value as the researcher might wish, but rho is only +.48, and tau turns out to be a puny +.11. The orderings remain the same; clearly the statistical manipulations carry something of their own into the evaluation. This particular example may be an unfair representation of the kinds of discrepancies which one would ordinarily come across in the analysis of psychological data, but by its very deviation it serves to underline the importance of considering rather carefully the auxiliary hypotheses from statistical theory introduced into a research report. Unexceptionable truth, even in the protocol language of a science, is not easily come by—the use of statistics, like the use of numerals and of instruments, brings with it a group of assumptions which are relevant to the interpretation of what we often call "raw data." Many times, the findings of a study are so clear-cut that any statistical analysis will carry conviction or so ambiguous that the most assiduous exploration of novel devices will not take rejection probabilities beyond the .05 level, but there remain the indeterminate number of studies where choice of statistical operation may occasion important variation in the interpretation of results. Psychologists of pre-*t*-test age will remember the data that were filed away as "insignificant" because the critical ratio was not 1.96 or larger.

There is another variation in the assessment of statistical statements which warrants at least passing attention, and that is the tendency for some selected statistics to carry a halo of convincingness which is not necessarily justified by reason or arithmetic, but rather seems to survive as a professional superstition. In its most general form, this prejudice can be seen in the opposition of "correlational" to "experimental" studies. To borrow a jargon word from the probability theorists, this is hardly an orthogonal comparison—"experimental" is a term properly applied to research method; "correlational" is a word descriptive of a set of statistical tests, which may or may not be appropriate to experimentally obtained results. The flaw in this supposed disjunction is sharply shown by a little arithmetic juggling. Almost any set of data which is treated by the statistics of differences (*t*-test, *F*-test, and so on) can be recast to develop a correlation coefficient. This would be an interesting side light but too trivial to deserve emphasis were it not for the prejudicial attitude of at least some psychologists toward these magic numbers of the statistician. To put the issue in better focus, consider the hypothetical results of an experimental study shown in Table 4. Assume that the numerals in each column represent number of trials to some criterion of learning and that the columns themselves indicate four levels of some antecedent condition.

Table 4

FICTITIOUS DATA FROM A HYPOTHETICAL ANIMAL LEARNING EXPERIMENT

(See Text for Explanation)

	Groups			
	1	2	3	4
	3	12	15	10
	4	13	14	25
	8	18	22	27
	12	8	19	19
	15	15	7	15
	—	—	—	—
Totals	42	66	77	96

The customary technique for assessing these data would likely be an analysis of variance, with the following outcome:

Between-groups mean square	101.67
Within-groups mean square	30.375

$F = 3.347$, significant at the .05 level.

This is not an overwhelming difference (the required F at the five-percent level is 3.24), but it is a respectable member of the set of results which are published in psychological journals of impeccable standing. But suppose that the data are set up to provide an index of correlation, and that the coefficient computed is +.48.[16] Presumably this numeral represents something approximately like an F of 3.347, but it would be surprising to find a responsible experimentalist submitting a research report that stated "There is a correlation of +.48 between amount of food animals are prefed and the number of trials it takes them to reach criterion level of learning." To the degree that it is a matter of style or the more pertinent matter of permitting easier comparison of outcomes, the prejudice illustrated here is inconsequential. To the degree that it represents the infusion of data with the surplus aura of a prestigious statistical device, it is at best sloppy

[16] It is, using Kendall's (1948) tau, and taking the column dimension as twenty ranks, tied four times in groups of five each. The "response measure" is ranked in the usual way.

thinking. Statistical tests, too, are applied in context, and only when the relationships among empirical considerations, theoretical issues, and the special characteristics of the statistic employed are understood can optimal interpretation of protocol sentences be made.

THE RECONSTRUCTED DATA OF PSYCHOLOGY

This chapter opened with a promise to talk about the parts of the language of psychology which are highly accepted, a promise which led somewhat paradoxically to an extended exposition of the physics of instruments and the mathematics of measurement and statistics. Yet, if the general premise that science is an interlocking directorate of ideas, techniques, and observations is accepted, the diversion to other fields of study is not surprising. Psychologists must use whatever they need in their attempt to anticipate animal and human behavior, even if this borrowing precludes a simple and reassuring definition of "datum." It is not enough to say, "Event A is related to Event B"; from the several considerations about auxiliary hypotheses which have been adduced earlier, it follows that the typical data sentence in psychology is more accurately expressed in the following way. *Granting auxiliary hypotheses about instruments, measurement, and statistical treatment, the relationship "Event A is related to Event B" is demonstrated to degree* x.

It should be emphasized once more that this representation of "datum" in psychology is not prescriptive for the writing of research reports or the training of psychologists, but rather it is an attempt to describe what elements beyond simple observation enter into the psychologist's statement of his findings. In those cases where the expected results are obtained and at a high level of statistical significance, there is scarcely a need to examine one's ancillary assumptions; more often, the *failure* of a relationship to be demonstrated is the goad which sends a researcher back to a reevaluation of his procedures and implicit hypotheses. Nevertheless, in both instances the researcher's observations of common reality make up only a part of the accepted protocol language of his science.

However complicated some of the associated premises may be in the psychologist's presentation of his findings, sentences of the sort described in this chapter are usually safely on the near side of acceptability. Controversial terms like "drive," or "id," or "intelligence," or "cause" have not yet come on the scene. These are words in the *theory language* of psychology, that collection of sentences which aims to make sense of regularities expressed in the protocol language. For some psychologists (Skinner, 1950), this next step into the range of theoretical abstraction may be unnecessary or at best premature for psychology, but most workers in the discipline continue to seek out broader generalizations than the protocol language will provide. Theories in psychology go beyond the irreducible minimum of unambiguous communication of empirical relationships and become, in a sense, commentaries on data.

SUMMARY

The language of psychology contains statements which are easily understood and acceptable, for example,

"On the average, four-year-old American boys weigh 38.1 pounds."

Ordinarily, statements of this order are not thought to be "theoretical," but rather represent "raw data" or "facts." In the present chapter, sentences of this "factual" character have been examined, and the notion of *protocol language* has been expanded and refined.

In the examination of protocol statements, a classification was set up to distinguish statements of recognition, narrative statements, instrument statements, numerical statements, and statistical statements. Although important differences among these kinds of sentences can be studied, they share a critical characteristic. All of them require that the researcher look closely at certain *auxiliary hypotheses,* assumptions he must make but which are oftentimes not tested directly by his research. The operation of auxiliary hypotheses in the expression of even the simplest protocol statement precludes any easy definition of "fact" or "datum." It seems reasonable to conclude that the status of protocol statements in psychology can be properly assessed only when they are put in relation to a more extensive explanatory system.

chapter eleven

Explanation in psychology: I. The problem of induction

THE EMPIRICAL SCIENTIST, EQUIPPED WITH AN effective protocol language, can proceed to the description of particular empirical events with a good chance that he will be understood by his colleagues. In well-developed areas of study, there usually is a set of stable language conventions which assure relatively unambiguous communication of the conditions, procedures, and results of a research. Pavlov, for example, after outlining his techniques and measures, could present his results in a form illustrated by Table 5, confident that his readers would know what he had done and what he had found out. This use of language for the precise documentation of experimental results represents an important part of the making of science, and stands on occasion as a model for all of science. This model would confine science to established fact, free of speculation, theory, and metaphysics. As we have seen, even the most "obvious" of protocol statements rests on untested assumptions, but a reasonable case could be advanced in defense of the position that some of these assumptions have trivial empirical implications, and that it is hairsplitting to refuse the appellation "scientific fact" to reliable descriptions of particular research outcomes. If this point is granted and if the scientific enterprise is seen as scientific fact-finding, then one could

Table 5

PAVLOV'S REPORT OF THE BEHAVIOR OF A DOG DURING EXTINCTION TRIALS

(Adapted from Pavlov, 1927, p. 53)

Stimulation Applied at Intervals of 4 Minutes

Time, P.M.	Amount of Saliva Secreted during 1 Minute, cubic centimeters
12.10	0.7
12.15	0.4
12.20	0.3
12.25	0.1
12.30	0.0

presumably collect the observations of psychologists into a handbook which would detail meticulously the results of all the research on human and animal behavior performed over a period of years.[1] The resulting catalog would certainly be cumbersome, but it would permit the researcher to operate safely within the well-established limits of his protocol language, and to avoid as well the dangers of unsupported speculation.

However attractive this procedure may appear at first glance, it takes only the briefest look at the history of empirical science to learn that researchers rarely if ever stop with a recitation of their observations. Rather, there is almost invariably found an immediate generalization from the obtained results, an expression of the findings which extends far beyond the local and particular observations that the researcher made. From the results cited in Table 5, together with similar sets of data, Pavlov drew the following conclusion: ". . . another important factor in determining the rate of experimental extinction is the length of pause between successive repetitions of the stimulus without reinforcement" (Pavlov, 1927, p. 52). It is clear that this statement is not meant to be restricted to the single occasion on which a particular dog salivated; it is, in fact, unlimited in its extension across species, reflexes, and durations of intertrial pauses.

---

[1] Published "handbooks" in psychology do not usually have this catalogical character, but make free use of theory and generalization. That an enumerative presentation is not impossible, however, has been demonstrated by the publication of a book (Ferster and Skinner, 1957) which comes remarkably close to the *datum omnia vincit* position sketched here.

With scarcely an exception, the conclusions of all studies of behavior express a similar expansion beyond the researcher's observations to an indefinite universe of events. We speak not of "the rats in this study" but of "organisms"; not of "running this alley" but of "response"; not of "college sophomores" but of "small groups." With remarkable unanimity, scientists are willing to lay down inclusive dicta about events which they have not observed, even about events which could not have been observed (e.g., those in the future). It seems fair to say that the psychologist is not interested in the unelaborated statement of research findings, no matter how "scientific" and reliable it may be, but rather his concern is with the *statement of laws,* with the expression of regularities in the world which includes far more than he can justify by an enumeration of his observations.

This shift from a reliable and limited set of observations to an extended and often infinite set of events, is an essential part of the work of scientists, and an understanding of science-making requires that we examine rather closely this complicated process of shifting between the particular and the general. Classically, this problem of abstraction has been treated under two headings: deduction and induction. In the deductive method, general principles are proposed and statements about particular instances are drawn from them in a logically systematic fashion; in the case of induction, arrays of particular instances in some way lead to or generate general statements. The present chapter will deal with the intricacies of the problem of induction, that is, of the route from data to generalization.[2] A discussion of deductive techniques will be postponed to Chapter 12, although it can be anticipated that analysis of the two methods will reveal some similarity and overlap.

THE COMMON BASIS OF INDUCTION

The ubiquitous occurrence of inductive leaps from data to laws should startle those who see science-making as a particularly surefooted and careful activity. On what grounds can Pavlov go from

---

[2] Because the word "induction" has ambiguous status in some scientific discussions, an important caution must be entered here. In the immediately following pages, our concern will be exclusively with the way in which human beings go from a set of observations in the protocol language to generalized statements. This treatment does not include such matters as "clinical inference," which involve deductive considerations or questions of general plausibility.

the behavior of dogs to an assertion about "factors determining extinction"? Why should a researcher on nonsense-syllable learning in college students write so easily about the advantages of distributed over massed training? In these and countless other cases, an apparently audacious leap is taken from a narrowly circumscribed set of observations to a generalization which is, at the very least, unbounded by considerations of time. This characteristic of timelessness seems nearly universal in inductive generalizations; no matter what other dimensions are involved, scientific conclusions carry an implication of "always." This escape from the constraints of time, and from other abstractions involving species, conditions, and behavior, seems on examination to be not only audacious, but supererogatory as well. There is, of course, wide variation in the breadth of generalization made by researchers. Oftentimes, the author of a research report will state very carefully the restrictions on his conclusions which are required by the limited nature of his observations. Nonetheless, there is usually some extension beyond the protocols of the research. An unkind critic might set up the following reconstruction of the scientist's reasoning as he draws an inductive generalization:

1. On September 6, 1954, the following observations were made. Twenty human subjects who had 30 seconds between presentations of paired nonsense syllables were able to recite the entire list four trials earlier than twenty subjects who had only 5 seconds between presentations.
2. I think my subjects are like other organisms; I think my set of nonsense syllables is like any other set; I don't see any reason why this effect should vary from time to time; I think that my choice of times is a typical one.
3. *Therefore,* distributed practice results in more effective learning of nonsense syllables than massed practice.

Why, the critic may continue, should a reliable observation be extended on the basis of the researcher's opinions about some rather doubtful issues? It would seem far more rigorous and much more in keeping with the demands of precision simply to state the facts and leave out the scientist's prejudices about what the facts may mean in some larger speculative framework. Such criticism of the inductive operation raises several problems for the empirical scientist.

Among the questions which deserve further examination are: Why does the scientist make inductive generalizations? What are the antecedents or determinants of inductive behavior in human beings?

Beyond these first questions of *psychological* justification for induction, is it possible to state rigorously a set of rules for drawing appropriate generalizations from sets of data? It is this last question which has concerned the philosopher in search of a warrant, that is, a justification, for inductive inference.

The most straightforward answer to the question about the scientist's "need" to generalize is to admit that the foregoing discussion is predicated on a faulty premise. The aim of research is not simply to assemble defensible protocol statements but is also to anticipate what will happen in the future. Inductive generalization cannot be understood unless the anticipation function of science is faced frankly. The elevation of his findings into a timeless expression represents in shorthand the scientist's commitment to the proposition that, all else equal, what has happened will happen again. Further, the generalization is a warrant for action: Having found that A is related to B in a certain way, one may act in the reasonable belief that on next encountering A, one will also encounter B.

Inductive generalization, then, is one of the ways in which the predictive character of science is expressed, and on the most general of levels, the behavior of the systematic researcher is like that of the ordinary citizen. The assertion "The sun has come up every morning in the past" is not just an encapsulated bit of information; it is the ground for belief that the sun will *always* come up in the morning, and that an alarm clock can be set for tomorrow in the reasonable expectation that there will be light enough to begin the day's work. The most highly confirmed inductions, those which have to do with astronomical motion or the stability of objects, for example, are so much a part of our everyday action that we are scarcely aware that we are acting in line with them. The peculiarities of inductive behavior are more forcibly presented in those instances where there is less-than-certain anticipation or where there is disagreement among people on the proper form of the generalization. For statements like "Sloe-eyed girls are sexy" or "The best way to get ahead is to let people know how good you are," there is usually an attempt, systematic or not, to examine rather sharply the grounds for the generalization. It is in the study of such less-than-perfect generalizations that we can cut through to the core of the inductive problem. Before this study is undertaken, however, we can note several broadly drawn characteristics of induction which apply to common everyday activity and to the behavior of the scientist as well.

First, inductive generalizations, whether or not their source is in systematic study, can be cast in the *form* "Events in the class A stand in relation *r* to events in the class B," or more simply "A *r* B." Such a statement is different from the similar expression given at the end of the preceding chapter as a description of "datum" in that the generalized form of the statement is not bound to a particular set of observations, but has as its range of coverage a broad stretch of events, some of which at least have not been examined (again, primarily those in the future). It is obvious that there is wide variety in the ways these generalizations may be stated, from the simplest universals like "The sun always comes up" to complex inductions like "It is unwise to drink martinis and beer at the same party, but on occasion it is necessary in order to avoid offending the hostess," or "The analysis of dreams will be therapeutically effective except when the patient is relating dreams merely to postpone examination of transference problems," or "Partial reinforcement results in more trials to extinction than does continuous reinforcement"; it is characteristic of all of them to share the generalized "A *r* B" form.

A second dimension along which inductive generalizations may be examined is the *degree of belief* with which they are held. A number of issues are interlaced here, and their examination will occupy us throughout the present chapter, but a starting point in the analysis of them is the *behavior* of belief. What behavioral indices can be used to assess commitment to an inductive generalization? One such index was alluded to in an earlier chapter, where it was pointed out that Everyman and Scientist alike are surprised when an anticipation or prediction is not confirmed. A related criterion for degree of belief, which can be developed out of the earlier discussion of the function of anticipation systems, is the *willingness to take action* on the basis of an inductive generalization. Certainly, the physiologist who discovers a particularly virulent bacillus will immediately modify his handling of the cultures, and a researcher who is certain about psychokinetic effects would waste no time in getting to Las Vegas. It is somewhat more difficult to evaluate degree of belief by the "action" criterion in the case of scientific research without obvious application to everyday living; for this instance, the researcher's degree of belief may be best shown by the willingness to submit his findings to public examination or to invest in another experiment.[3] It is an empirical problem, and a complicated one at that, to determine what measures of be-

---

[3] The problem of belief is closely related to questions raised in modern decision theory as treated, for example, by Luce and Raiffa (1957).

havior will serve as the most fruitful index of conviction about an inductive generalization. What is of paramount importance to an understanding of the language of science is the rather disturbing implication that an appeal must be made to factual considerations about human behavior in order to make sense of inductive generalization.

Certainly a major characteristic of induction is its *dependence on the experience of the generalizer.* This assertion, which stands at the heart of empirical science, was made in dramatic and convincing form by David Hume some two centuries ago. In his *Enquiry Concerning Human Understanding,* Hume posed a set of problems which nag at philosopher and scientist alike, and it remains an open question whether or not the impact of his overturning of ancient dogma has even yet been fully assimilated. Hume started with the obvious evidence of inductive generalization by human beings:

> The hearing of an articulate voice and rational discourse in the dark assures us of the presence of some person: Why? because these are the effects of the human make and fabric, and closely connected with it. If we anatomize all the other reasonings of this nature, we shall find that they are founded on the relation of cause and effect, and that this relation is either near or remote, direct or collateral. Heat and light are collateral effects of fire, and the one effect may justly be inferred from the other. (Hume, 1748 [1939, p. 599].)

After discussing the weakness of any attempt to understand this kind of inductive leap by appeals to pure reason or a priori and necessarily true propositions, he proposes the following solution:

> This principle [which explains generalizations about relationships between events] is *custom* or *habit.* For wherever the repetition of any particular act or operation produces a propensity to renew the same act or operation, without being impelled by any reasoning or process of the understanding, we always say, that this propensity is the effect of *custom.* By employing that word, we pretend not to have given the ultimate reason of such a propensity. We only point out a principle of human nature, which is universally acknowledged, and which is well known by its effects. Perhaps we can push our inquiries no further, or pretend to give the cause of this cause; but must rest contented with it as the ultimate principle, which we can assign, of all our conclusions from experience. It is sufficient satisfaction, that we can go so far, without repining at the narrowness of our faculties because

> they will carry us no farther. And it is certain we here advance a very intelligible proposition at least, if not a true one, when we assert that, *after the constant conjunction of two objects*—heat and flame, for instance, weight and solidity—*we are determined by custom alone to expect the one from the appearance of the other.* (Hume, 1748 [1939, p. 609]. Italics ours.)

For all the simplicity and apparent good sense of Hume's proposal, his conclusion that our most fondly held generalizations are based merely on repeated conjunctions of events was not warmly welcomed, either by his contemporaries or by his philosophical successors. A good part of the history of post-Humean academic philosophy can be understood as an attempt to escape the practical and intellectual implications of the *Enquiry*.

Hume's skeptical manifesto also sets a problem for the psychologist interested in the determinants of inductive behavior; it leads us back to the set of questions posed earlier. What are the *antecedents* of inductive generalizations, the prior conditions which Hume summarizes as a "principle of human nature"? How can the inductions, once made, be justified? It is to the first of these questions that we must turn now in discussing the *psychological* grounds of induction.

THE PSYCHOLOGICAL GROUNDS OF INDUCTION

When the "problem of Hume" is put in psychological dress, it becomes apparent at once that asking "On what basis do men make inductive shifts?" is scarcely less than asking "Why do men behave the way they do?" The psychological roots of generalization, inside or outside the laboratory, lie deep in the standard problems of the student of behavior—perceptual capacity, learning history, and motivation, to name but three. The very complexity of the empirical issues involved may have contributed to the persistence of the problem of induction as a philosophical puzzle and to the failure to find a "solution" in the face of repeated attempts. In fact, so much of psychology can be seen as a study of the basis on which organisms make anticipations (i.e., predictions based on some sort of inductive shift) that the study of induction as a special kind of behavior has hardly been outlined as a research problem. As Leeper (1951) has pointed out in a review of research on inductive concept formation, "[the process] includes not merely the traditional concept formation experiments with human beings, but also conditioning experiments, discriminating experiments, and many trial-and-error experiments with animals." In short, the making of inductive shifts from a limited set of particulars to a wider generalization is an everyday matter for us all; the systematic study of the determinants of this activity will encompass much of what is considered to be the field of psychology.

It would be congruent with our earlier treatment of vocabulary learning if we could assume that human beings learn to put sentences together in much the same way that they learn to name objects. In the presence of a dog, both the response "dog" and the response "four legs" may be elicited. The reinforcement of this concomitant elicitation of two sets of responses, coupled with the acquisition of intraverbal control of such words as "has," may eventually lead to the sentence "A dog has four legs." The case for the learning of syntax by reinforcement, appealing as it may seem in the context of our previous discussion of vocabulary acquisition, is in fact quite inadequate to account for even the simplest kind of language learning. Bruner (1957b), among others, has pointed out that if all sentences were learned by some such process the number of possible conjunctions would be so vast that "our lives would be far too short to master even the simple prattle of a child." It will be seen as we proceed with our discussion of the inductive process that human beings appear to learn language and its syntax by acquiring rules and structures which organize the vocabulary into useful units. This conclusion does not imply that the simple reinforcement model is never applicable. However, it seems rarely operative beyond the very early language acquisition of the child.

A general paradigm for the empirical study of induction which is more-or-less neutral theoretically might include a consideration of *input,* that is, what information is supplied to the organism; of *organismic capacity,* that is, the perceptual competence, learning history, and motivational level of the generalizer; and of *output,* that is, the behavior used as an indication of inductive generalization. Under variations of this paradigm, there have been a number of empirical attacks on the problem of what makes people draw conclusions from sets of particulars.

The Experimental Study of Inductive Generalization

The most extensively used research model has been that of *concept formation,* in which subjects are presented with materials that the researcher has organized to represent instances or examples of some class. Typically, the task demands that the subject "discover" the characteristics of the presented material which will permit him to describe correctly the notion or concept that the researcher has built into the instances. For example, in an early investigation by Smoke (1932), subjects were presented with drawings to which the experimenter had attached nonsense "names." A *wez,* to take one of Smoke's figures, was "two straight lines of equal length that touch end together with a dot equidistant from the free ends of the lines." After exposure to a series of examples of *wez,* subjects were asked to describe and to reproduce the figure to which they thought the word referred.

In varying degrees of complexity and with manipulation of such aspects of the task as relation of positive to negative instances, number of instances encountered, or number of attributes used, this research design for the study of concept attainment has contributed substantial information about the relationship between input and the generalizing behavior of human beings. Bruner et al. (1956) have presented an extensive study of some aspects of the concept-formation process. They indicate that different types of concepts require different approaches or strategies for adequate or even possible solution. Furthermore it appears that different individuals may in fact use different strategies for the solution of the same problem. Hovland also has called attention to the idiosyncratic way in which people tackle traditional concept-formation problems.

> What is quite unclear from [a study of negative and positive instances] is *S*'s expectations as to the type of concept model to be employed and as to the number of characteristics of the stimulus figure which might be relevant to the concept-formation task. Without some common understanding on the part of *E* and *S*, it is difficult to define what information is conveyed by each instance. (Hovland, 1952, p. 461 f.)

Concept formation is not a simple process but is dependent on a wide range of variables; it is the very generality and complexity of the problem of generalizing behavior which make a precise empirical and conceptual analysis difficult to achieve (see also Bruner, 1957c).

An interesting variant of the general research paradigm, and one that may represent somewhat more realistically the way in which people generalize, derives from recent work on *attitude change.* In general, it is the aim of this research to investigate the characteristics of input (the communication) and of the organism (e.g., personality variation) which result in a change in the predictive generalization under which the organism has been acting. Once more, a specific study can illustrate the direction of this research line. Janis (1954), in an investigation of the effects of a communication on subjects' opinions about a future event (e.g., How long will it be before a cure for the common cold is discovered?), examined his findings in an attempt to discover whether there existed any striking personality differences between the people who changed their opinions markedly and those who were resistant to the communication. His discovery that level of self-esteem was an important variation between the groups is interesting in its own right, but the study is pertinent to the present discussion in illustrating a research technique which may be used to tease apart the skein of variables which influence the making of inductive generalizations.[4]

On a somewhat different level of empirical analysis, there is a further group of studies which brings to the laboratory a prototype of the circumstances involved in inductive inference. Subjects are required to predict which of two alternatives is likely to occur, in an experimental setting where the researcher sets up different likelihoods of occurrence for the alternatives. Galanter and Gerstenhaber (1956) have suggested that the sort of inference made by different subjects given the same information will vary as a function of *cost,* that is, on the basis of how much the decision means to the subject. In studies of this hypothesis, they have shown that human subjects will change their predictive behavior about the operating characteristics of a "machine" when the payoff for making a correct prediction is changed. In the context of an empirical study of the making of inductive generalizations, this and related work on the prediction of alternatives bring to light another group of variables to be dealt with in any "psychology of induction."

Even as fleeting a glance as we have taken here, and these approaches to the problem are drawn almost haphazardly from the ones eligible, brings to a sharp focus two general conclusions about empirical studies of inductive inference. First and foremost, *the problem is open.* The research done to date has not led to a simple and inclusive theory about the behavior of induction. So much depends on the particular mode of research employed and on the underlying theoretical model

---

[4] Recent summaries of research by Hovland and his associates (1953, 1957) give an overview of studies in opinion and attitude change.

in use that we must withhold acceptance of any general formulation of the problem. Secondly, and within the limitation implied by the first conclusion, the behavior of induction cannot be optimally conceived as dependent in a simple way on input, without regard to the characteristics of the generalizer and the specific circumstances under which the input is delivered. For the simplest cases, there is evidence of an active selection and rejection of alternative generalizations, with parallel test of their "success" as new information is provided. Although in some simple learning studies, the making of "predictions" can be fruitfully related to input alone (e.g., schedules of reinforcement), the analysis of only slightly more complex cases (e.g., learning to learn) requires hypotheses about the organism's history, motivation, and perceptual skills.[5]

The few illustrative cases which have been cited suggest that inductive behavior does not occur merely as a function of a series of instances acting on a neutral inducing organism. Inductions take place within the framework of an active organism with a well-developed view of the world, with particular personality characteristics, strategies, and prototheories. Evidence is evaluated against the background of prior experience, prior inductions, and prior theoretical systems. Events never impress themselves on a *tabula rasa* which then magically produces a generalization, but rather they interact with the complex network of thoughts and behaviors that are the observing scientist. Even the most elementary inductive generalizations depend on the context in which they function; both the erection of the generalization and its test are related to other generalizations or anticipations operating when information is delivered to the generalizer.

One of the most puzzling aspects of the psychology of induction is the tendency, at least by adults, to make inductive leaps after very few instances. In the extreme case, one instance frequently is sufficient for the generalized shift. At the very least, the experienced individual tends to make guesses, or form hypotheses, as soon as an event has occurred. Subsequent events only serve as evidence for the confirmation or rejection of these guesses. To this extent then, the history of the organism may frequently lead him to use deductive strategies (see Chapter 12) in situations which seem to call for induction.

---

[5] Krech and Crutchfield (1958) provide a useful introductory discussion of the role of perception in the drawing of inductive inferences. For a more extended treatment, see Allport (1955) or Humphrey (1951).

The Work of Jean Piaget

The thinking of children is an extensive source of hypotheses about the building of inductive inferences and about the errors which may result from an inadequate background of supporting generalizations. Piaget, in a lifelong investigation of the determinants of human thought, has presented in a group of publications (e.g., 1929, 1930, 1951, 1953, 1954) the most ambitious and most nearly complete scheme for understanding how we get from the chaos of particular events to an abstract and effective construction of the world. In brief, Piaget's exposition runs along the following lines. As the child develops, there is an increasing differentiation and structuring of his environment. This structuring takes place as the child comes into active contact with presented stimulation. From his study of this intricate development, Piaget has extracted two fundamental themes—the universal operation of certain modes of thought and the central importance of "mental structures."

In elaboration of his first theme, Piaget maintains that human beings, at every stage of development, bring to bear on the problem of structuring the world two basic processes, which he calls *assimilation* and *accommodation*. The assimilative function is seen in the organism's attempt to understand the world in terms of his available response system; in Piaget's words, "the universe is embodied in the activity of the subject" (Piaget, 1953, p. 43). When the young infant is presented with a new toy, for example, he tries to assimilate it to his present activity, that is, he "tests" whether the toy is good for sucking, or grasping, or shaking. Similarly, the adult presented with a novel stimulation—say, a new mechanical device—will attempt to fit it to what he already knows of similar contrivances. Stated in its most general form, the notion of assimilation implies that the organism will generalize to a new experience whatever responses are available to him; to the degree that a certain response is successful, to that degree will the new experience be "understood" or "known." If no response is available to the organism that "fits" the experience, then no change, no new knowledge, will be possible. Clearly, a second principle must be included to account for change in the organism, and it is accommodation which is assigned this function. Presumably, in his essays at assimilating or incorporating a new object or event, the organism will vary his activity somewhat; in the course of such variation, he may hit on a new response pattern which permits him to use or recognize or understand the object. This variation in available response patterns as a function of demands of the environment Piaget calls accommodation.

The business of adaptation to the world, then, is a rather delicate balance between assimilation—doing what has been done in the past—and accommodation—the change of a response to fit the presented stimulation. Piaget, particularly in his work on the very young child (1951, 1953, 1954), presents a convincing picture of the development of human thought as the simultaneous operation of these inherent modes of behavior. A somewhat more conventional statement of Piaget's position would emphasize his assignment of particular properties to the human input-output system as it makes inductive generalizations. He has gone beyond similar attempts to characterize the operations of human thought, first in stating a set of rather explicit hypotheses, and second in adducing a rich collection of behavioral evidence in support of these hypotheses.

Piaget's second theme—the central importance of mental structures—follows closely from his proposals about assimilation and accommodation. At any particular time in the development of a human being, there exists a certain balance between organism and environment; that is, it is possible to describe the range of environmental events toward which the organism responds reliably, and to state how "accurately" this response system reflects the environment.[6] It is to these balance points or organized stimulus-response systems of more-or-less stable character that Piaget applies the term "mental structure." A simple example of what he means can be seen if we refer again to the development of the child's concept of the permanence of inanimate objects. The human infant, in the first months of life, behaves as though an object moved out of his visual field ceases to exist—he is not distressed at the disappearance, he does not search for the object, he will turn to some other activity if the object is covered, and so forth. Such a phenomenon is for Piaget a different "structure" from that represented by the child's behavior a few months later, when he will search actively for an object out of view, remove obstacles, and so on. The importance of this conception and its relevance to a treat-

---

[6] It is an inevitable condition of Piaget's theory of thought that this evaluation of "accuracy" or success must be made in terms of development toward some higher, more successful group of responses. It is doubtless for this reason that his interest was drawn to the study of ontogenesis, i.e., to the faulty and incomplete thought structure of children.

ment of inductive inference can be seen more sharply if we consider a parallel example in the behavior of older children.

Piaget and Szeminska (1941) presented to young children an array of eggs and an equal number of eggcups; the task set for the subjects was to state whether there were more eggs, more eggcups, or an equal number of each. It turned out that this judgment varied according to the arrangement of the objects; when there was an egg opposite each cup, the children judged the two arrays to be equal in number; when the eggs were crowded together, so that they occupied a shorter line, the children reported that there were more eggcups. Conversely, when the eggcups were brought close together and the eggs spread out, the children's conclusion about relative number was reversed. Surprising as this variation in the judgment of number with an "accidental" change in the environment may seem to the adult, Piaget and his colleagues have demonstrated that the behavior of induction, even along such elemental dimensions as number or volume or extent, depends on the developmental level of the generalizer, and that prediction about what inference will be made from a set of particulars demands some knowledge of the "structures" which guide the organism's action. Piaget's interest has been confined rather closely to a study of thought development in children, but his formulation can be readily extended to other cases in which there is variation in the structure available when a demand is made for an inductive generalization.

In his discussion of the child's concept of space, Piaget draws the analogy between children's thinking and the development of a scientific system:

> . . . one may compare the "distant space" of the child . . . with the celestial space of the uninformed adult or of immediate perception. The sky seems to us a big spherical or elliptical cover on whose surface move images without depth which alternately interpenetrate and detach themselves: sun and moon, clouds, the stars as well as the blue, black, or gray spots which fill the interstices. It is only through patient observations relating the movements of these images and the way they mask each other, that we arrive at the kind of elaborating subjective groups which satisfied mankind until the constitution of objective groups was made possible by the Copernican image of the earth and of the solar system. (Piaget, 1954, pp. 144–145.)

The symmetry suggested in this passage between ontogenetic and scientific development can be found throughout Piaget's writings, and his treatment of the issues involved may represent a crucial advance in our understanding of what goes on when men make inductive shifts.

Piaget began his investigations with a theoretical prejudice and a source of data quite different from those used by other psychologists concerned with the behavior of induction, yet his results support and extend their findings in striking ways. His discoveries fortify the conclusion reached earlier that inductive inferences are made in the context of prior generalizations under wide variations of skill, knowledge, and motivation of the generalizer.[7]

THE LOGICAL PROBLEM OF INDUCTION

If this tentative conclusion is taken seriously and much of the "problem of induction" is seen to be an open empirical issue, what then remains as the *logical* or *formal* problem of induction? The practicing scientist is likely to be impatient with an exposition of the epistemological questions at issue; rightly or wrongly, he is convinced that his procedures will not change nor will his conclusions be in great jeopardy, no matter what the philosophers decide. There are, however, two questions which warrant attention to the philosopher's statement of the problem of induction: What can be learned from a study of current philosophical analysis which will clarify or aid empirical work? and: To what degree are "formal" treatments of the subject elliptical statements about empirical (largely, psychological) matters? The first of these questions concerns the justification of inductive inference; the second asks whether there *is* a logical (i.e., nonempirical) problem of induction.

Many of the philosophical answers to Hume's skepticism have been more-or-less well-disguised attempts to wriggle away from the problem, usually by assigning some superordinate characteristic to the universe (e.g., the Postulate of Limited Variety) or to the workings of human thought (e.g., Harrod's (1956) Principle of Experience). This too-quick summary may appear to disparage a great deal of hard and complicated work, but as Goodman states:

---

[7] For another discussion of problems related to human induction, particularly in mathematics, see Polya's *Mathematics and Plausible Reasoning* (1954).

> The typical writer begins by insisting that some way of justifying predictions must be found; proceeds to argue that for this purpose we need some resounding universal law of the Uniformity of Nature, and then inquires how this universal principle itself can be justified. At this point, if he is tired, he concludes that the principle must be accepted as an indispensable assumption; or if he is energetic and ingenious, he goes on to devise some subtle justification for it. Such an invention, however, seldom satisfies anyone else; and the easier course of accepting an unsubstantiated and even dubious assumption much more sweeping than any actual predictions we make seems an odd and expensive way of justifying them. (Goodman, 1955, p. 65.)[8]

Recently, however, there have been launched a number of more energetic assaults on the problem, most of which start from a recognition that Hume's wrenching conclusion cannot be side-stepped. Goodman puts the matter in this way:

> If the problem is to explain how we know certain predictions will turn out to be correct, the sufficient answer is that we don't know any such thing. If the problem is to *find* some way of distinguishing antecedently between true and false predictions, we are asking for prevision rather than for philosophical explanation. (Goodman, 1955, p. 65.)

What is needed is a statement of rules or "canons of induction" against which particular kinds of predictions can be evaluated.[9] Goodman, together with those of his philosophical colleagues who have gone far enough into the problem to be well stuck, is sensitive to the fact that no such set of rules for valid inductive inference is presently at hand. What recent philosophical treatments have achieved is a narrowing down to the search for general principles which will have the explicit and detailed statement of the sort that make rules of *deductive* inference so powerful, and which will at the same time reflect accurately the inductive procedures of empirical science. Carnap, in his *Logical Foundations of Probability* (1950) opened the way for a new treatment

---

[8] For an expert discussion of the most important answers to Hume, see von Wright's *The Logical Problem of Induction* (1957). Hempel (1945) and Braithwaite (1953) have also dealt with the problem in a lucid fashion.

[9] The most ambitious attempt to provide a system of rules for inductive inference was made by Mill (1843). Its promise and its inadequacies have been reviewed in damaging detail by Cohen and Nagel (1934).

of the old problem of induction, and his remains one of the most significant philosophical contributions to the problem. For other modern analyses, see Hempel (1945), von Wright (1957), and Braithwaite (1953). In the present exposition, Goodman is taken as representative because he has put his case in a form which permits us to avoid the intricate detail of a precise logical analysis, but this emphasis on one current position should not be taken as evidence that there are no disagreements among philosophers of science.

In his detailed review of attempts to resolve the problem of induction, Goodman points out that they all rest on a syntactic base; in other words, the basic issue has been one of stating the relation between statements of evidence and the proposed inductive generalization. Given an evidence statement, e.g., "This copper wire conducts electricity," what is the increase in confirmation of the inductive shift "All copper wires conduct electricity"? Goodman rather gleefully notes that whatever proposal is advanced to account for cases of this order applies equally well to evidence-generalization pairs like:

"A member of my audience is a third son."
"All members of my audience are third sons."

Proceeding with this technique of absurd outcomes, Goodman successively criticizes alternative proposals and comes at last to the core of his revision of the model for inductive inference—the notion of *entrenchment*. In brief, entrenchment is an extrasyntactic criterion for the selection of an inductive generalization; it brings under examination not only particular evidence statements, but the *history of use* of the generalization as well. In order to decide what is a credible induction and what is not, it is necessary to take into account how often in the past similar inductive generalizations have been made. Those generalizations will be selected which are couched in terms having a stable history of use, i.e., "a more impressive biography." In other words, we tend to accept those terms that we have habitually used in making generalizations. The effect of this proposal is to set the logical problem of induction in a new frame. No longer is the issue to be bounded by the relationship between bits of evidence and a proposed induction; the field is widely broadened to include a "biography" of the terms used in inductive generalizations. From this point of departure, Goodman goes on to analyze in greater detail the way in which degree of entrenchment determines the selection of generalized statements, always in the context of linguistic analysis, asking what grounds for acceptance there are outside the accumulation of particular instances of evidence.

> . . . the roots of inductive validity are to be found in our use of language. A valid prediction is, admittedly, one that is in agreement with past regularities in what has been observed; but the difficulty has always been to say what constitutes such agreement. The suggestion I have been developing . . . is that such agreement with regularities in what has been observed is a function of our linguistic practices. Thus the line between valid and invalid predictions . . . is drawn upon the basis of how the world is and has been described and anticipated in words. (Goodman, 1955, p. 117.)

The position outlined by Goodman is hardly a final answer to the problem of Hume, and by no means has it been clasped to the bosom of the philosophical community. His restatement of the problem of induction is more striking when seen in apposition to the psychological premises discussed earlier. Just as the investigator of inductive behavior has come to recognize the importance of contextual and historical constraints on the way people make inductive shifts, so Goodman proposes that the formal attack on the problem of induction be widened to include contextual and historical considerations. From either point of view, a staggering array of problems remains; those which press on the psychologist are paralleled by the philosopher's struggles to state the conditions under which a term may be said to be more-or-less well entrenched, the rules which govern presently ambiguous cases, the role of inductions of higher order (Goodman's "overhypotheses"), to cite but a few.

The apparent promise of this philosophical restatement of Hume's insight that historical considerations are relevant to the problem of induction must be evaluated rather carefully. Goodman's notion of "entrenchment" seems related to "degree of belief," which has been seen to be only one of the variables affecting inductive behavior. Moreover, any "solution" of the problem of induction which has empirical implication must stand or fall as a result of empirical test. It is unlikely that one single, simple set of antecedents such as number of prior generalizations will satisfy the empirical questions about induction stated earlier in this chapter. Goodman's suggestion enters the market place of hypotheses about induction and must be judged on the same grounds as other hypotheses are judged. What should be heartening to the practicing scientific worker is the progress being made toward formulations of the inductive puzzle which are meaningful when judged against what he does in the field or in the laboratory.

In spite of this progress, however, the answer to the first of the questions posed earlier—Can the researcher learn anything from a study of current philosophical analysis which will clarify or aid his empirical work?—must be a guarded "No." The procedures of science are in fact the starting point and testing ground of the philosopher's quest; the researcher restricted to inductive procedures bearing a philosophical imprimatur would be strangled. Yet, this reservation cannot be taken as a recommendation to ignore the philosophers of science. Their nineteenth-century role as sweepers-up and sorters of science has been changed in some ways to that of guide and vanguard. Recent advances in the development of the apparatus of deductive logic stand in evidence of the peculiar and important place philosophical analysis has in the work of empirical researchers. An attempt to answer the second of our questions—Is there a nonempirical problem of induction?—will illustrate even more sharply the function of a philosophy of induction.

When the philosopher of science writes about induction, or indeed about any problem which has implications for human action, he is performing in several roles. First among these is his place as Theorizer General to the empirical sciences. For example, many of the disquisitions put forward by the English philosophers of empiricism, from Locke to Ryle, can be translated into statements which permit empirical test. The analysis of perception and memory, to take well-studied cases, has moved progressively from speculative presentation by the philosopher to empirical analysis by the psychologist. Similarly, at least some of the problems outlined in the philosopher's entanglement with the problem of induction fit very well indeed into an empirical treatment. The importance of the philosopher's theorizing about testable matters must be evaluated according to the same canons that apply to other theory construction—chiefly, that the proposals lead to testable and confirmed statements about reality.

There is a second job which the philosopher of science tackles, and it is one which precludes any offhand evaluation of his work. For the sake of brevity, this job may be called *reconstruction and extension of the procedures of empirical science.* To understand this unique task, let us recall two analogous instances in the history of mathematics. When some unknown Mediterranean thinker began to play with the possibility of reducing the results of land survey to a simple set of symbols, he could scarcely have anticipated that he was taking the first step toward the development of a formal system of geometry. Moreover, had they known of his activities, the ordinary surveyors would almost certainly have been amused; then as now, the practical man of science would maintain that the solution to the problem was to get out plumb line and cord to see what really happened. Apposite to this example and nearer to us in time, the first attempts by Pascal and Fermat to discover the laws of chance must have met with some puzzlement on the part of the practical dicemen and cardsharps who posed the problems. But here as in the case of geometrical beginnings, what started out as a reconstruction or formalization of events well known to nonmathematicians resulted in the formal (i.e., nonempirical) extension of these reconstructions to symbolic systems of enormous power and of utility to the practical researcher.

It may be suggested that the philosophy of induction stands in an early stage of philosophical reconstruction and extension. At the moment, only a beginning has been made in the first task of formalizing the procedures of science, that is, of building a relatively simple reconstruction of what the researcher does in his normal routines of induction and test. The philosophers of science may, in the future, succeed in this endeavor, and even go on to enrich the scientific method by nonempirical extensions of their formalization of inductive techniques. In the meantime, however, the empirical worker will continue to make his inductive shifts with plumb line and cord.

SUMMARY

The psychologist, when he reports his observations of behavior, almost invariably extends his statement of conclusions beyond what he has shown to be the case; he *generalizes* his findings to encompass observations which he has not made. This extension beyond the demonstrated instance, mirrored in the behavior of other empirical scientists and of men at large, has teased generations of philosophers and psychologists. By what right, on what grounds, can we go from an array of particular instances to a general statement of principle or law? The modern history of this puzzle developed from and seems always to return to Hume's assertions that no a priori warrant for induction is free of contradiction and that the basis of generalization is human habit.

The psychological problem involved is so general as to be almost coeval with the explanation of behavior, but there are a number of contemporary formulations of it, notably that of Piaget, which promise to supply an effective statement of the circumstances under which men make inductive generalizations.

The problem for the philosopher has had a complex history, pitted by rhetoric, false starts, and apparently a general depression in the face of Hume's skepticism. Currently, however, there is abroad among philosophers of science a renewed interest in inductive generalization, with an important shift in focus from "How can we provide a formal warrant for induction?" to "What is the most effective symbolic reconstruction of the procedures of science?"

Whatever stance is taken in the study of induction, philosophical or empirical, there is an increasing recognition that the making of inductive shifts cannot be fully comprehended as an isolated development from evidence to principle. Inductive inferences, in science as in other human action, take place in the context of an elaborate set of presuppositions which direct the course of generalization in ways that we are only beginning to understand.

chapter twelve

Explanation in psychology: II. The problem of deduction

THE INABILITY OF PHILOSOPHERS AND PSYCHOLOGISTS to propose a workable set of rules for inductive inference poses a critical problem for any attempt to understand the language of psychology. Without a canon of induction which establishes unequivocal procedures for drawing appropriate generalizations from a collection of data, how are we to proceed to the essential work of explanation and prediction? The absence of a warrant for induction would seem, at first glance, to open the way for a limitless universe of possible generalizations, a veritable cafeteria of theories. Stated in the most disturbing way, if there is no systematic procedure for establishing an inductive shift, then one summarizing formula is as good as the next.

Although this depressing theme has appeared frequently enough in some metaphysical contentions, the lack of an inductive directive has not in fact led to an imaginative proliferation of generalizations among empirical researchers. On the contrary, there is remarkable homogeneity among scientific specialists in drawing conclusions from an array of observations. Given data about the behavior of rats in a T-maze, or of human beings on an aptitude test, different psychologists will, as a general rule, make much the same kind of summarizing statements. Even without an explicit rulebook for the making of generalizations, it is obvious that important constraints restrict the invention of explanatory or generalized statements.

The operation of constraints on the free invention of explanations has been alluded to earlier in our discussion of the contextual character of human induction. As we turn now to a closer examination of the context of scientific generalizations, it will become apparent that particular sets of observations or particular groups of protocol statements are evaluated against widely held general principles. The interpretation or explanation of protocol statements depends in large measure on their congruence with what we believe. The researcher does not ask "Is this a possible generalization?" but rather, "Does it fit?" In the pages to follow, we will pose a group of questions which grow from this problem of *fit,* of agreement with believed-in general propositions. The first issue to be faced concerns the nature of the congruence between protocol statements and general principles, together with an examination of deduction in psychological theory. There will follow in Chapter 13 a discussion of the sources and uses of scientific explanation. Finally, the induction puzzle will be reopened in a treatment of confirmation and choice of psychological theories.

DEDUCTIVE SYSTEMS AND PLAUSIBLE SYSTEMS

During the seventeenth century, an ancient and attested belief that the corpse of a murdered man bled in the presence of his killer came into question. Doubt among physicians and natural philosophers did not derive from a series of well-controlled experiments, but rather from a weakened commitment to a theory about "sympathy and antipathy," which postulated a tendency for like to seek like. When this theory was abandoned, the special case of the murderer's effect on the blood of his victim was no longer tenable. Without empirical refutation of even inelegant form, the empirical generalization faded from the books of science; with no change in the observational grounds for the inference, it was abandoned because it did not fit with prevailing theories. It was in the same period of rapid change in men's structuring of their world that the relationship between the moon and terrestrial tides was submitted to argument. Many competent scholars, fully aware of the correlation between tidal change and lunar phase, could not accept the postulation of a causal relationship because of its inconsistency with the superior premise that there was no action at a distance.

Repeatedly in the history of science there can be found cases of two general types—abandonment of an empirical generalization with a change in theoretical stance, and reluctance to accept an empirical generalization which does not gibe with preconception. In the latter case, the most careful research is often no guarantee of conviction. Galileo's publicized contention with his colleagues and the ecclesiastical authorities of Rome is perhaps the best-known example of human resistance to the empirical generalization which runs counter to widely accepted principles, but many equally dramatic instances abound. Redi's demonstration that venom was the fatal agent in the bite of vipers was rejected by scholars who were convinced that the malevolence of the snake was central. Similarly, Jenner's introduction of cowpox virus as an agent against smallpox has been ridiculed and fought against from its first application down to the present day, and Freud's descriptions of infantile sexuality were cast away in horror by professional colleagues for whom the principle of childish innocence was an overriding consideration.[1] Human knowledge appears at any given moment to encompass more-or-less adequately the phenomena we observe, and whatever explanation we have functions until an original thinker jogs us. For this reason the more obvious and telling examples of the importance of congruence between data and principle must be drawn from past and often ill-remembered scientific errors. But whether our cases are selected from medieval or from modern science, the lesson is clear: The acceptability of a generalization depends not merely on the repeated observation of its instances, but as well on its plausible relationship to other general statements.

When we ask for an *explanation* of a phenomenon, we are expressing a demand for the context of general statements into which the phenomenon may be fitted. The variety of explanatory relationships which can be advanced is quite large, running from introspective assertions such as: "I married Myrtle because I like redheads," to what have been called in the philosophy of science "mere empirical generalizations" such as: "The swans in my pond have long necks because all swans have long necks," to explanatory schemes containing words which are far from the protocol language, such as: "He joined the

---

[1] The case of the Greenwich observer (Chapter 3) presents evidence that the reluctance to give up basic principles is not always unjustified; what often require changing are auxiliary assumptions.

Lions because he has a strong affiliative need." For all their apparent differences, these "explanations" share the characteristic of making the statement to be explained an instance of some wider generalization; they all involve in a more-or-less rigorous way the *deduction* of the statement to be explained from one or several general statements. In its simplest paradigmatic form, this procedure can be seen as a conjunction of a generalization and a condition, from which conjunction one may deduce the statement to be explained. Thus, for the second case given above,

Law: All swans have long necks.
Condition: The animals in my pond are swans.
Deduction: The animals in my pond have long necks.

Although this conclusion may seem unremarkable in itself, it represents fairly the general deductive tactic of science. A statement summarizing a group of observations stands in two relations—one "downward," as it were, to the observations on which it is based; the other "upward" to the general statements which lead in a chain of deductions to the summarizing statement. This second relation of "deducibility" provides for scientific statements the context and fittingness so important in determining the acceptability of an empirical conclusion. At one time in the history of man, thunderstorms were "explained" as evidence of anger in animistic deities; at a later period, the action of witches "explained" such storms; at the present time, our explanatory treatment of the phenomenon involves notions such as high-pressure areas, cold fronts, and the like. All of these meteorological theories aim at the plausible placement of the phenomenon in an existing system of general principles.

The examples which have been cited may seem a rather heterogeneous collection of "deductive systems," and it is reasonable to suspect that there are important differences between the "explanation" which depends on the color of Myrtle's hair and the "explanation" of thunderstorms which requires a sophisticated knowledge of the movement of air masses and temperature gradients. In order to understand the ground of these differences in explanatory mode, it is helpful to make a tentative distinction between *deductive* and *plausible* systems. At their worst, plausible systems scarcely deserve the honorific label "explanation"; the affection of Myrtle's husband for redheads could not have led in any reliable way to the "deduction" that he would actually marry her. And yet, explanatory systems of this reduced form often meet two basic requirements of plausible reasoning. First, as has been noted already, they include a generalization of wider scope than the statement to be explained, and second, they provide some sort of satisfaction to the explainer, some feeling of having properly answered the question "Why?"

In everyday discourse, plausible systems of remarkable diversity and rigor are put forth in explanation of observed phenomena. Juvenile delinquency is ascribed to urban development, family breakdown, or John Dewey; ice storms are blamed on the H-bomb or on secret maneuvers of the Russians; recessions are "deduced" from too high taxes, the failure of confidence, or the stupidity of the opposition party. In each of these cases the explainer, and sometimes even his audience, reaches a level of satisfaction with the explanatory scheme which diverts or postpones another "Why?" In spite of occasional wide consensus, however, these plausible explanations do not measure up to the usual demands of scientific precision.[2] Their inadequacies, in common speech or in empirical research, can be better evaluated if we first put under study *deductive systems* in science, and then return in Chapter 13 to an examination of plausibility against the criteria for deductive rigor.

THE FORM OF DEDUCTIVE SYSTEMS

Unlike plausible systems, where there is oftentimes some option available as to which general principles will be used and even some choice as to the style of "deduction" employed, a fully worked-out deductive system in science does not permit this latitude. The rules for such a system must be clearly understood, so that they can be used in unequivocal fashion. As we have previously noted, the language of logic provides all science with a well-developed set of such invariant rules. Given these logical tools together with other rules for the manipulation of the symbols of the system, only those statements will then be allowed which the rigorous application of these rules permits.[3] Viewed as a game on paper, the deductive system starts with the writing down of a series of initial sentences, and proceeds from "move"

---

[2] It will be recalled from Chapter 1 that plausible explanations (e.g., "All fat men are jolly") also frequently suffer from vagueness of their constituent terms.

[3] It should be noted that, for the moment, the symbols of deductive systems will be treated as free of empirical reference, that is, as having only intraverbal status. The discussion of deductive systems which follows here is based in part on Braithwaite's (1953) sensitive and detailed exposition of scientific explanation.

to "move" as the rules of the game prescribe. Suppose, for example, that the initial statements (I) of a deductive system are as follows:

I1. If $K_1 >$ [is greater than] K_2, then $A_1 > A_2$.
I2. If $L_1 > L_2$, then $B_1 > B_2$.
I3. If $M_1 > M_2$, then $C_1 <$ [is less than] C_2.
I4. Z is some function of A, B, and C such that:

a. If ($A_1 \oplus$ [combined with] $B_1) > (A_2 \oplus B_2)$, then $Z_1 > Z_2$.
b. If $(A_1 \oplus C_1) > (A_2 \oplus C_2)$, then $Z_1 > Z_2$.
c. If $(B_1 \oplus C_1) > (B_2 \oplus C_2)$, then $Z_1 > Z_2$.
d. If $(A_1 \oplus B_1 \oplus C_1) > (A_2 \oplus B_2 \oplus C_2)$, then $Z_1 > Z_2$.[4]

If it is further assumed that certain mathematical manipulations are permitted in the system—in this case from the algebra of inequalities—it is possible then to "make predictions," that is, to write down a further series of statements which are permitted by the rules of the deductive system. Let us now apply this system to a set of specific

[4] This example may seem appallingly symbol-ridden and esoteric to anyone lacking some familiarity with symbolic notation. However, to the logician it will be even more unnerving in its simplicity—a simplicity which carries with it a host of errors. The illustrative intention of the example would be blunted by a fully rigorous statement, but for the interested reader the following points of clarification can be added.

The formal theory deals with a certain class T of otherwise unspecified individuals or elements (later to be interpreted as variables in certain kinds of experiments). It deals with certain quantitative characteristics of those elements. The elements are represented by function symbols "A", "B", "C", "K", "L", "M", "Z". The domain of arguments for these functions is T; their values are real nonnegative numbers. Thus, A assigns to every element x of T a number Ax. Let x and y be variables ranging over T. Then I1 says:

$$(x)(y)[(Kx > Ky) \supset (Ax > Ay)]$$

Similar restatements can be made for I2 and I3. The statement I4 requires analogous restatement, e.g., Z is a function over T whose behavior is connected with that of functions A, B, and C. Thus I4a says:

$$(x)(y)[([Ax \oplus Bx] > [Ay \oplus By]) \supset (Zx > Zy)]$$

It also introduces the more difficult problem of dealing with $\oplus$. For an understanding of the examples presented it is necessary that $\oplus$ be associative, commutative, and interpreted in such a way that for all elements in T, $Ax \oplus Bx > Bx$, and $Ax \oplus Bx > Ax$.

Having indicated the outline of the proper statement of the theory, we shall carry through the example in the abbreviated form.

instances. In order to do this we must specify particular values (indicated by Greek letter subscripts) for *K*, *L*, and *M*, which are variables of the system. This specification may be indicated by the statement of the following three conditions (C).

C1. $K_\alpha > K_\beta$.
C2. $L_\alpha > L_\beta$.
C3. $M_\alpha > M_\beta$.

On the basis of these specifications we are in a position to ask what the system will "predict." Without any additional assignment of values, the rules of the system enable us to ask about the resultant values of *Z*. Thus, we may ask for each of the following questions (Q) whether the combination of *K*'s, *L*'s, and *M*'s on the left will result in a higher value of *Z* than the combination on the right.

Q1. $K_\alpha L_\alpha$ versus $K_\beta L_\beta$.
Q2. $K_\alpha M_\alpha$ versus $K_\beta M_\beta$.
Q3. $K_\alpha L_\beta$ versus $K_\beta L_\alpha$.
Q4. $K_\alpha M_\beta$ versus $K_\beta M_\alpha$.
Q5. $L_\alpha M_\alpha$ versus $L_\beta M_\beta$.
Q6. $L_\alpha M_\beta$ versus $L_\beta M_\alpha$.
Q7. $K_\alpha L_\alpha M_\alpha$ versus $K_\beta L_\beta M_\beta$.
Q8. $K_\alpha L_\alpha M_\beta$ versus $K_\beta L_\beta M_\alpha$.

For Q1, Q4, Q6, and Q8, it follows that the set of conditions represented on the left will produce a larger *Z* than that represented on the right. For Q2, Q3, Q5, and Q7, the only inference possible under the rules given is that differences in *Z* are indeterminate.

With the addition or revision of initial statements (I) a different set of moves can be made. Similarly, by changing the rules for manipulation of symbols in some regard, it is possible to obtain different outcomes at the "prediction" level. This kind of deductive game, although it is not without an appeal of its own, clearly does not represent a scientific system. Until the symbols are given some *interpretation,* i.e., until they are set in some relation to a protocol language, the game remains a matter of shuffling and reshuffling notations which are empirically vacuous.

Such empty deductive systems—notational games with rules—are called *calculi* (Braithwaite, 1953); their relationship to a system of *empirical* explanation can be seen most readily by trying out interpretations for the symbols "*K*", "*L*", "*M*", "*A*", "*B*", "*C*", "*Z*", and

"⊕".[5] From the many interpretations which could be given this calculus, we will select for further examination one possible version with relevance to contemporary psychology.

An Empirical Interpretation

An investigator studying the behavior of rats running an alley might reasonably have the notion that response strength is a joint multiplicative function of incentive, habit, and drive. In turn, incentive may be hypothesized as positively related to amount of reward on each trial, habit as positively related to number of trials in the apparatus, and drive as negatively related to amount of food given the animals in daily maintenance. This system of explanation for the animals' behavior represents an interpretation of the calculus described earlier, where the following translations are made.

K: Amount of reward.
L: Number of trials.
M: Amount of food provided in maintenance ration.
A: Incentive.
B: Habit.
C: Drive.
Z: Response strength.
⊕*:* Multiplication in the usual arithmetic sense.

If, moreover, the conditions obtain which were specified for "prediction" in the original calculus, namely:

C1. $\text{Reward}_\alpha > \text{Reward}_\beta$,
C2. $\text{Number of trials}_\alpha > \text{Number of trials}_\beta$, and
C3. $\text{Maintenance ration}_\alpha > \text{Maintenance ration}_\beta$,

then, under the rules of the calculus and under the empirical interpretation given, the following predictions (P) based on the questions (Q) of page 220 can be made, among others:

P1 (Q1). Response strength is greater when Reward_α occurs for Trials_α than when Reward_β occurs for Trials_β.

---

[5] A complete interpretation of this calculus would require as well some specification for the use of ">", "( )", "if . . . then", and so on. For the present limited exercise, these symbols may be taken as having the use assigned them in mathematics or logic.

P3 (Q3). Differences in response strength are indeterminate when Reward_α occurring for Trials_β is compared with Reward_β occurring for Trials_α.

Similar statements can be made, *in the interpreted system,* for each of the "predictions" of the calculus.

It is worth repeating that an abstract calculus is neutral in regard to the specific empirical translation made. For instance, a child psychologist could impose on the scheme an explanation of sibling rivalry in which the *K-A* relationship has to do with age and discriminatory capacity, the *L-B* relationship with parental consistency and social prediction, the *M-C* relationship with severity of punishment and the ability to inhibit aggression. For this case, as for any other, the implications built into the calculus hold for the interpreted system.

The scientific utility of an explanatory matrix, however, is not guaranteed by a rigorously stated calculus. The important work of interpretation is not a matter of haphazard substitution of psychological words for symbols, but depends on the ingenuity and knowledge of the theorist (see Chapter 13).

Whatever example is taken as prototypical, we may ask: What is the place of a calculus and an empirical interpretation of it in the procedures of scientific explanation? Certainly at first inspection, there seems to be represented in the preceding pages an enormous technical apparatus for grinding out some fairly obvious conclusions, almost a Rube Goldberg view of science. How accurate a reconstruction of psychological theory is given by the calculus-with-interpretation view of explanation?

Without doubt, this portrait of scientific explanation does not jibe with the *behavior* of scientists; it is ludicrous to imagine a researcher inventing a deductive calculus and then seeking out an interpretation which will be empirically sensible. There is reason to believe that this procedure is almost precisely upside-down to the behavior of the theorist, as will be seen in Chapter 13. However, in attempting to comprehend the function of a deductive apparatus in science, it is well to recapitulate briefly the arguments which led to the sample calculus just presented. In brief, the observation of an event, described adequately in the protocol language of science, tends almost always to be followed by the question "Why?" from the researcher himself or from a critical colleague. One of the implications of this "Why?" is, "Into what context can I fit this protocol sentence?" or more precisely, "What general principles can be adduced to explain this protocol sentence?" The fully stated deductive system, a calculus with its interpretation, is one of the available answers to these questions. The theorist states, as precisely as he can, the premises of a system and the rules for manipulating it which lead to the "prediction" statement which evoked the question "Why?" The apparent circularity of this operation, together with the cumbersomeness of explicit deductive systems, forces us to examine what justifications may exist for using this weighty machinery.

The Context of Generalizations

In addition to the evocation of satisfaction which it shares with plausible explanation, a deductive system meets the requirement for communicability of scientific systems. In earlier chapters, the central place of communicability in definition and the introduction of constructs was stressed; in the present context, the argument must be broadened to include the *relationships* among scientific terms. The sin of omission in the use of definitions *in vacuo* is the failure to make explicit the rules for manipulating constructs *within systems* (see Chapter 4). In an explanatory system, it is not enough to state the observational circumstances under which a term like "drive" may be said to be meaningful; it is also necessary to state how this term will function in a deductive network. If psychology is to go beyond classificatory statements ("All ectomorphs dislike cold baths") and two-term functional statements ("The more practice, the more skill"), then the explicit specification of interrelationships is an unavoidable requirement. Once this demand is accepted, the place of a calculus with its interpretation is more easily comprehended. For one, the public expression of initial statements—the basic theoretical notions—and the rules for their manipulation provide an opportunity for the theorist to determine whether or not his explanatory scheme does produce the prediction he is seeking. Even in as simple a case as we have proposed for animal learning, it is by no means uninteresting that the system permits no prediction for the high-Reward–low-Trials condition. In more complicated explanatory attempts, it becomes increasingly difficult to find out what the implications of a theory are without an explicit expression of its initial statements. There is gain for the scientific enterprise when an explanation is found to be faulty; there is little such gain when no apparatus exists for deciding whether or not a sought-after prediction is deducible from the theory.[6]

The explicit statement of context, i.e., the public statement of an explanatory system, has several by-products that increase the payoff for the labor of deductive maneuvering. It has often been noted that a deductive system only gives back in predictions what the theorist has put into his initial statements, but it would be incorrect to conclude from this that nothing new results from the deductive game. A deductive system, reduced to a form which permits relatively rapid derivation of implications, will oftentimes produce a sentence which the theorist did not anticipate in his original layout of the scheme. This characteristic of "psychological novelty" serves the important function of guiding the researcher toward relevant empirical tests of his explanation; it tells him, in a sense, what the next step in research should be.[7] The legend notwithstanding, Galileo's work on gravitational effects was not carried out by dramatically dropping balls from the Tower of Pisa; the inadequacies of his clocks required that the bulk of his research be performed on the much more prosaic inclined plane. One may reasonably suspect that this shift in procedure was possible only because the principles under examination led to a wider range of implications than was at first suspected. Similarly, Pavlov's observations of salivation in dogs and Thorndike's observations of puzzle-box solutions by cats led to the statement of general principles which have generated a host of testable theorems. It is true, of course, that none of these innovators turned from his research to establish a detailed deductive system that would serve as a research Baedeker for his successors; the systematizer in science is not always the same man as the discoverer. What is to be learned from these cases, however, is that a collection of general principles will often lead to theorems or predictions which are not obvious when the principles are proposed. The only guarantee that these implications will be drawn and submitted to test comes from the explicit and public expression of the principles and the rules for their use.

The consideration that statements of general principles produce a dividend in psychologically novel outcomes also points to the ineptness

---

[6] A deductive system will "predict" events in the past as well as events in the future. The use of "prediction" in the present context is an abbreviation for the more cumbersome phrase "prediction or postdiction or both."

[7] The ability of an investigator to go on to the "next experiment" is convincing evidence for the operation of an explanatory scheme, whether or not he tells anyone else about it.

of a charge of circularity aimed at deductive procedures of explanation. The assertion that $K_\beta L_\beta$ results in a larger Z than $K_a L_a$ may serve to "explain" the outcome of an experiment the researcher is trying to understand; but the noncircularity of his proposal derives from the fact that *other* experimental outcomes are now predicted, and the general principles can be subjected to new tests. The generalization "All swans have long necks" applies not only trivially to the swans that the generalizer may have seen in his lifetime, but also predicts a morphological characteristic of swans for all time and for all observers. The club of the circularity argument can be wielded only in those rare cases when a deductive system is proposed to handle a single set of protocol statements, and is never again put to empirical check. Historical "explanations," such as a statement of the reasons for Caesar's crossing of the Rubicon, are often liable to fall into the class of perfectly empty explanatory circles, but the ordinary run of scientific principles, carrying words like "all," "every," and "in similar circumstances," break the circle by their reference to not-yet-examined instances.

Nowhere is the value of explicit deduction more forcibly borne home than in the revision of explanations. The forward movement of scientific systems toward more adequate treatment of observed phenomena requires that explanatory schemes be modified as new information is obtained. Changes in the set of initial statements have to be made which will permit deduction of new findings or understanding of results not predicted or incorrectly predicted by the original set. This work of change and addition is made materially easier if it is possible to follow the sources of an incorrect prediction up through an explicitly stated system, in order to discover where the explanation went wrong. If, for example, two initial sentences are involved in the deduction of a statement to be tested, and the test shows that the statement is untenable, the researcher can focus his attention on these two initial statements as the basis of error in the prediction. Thus, if it turns out that P1 from our animal-learning example is not confirmed by empirical test, it becomes necessary to examine I1, I2, and I4a of the system with a view toward revision. The failure of confirmation will not normally point to a single initial statement in need of change, but only to the group of initial statements which were used in making the prediction. It is the job of the theorist, then, to choose which of the principles he will repair; it is a cardinal virtue of explicit deductive systems that they assist the theorist in his decisions about where his explanation requires modification.

A closely associated gain from explicit statement can be seen at once. Assume that in the face of a negative result the theorist changes one of his initial sentences so that he is now able to deduce the disturbing result. To the degree that the changed principle is involved in other deductions, he has now made changes throughout the network. Not only will the system produce a different outcome for the invalidated prediction; it will also produce different predictions for other test situations. Within an explicit deductive system, the theorist may, more-or-less quickly, check to see whether or not he has, by his *"ad hoc"* change, built other errors into his explanation. To follow our example once more: Suppose, with the failure of confirmation of P1, the theorist of animal learning modifies I2 to read "If $L_1 > L_2$, then $B_1 > B_2$ only if $L_2 > Y$," Y being interpreted as some stated minimum number of trials.[8] This revision leads to new predictions for Q6, Q8, and for all other deductions involving I2. When they have been reassessed, it is possible to determine whether the change has altered the overall predictive efficacy of the system.

Protection against making a succession of *ad hoc* changes without reference to associated changes in related deductions is an important one in science. It is all too humanly possible to revise an explanation in order to undo a wrong prediction without taking into account the results elsewhere in the range of the explanation. As a consequence, there is a tendency for each new empirical finding to give rise to a new and narrowly limited "explanation." Scientific explanation is most nearly achieved when a large number of apparently divergent phenomena can be brought under a single deductive system; it subverts this goal to change the principles of an explanation in order to fit an observation without going on to enquire what new implications result at other places in the system. Quite frequently, and especially in theories of limited scope, these checks can be made without resorting to the kind of symbolic representation given in our example on page 219, but as a theory becomes more comprehensive, it becomes increasingly difficult to run off in one's head the revised deductions which follow on a change in initial statements.

One last advantage of the explicit statement of deductive systems can be seen if we note once more the communal character of scientific research. No single researcher can hope to investigate in a lifetime all the implications of his pet theory; its establishment or failure de-

[8] Translated somewhat loosely into laboratory language, this revised principle states that differences are not expected to appear in the early stages of learning.

pends upon the empirical studies of many investigators. The relevance of this work of several hands to a particular theoretical formulation can be determined only to the degree that a commonly understood system of principles has been stated. The domination of Hull's name in reference lists to experimental research in the years following 1943 is in large part ascribable, not so much to his unusual skill in inventing explanations, but rather to his relatively explicit statement of initial sentences. This statement permitted latter-day researchers to point out the relationship of their studies to Hull's principles. A public statement of theoretical context for research is a guard against fractionated and repetitious empirical studies; just as communication through the protocol language requires a sharing of definitions and observations, so the slow movement of the psychological community toward far-ranging and attested general principles requires an explicit statement of explanatory systems.

A caution should be entered in our consideration of fully explicit deductive explanation. Systems even as simple as that described on page 219 do not spring complete from the brow of the behavior theorist; the reconstruction of explanation and its justifications which have been proposed here are not held to be accurate representations of the daily procedures of science. Important research doubtlessly derives from principles as weak as "Somehow, the method of feeding infants is important in the formation of personality," or "What will happen to response strength if quality rather than amount of reinforcement is varied?" Explanatory schemes of great detail and precision are not the beginning of science, but rather the sophisticated statement of "where we are now." When the funds of ingenuity and information make it possible to set up a group of initial sentences and their manipulation rules, the advantages cited earlier can be seized. But in an area of study as diffuse and of as various antecedents as psychology, systematic statements of explanations may be slow to come, with plausible explanation and very limited theories holding the field. It may be expected from this consideration that for the time being the systematic collection of empirical generalizations, tied to protocol statements, will make up a large part of fruitful research in psychology. The lack of deductive systems, however, is no less a defect because it can be "understood" by appeal to the complexity of behavioral phenomena or the relative youth of psychological science; at some point in the course of psychological research, the fundamental goals of prediction and control of behavior can be achieved fully only by the presentation, test, and revision of explicit deductive systems.

THEORETICAL WORDS

The emphasis of the foregoing discussion has centered largely on the values to scientific communication of a public expression of explanatory proposals. In taking this tack, we have moved obliquely away from another group of questions, those having to do with the place of theoretical words in the language of psychology. Once these issues have been treated, the way will be clear for an evaluation of the present status of explanation in psychology.

The introduction of terms into the protocol language of psychology and their clarification by one or another of the definitional tactics described in Part I meet nowadays with relatively little contention among students of behavior. The operationist *Putsch,* supported from afield by the antimetaphysicians of the Vienna Circle and from at home by the pervasiveness of Watson's reinterpretation of psychology, had the advantage of bringing about agreement on the importance of reliable usage of protocol terms. Although psychologists continue their profitable infighting about what particular definitions are strategically powerful, there is reassuringly little misunderstanding of what a researcher is saying when he talks about his empirical procedures. This benevolent homogeneity does not extend to the invention and use of theoretical words. These orphans of the psychological language have been subjected to a buffeting of abuse which has ranged from attacks on Freud's mythological terms to halfhearted defenses of "explanatory fictions" to Skinner's dismissal of "imagined changes in fanciful worlds of . . . intervening variables" (Skinner, 1958, p. 99). Professional attention has further been focused on the status of theoretical words by a series of articles in the *Psychological Review* which followed on MacCorquodale and Meehl's (1948) discussion of theoretical terms in psychology (see Chapter 14). What peculiar attributes of theoretical words cause strong psychologists to blanch?

The major difference between words with theoretical status and words of the protocol language is that appropriate use of the former is largely dependent on intraverbal contexts and cannot be fixed by the specification of objects or events in the presence of which the use of these words is reinforced. Theoretical words are not tacts, and the conditions for their proper utterance include something beyond a regularity in the environment of things. This removal from palpability and the possibility of operational translation underlies in part the excitement occasioned in discussions of "id," "central excitatory state," "incentive," "reflex reserve," and so on. The honest user of these words, when pressed for a definitional chain that will lead down to the common world of objects and events, must necessarily demur (see Chapters 5 and 6).

It should be noted in passing that many of the theoretical terms of psychology suffer from disabilities that are not based on their syntactic function. A number of them (e.g., "sensation" or "thought") are reminders of the philosophical ancestry of psychology and have been tarred by the brush of association with low-prestige words like "will," "mind," and "image." Another group, closely related to the first (e.g., "dream," "fear," or "conscious"), grows out of the language of phenomenal description and their function in formal theories is frequently not clearly enough separated from their place in the common language of experience. Members of still a third group (e.g., "anxiety" or "reinforcement") have the paradoxical status of sometimes serving as protocol words susceptible to ordinary definitional refinement and at other times serving as theoretical words with the special problems attendant on this characteristic. None of the foregoing supernumerary disabilities is quite on the mark of the central difference between protocol terms and the words of systematic theory. This difference, as has been noted, depends on a variation in the conditions for appropriate use, a variation which has to do, not with the relation of words to things, but rather with the relation of words to words.

If a physicist were asked for a definition of momentum, it is unlikely that he would respond with "It's when something moving hits something else," nor would he usually demonstate by bringing two objects together. Far more likely is a response such as "Momentum is equal to the product of mass and velocity." This answer, which would be satisfying for the listener to the degree that he knew something about mass and velocity, is not the kind of definition that we have met with earlier. Rather, it is a specification for use *within a system of symbols,* that is, a statement about the proper relationships of the words "momentum," "mass," and "velocity." No direct and immediate call is made in this statement for a description of the observational circumstances under which the word "momentum" may be uttered. It is worthy of attention that this example is drawn from a relatively low-level physical principle; it would be possible for the explaining physicist to derive rather quickly a group of testable theorems the verification of which would support his formulation. Matters are inordinately more complex if one asks for a definition of "electron" or "wave." In these instances, nothing short of stating great chunks of physical theory would suffice for an answer. The distinctive nature of theoretical words is perhaps best illustrated by the extended statement necessary to answer such a demand for the "definition" of the central constructs of well-developed sciences. Neither the classical genus-species response of the schoolboy (e.g., "An elephant is a large quadruped with a long proboscis") nor the more elegant reduction sentence {e.g., "Put in water$(x) \supset$ [Soluble$(x) \equiv$ Dissolves (x)]"} will do when theoretical words are the subject of enquiry. In brief, *a theoretical word is to be used as the system of sentences containing it dictates that it shall be used.*

The special character of theoretical words can be seen in homelier guise by looking once more at the simple theory sketched on page 221. The term "habit" or "*B*" is clearly not available for operational definition or casting into the reduction-sentence form because it does not appear in a testable theorem, that is, at the P-level. If one is asked to define "habit," the correct procedure would be to state the system of sentences which include "*B*" and the rules for their manipulation; in other words, "habit" is defined by the theory which includes it.[9] It will be recalled from Part I that the psychologist's search for reliability in the use of his terms seems on occasion to have blunted his recognition that some words in the psychological language are incapable of simple reduction to the world of lever boxes and aptitude tests. Words like "superego" and "inhibition" are not unscientific because they are stiffly resistant to easy formulation in the usual definitional modes; they are important for explanation as a function of their relationships to other theoretical words and the resultant part they play in an eventual derivation of testable hypotheses.

With this understanding of the role of theoretical words, the importance of an explicit statement of a deductive system is emphasized once again. If theoretical terms in a system of scientific explanation can be properly used only if we know their relationships to other words in the system, then a careful public expression of the explanatory scheme is the sole guarantee that we know how to use the words, that is, that we know what they "mean." It is reasonable to believe that much current controversy among psychologists has its roots in a failure to understand the differences between the conditions for use of theo-

---

[9] In simple systems, paraphrase in a classical "definitional" form is not too unwieldy, as "Habit is that which is greater the greater the number of trials and which combines with incentive and drive to determine response strength." A more revealing exercise can be set up if an analogous restatement is attempted for "gene" or "nucleus."

retical terms and the conditions for use of words in the protocol language. Consider, for example, the rather bizarre case of the term "anxiety."

In Chapter 6, the term "anxiety" was taken as an example of the way in which the usages of the vernacular infuse scientific discourse, and further, of the sometimes casual way in which so-called definitions of a word are proposed without relevance to systematic context, that is, to theory. In order to understand the use of "anxiety" in explanations of behavior, it is not sufficient to point to a measuring instrument which carries this label; the word also appears in theoretical sentences and whatever predictions are made about the behavior of anxiety will depend in part on the structure of these sentences. For example, quite different implications will be drawn from the following contextual appearances of the term:

> An increase in unpleasure which is expected and foreseen is met by a *signal of anxiety;* the occasion of this increase, whether it threatens from without or within, is called a *danger.* (Freud, 1949.)
>
> It has been assumed . . . that subjects scoring at the extremes . . . of the anxiety scale . . . have different levels of D [the drive construct of Hull's theory] operative. (Spence, et al., 1954.)

The appropriate use of "anxiety" in explanations of behavior will depend not only on its status in the protocol language, but also on its relationship to other terms in theoretical statements.

This investigation of the several faces of "anxiety" demonstrates the complexities in so guileless a question as "What do you mean by 'anxiety'?" A satisfactory answer may be given by a statement of the circumstances under which normal adult Americans utter the word, or a definitional statement of the observations one must make in order to use the word in a reliable protocol language, or finally, a statement of the relationship of the term with other words in an interpreted deductive system of explanation. In the particular instance of poor overworked "anxiety" and in the general instance for many terms in the language of psychology, it is the third of these alternatives which precipitates controversy and a distaste for "explanatory fictions." Both the contention and the irritation derive from a failure to establish deductive networks which permit the evaluation of theoretical words. The pure empiricist of psychology is never in a stronger position than when he is pointing out the fluid quality of many theoretical constructs; as long as they float hazily above a well-established protocol language, so long will the theoretical words of psychology deserve the charge of unscientific multiplication of entities. William of Occam's razor was not meant to cut off theoretical discourse, but it continues to serve as a warning against haphazard shifts away from the solid base of empirical description.

THE GRAMMAR OF PSYCHOLOGY

In treating of the use of deductive systems in psychology, there has been presented an opportunity to understand how theories function as the grammar of a science. In the early history of an empirical discipline, much of the work of language analysis has to do with the setting up of categories, with the work of classification. This concentration shows itself in the proportion of effort expended in definition and the establishment of rules for the assignment of observations to different classificatory divisions. The emphasis of this book on words which are substantive or nominal in form reflects the fact that much of psychology is still in this diagnostic or Linnaean stage of development. With refinement of categorization, there is in the history of science invariably a gradual movement of interest to a statement of functional relationships among variables and among the theoretical words of a deductive system. The classification of chemical substances is succeeded by Dalton's statement of combination rules for elements, the early scattered observations of electrical phenomena are pulled together by Ohm's statement of a general principle, Darwin's interest in the flora of the Galápagos is followed by the hypotheses of natural selection, and so on.

The statement of interrelationships among the words of a science is its grammar, and an empirical discipline may be said to have a language system of its own when it goes beyond the invention and clarification of vocabulary to reach a systematic statement of the rules for using that vocabulary. Thus, from our earlier example, the sentence "If $K_1 > K_2$, then $A_1 > A_2$" is part of the grammar of psychology, given an explicit expression of the proper use of the terms "*K*" and "*A*". It can be said in general that *the grammar of a science is the calculus of its theories.* Just as the grammar of a natural language determines what sentences may properly be formed, so does a theoretical calculus prescribe the proper form for sentences in the theory, and, with the inclusion of rules for manipulation, the calculus also provides a statement of legitimate maneuvers in getting from one sentence to another.

There are several implications in this view of scientific grammar which deserve notice. The first arises in consideration of the familiar objection that very few theoretical formulations in psychology have presented explicit and complete calculi. Are they then without a grammar? The answer to this question brings us full circle to the discussion of the vernacular with which Part I began. Of course, psychological hypotheses and hunches without an explicit calculus are grammatical, but they are rooted in the grammar of the common language. Sentences are permitted which are permitted in the common language, and types of derivations are permitted which have grown to be accepted in the community of rational users of the language. For many of the hypotheses of a science of behavior, this commitment to the methods of the vernacular is not costly; most, if not all, of the derivations presented in our animal-learning example could be made by any reasonably intelligent adult, even without the apparatus of formal expression. But the ambiguities of the vocabulary of common languages are more than matched by the ambiguities and limitations of natural grammar. Several examples may serve to illustrate the difficulties derived from the use of common-language forms.

It is not an uncommon practice in clinical psychology to construct a test which aims at detecting some aspect of behavior held to be important for prediction. Thus, people who have a strong motivation to achieve are found to perform distinctively on a test of achievement need ("For every person, if he has a high achievement need, then he will have a high test score"). Once the test has been devised, high scores on it are used to select for study people with marked tendencies to achieve ("For every person, if he has a high test score, then he has a high achievement need"). The latter assertion is often assumed to be implied by the former, when it is in fact an independent empirical assertion subject to test. This practice, which appears innocent enough and is certainly common, leads logically to an assertion which few test-constructors would be willing to maintain: "A person has a high achievement need *if, and only if,* he has a high score on the test."

A second illustration of ambiguity in natural grammar comes from the use of the connective "or." In English, this word can express mutually exclusive alternatives (e.g., "You wash your face or you'll get no candy") and it can express a pair in which both members may be attained (e.g., "You can buy the regular pack or the crushproof box"). The variation in this usage makes a specifiable difference in the deductive use of "or" (see Quine, 1950). Frequently, difficulties of this order can be guarded against by careful statement even in the vernacular. Of greater interest to the psychologist are ambiguities such as the one contained in the calculus on page 219. There, in line with most contemporary theorists, the rule for combining different terms has been left more-or-less open in the expression "combined with." In order to attain further precision in prediction, this formulation must be given an interpretation which permits unambiguous solution of the function. Reflection on possible reformulations of "combined with" will carry us to another important implication of considering calculi as the grammar of science.

It has been repeatedly and correctly asserted that one of the marks of the scientific method is its use of mathematical devices, from arithmetic to differential equations and beyond. Mathematical rules for the manipulation of symbols function as an important part of the grammar of science; although they may on occasion be taken for granted, mathematical postulates are essential to the statement of a calculus. Thus, the series of I-statements cited earlier may be revised to read:

I1. $A = 100(1 - 10^{-.04K})$.
I2. $B = 100(1 - 10^{-.20L})$.
I3. $C = 100 - 100(1 - 10^{-.35M})$.
I4. $Z = A \times B \times C$.

This set of modifications, although it does not change the determinate predictions of page 220, widens enormously the range of test situations and makes possible much more detailed predictions at the P-level. Once the general outline of a theoretical relationship has been stated, the most important succeeding changes are largely in the mathematical part of the calculus. Psychological theory, to be sure, is barely up to statements using simple forms such as the algebra of inequalities, but it would be depressing indeed if this were taken as a permanent limitation on the discipline. The great insights of creative thinkers in psychology must ultimately be given an expression which provides test situations of subtlety and precision. It is this dominance of mathematics in science which so strongly supports the use of an interpreted calculus; once an explicit statement has been made, the system can be submitted to the flexible and comprehensive techniques of mathematical formulation.

The role of deduction, of a calculus with its interpretation, can now be stated in a summary fashion. The formality of the scheme and its obvious distance from the present-day activities of psychologists require

Table 6

A SUMMARY STATEMENT OF DEDUCTIVE PROCEDURES IN THE USE OF A THEORY

Procedure	Partial Example (see pp. 218–222)
Statement of a calculus and appropriate rules for inference	If $K_1 > K_2$, then $A_1 > A_2$. Algebra of inequalities applicable.
Interpretation of the calculus	Let "K" be interpreted as "amount of reward"; let "A" be interpreted as "incentive."
Statement of conditions	$K_\alpha > K_\beta$.
Derivation of predictions	$A_\alpha > A_\beta$, and, all else equal, $Z_\alpha > Z_\beta$.
Interpretation of the predictions (definition)	This step may involve any of the definitional maneuvers described in Part I. For example, a nominal form would be: Let "K_α" stand for "4 pellets" and "K_β" for "2 pellets," etc.

the iteration of an earlier caution: This reconstruction is not meant either as a prescription for proper conduct of the researcher or as a portrait of twentieth-century psychology; it is rather a proposal for an ideal explanatory canon. The review presented in Table 6 can be taken as the expression of a goal, against which less rigorous systems of explanation can be evaluated.

SUMMARY

An important part of the work of science consists of placing empirical generalizations within an explanatory context. In its simplest form, this procedure includes the statement of a general principle or a set of general principles from which one can "deduce" the statement to be explained. Oftentimes, explanatory schemes are no more than plausible, that is, they carry conviction of a sort, but do not contain clear and explicit rules for making predictions. A fully worked out deductive system, on the other hand, expresses publicly the initial statements of an explanation and the rules for their manipulation and the deduction of testable predictions. There are a number of gains to be derived from such precise and detailed expression; among them, the ease of using mathematical manipulations in theory, the assistance provided in the revision of explanations, an increase in communicability of findings from one laboratory to another, and, of central interest to all theorists, the basis for a proper use of theoretical words.

Explicit deductive systems are not easily come by, and their development in psychology has been slow and uncertain. Nonetheless, one of the goals of a science of behavior is the unequivocal statement of explanatory systems which will permit the accurate prediction of animal movement and speech.

chapter thirteen

The sources and uses of explanatory systems

IF THE PRESENT PSYCHOLOGICAL SCENE IS SURveyed from the rarefied heights of a demand for fully explicit deductive systems, it is obvious at once that few existing explanatory proposals in the study of behavior match the ideal statement outlined in Chapter 12. Aside from the recent work on mathematical models for behavior (e.g., Bush and Mosteller, 1955), there is a very limited number of psychological theories which measure up to the standards of explicit and precise statement of a calculus of explanation and its empirical interpretation. This circumstance is the occasion neither for a rejection of deductive techniques of explanation nor for an attack on psychology as unsystematic or unscientific. Rather, the portrait of a deductive system sketched in the preceding pages provides an opportunity to examine present-day psychological theory with an eye on its deviations from an exemplary expression and a further opportunity to go on to a statement of the functions of plausible systems.

It is possible to review current explanations in the light of rigorous deductive requirements and to state, at least roughly, the degree of coherence between the ideal and the real. Somewhat surprisingly, it is not in the expression of initial statements that most behavior theories are weak. Although they are usually stated in an interpreted form, that is, in the language of the theory, the major premises of psychological explanations can be readily found in the theorist's exposition. The following sentences can be taken as examples of initial statements of three psychological theories.

> The ego pursues pleasure and seeks to avoid unpleasure. (Freud, 1949, p. 16.)
>
> The organization of reciprocal relationships between two counteracting functions or neuromotor systems is ontogenetically manifested by somewhat periodic shifting of ascendancy of the component functions or systems, with progressive modulation and integration of the resultant behavior patterns. (Gesell, 1954, p. 349.)
>
> Wherever a psychological need exists, a system in a state of tension exists within the individual. (Lewin, 1938, p. 221.)

Statements of this order are analogous to the interpreted I-statements of Chapter 12, and taken with other premises of the theories in which they appear, they are aimed at the derivation of testable hypotheses about behavior. Recent reviews by Hilgard (1956) and by Hall and Lindzey (1957) have provided, for the fields of learning and personality, excellent summary presentations of the initial statements of several psychological theories. An examination of these surveys will show that, although there is great diversity, there is rarely any serious doubt about what the theorist intends to be the fundamental postulates of his explanation.

The relative clarity and explicitness shown in the statement of initial premises in current psychological theory are not so easily illustrated when one turns to a consideration of the *relationships* among initial statements, that is, the rules for manipulation of postulates. For example, we may ask of the theories illustrated above: When these initial sentences are used in the theory, what are the rules for making a deduction? What is the function of "pursues," or "is manifested by," or "exists in"? These are not questions of definition in the ordinary sense, but rather demands for a statement of the way in which the sentences of the theory are to be manipulated. No requirement is made for defining or pointing to "ego" or "tension," but in order to apply the explanation it is necessary to know the calculus —the grammar—of the theory. It should be apparent at this point that such a calculus need not be tricked out in the costume of mathematics or forced into a symbolic mode like that presented on page 219;

a more reasonable criterion for a theoretical calculus is that competent colleagues be able to draw the same inferences from the set of initial statements without having to call on the special knowledge or insight of the theorist. This requirement for deductive systems is so rarely met in psychology that it deserves special emphasis. If no specification of manipulation rules is made for the initial statements of a theory, the researcher is limited to segmental tests, that is, to tests of individual sentences of the theory, under that most popular of disclaimers, "all other things equal." However, when the operation of two or more theoretical sentences is under examination, e.g., the relationship of "ego" and "superego" or of "tension" and "valence," it is necessary to state a calculus for all sentences containing these terms. Such a procedure immediately entails the consideration of "other things."

Once the psychological theorist has scrambled somehow over the bridge between his initial statements and his testable predictions, he is once more on relatively solid ground. In the work of definition, the techniques reviewed in Part I have stood the researcher in good stead. Although he may not always be able to say whether he is using a nominal definition or a reduction sentence, he can frequently trace for his audience the links between the words in his hypotheses and the observations he will make to test them. The metaphor of the bridge is not inapt; on one side are the sweeping speculations of creative men, on the other the basic scientific endeavor of testing hypotheses. The chasm in between—the route from premise to theorem—is where psychological theories are most in need of engineering.

The general point under consideration in this survey of deficiency can be made in another way by posing the following question to a theorist of behavior. Under what set of circumstances would you doubt the correctness of your theory? If a deductive system is even moderately explicit and precise, the theorist should be able to specify test situations which would fail to confirm his explanation. If he is unable to do so, or if he is always and easily ready to "reanalyze" his "deduction" as soon as the data are in, then one may reasonably be suspicious whether anything more than a plausible system underlies his explanation. This does not mean that the theorist, once he has proposed an explanation, is barred from revising it in the light of new knowledge. It does imply that the explanation be communicable enough in all its aspects to permit the designation of circumstances which could cast doubt on its validity. One of the continuing attacks against psychoanalysis, for example, has been based on just this issue—it seems to the uncommitted psychologist on occasion that no matter what findings are obtained in the study of human personality, there is near at hand a psychoanalytic "explanation" for the data. The justice of this attack, on psychoanalysis and on other theoretical forays as well, can only be evaluated when the theories are expressed in a way which lends itself to the public derivation of testable predictions.

THE FUNCTIONS OF PLAUSIBLE SYSTEMS

Through much of the preceding discussion of explanation in psychology, the emphasis has been on failures, deficiency, and omission. The absence of a simple technique for induction and the inadequacies of deductive explanations of behavior bring us to some long-postponed questions. What is the status of explanation in present-day psychology? What are the uses of plausible systems? The answer to these questions can be made under three quite general headings—the evocation of satisfaction, the statement of reliable generalizations, and the grounds for further research.

It will be recalled from an earlier discussion of plausibility that one of the marks of a plausible explanation is its tendency to satisfy the explainer or his audience, to answer in some sense the question "Why?" Quite apart from its accuracy as a way of predicting events, a plausible explanation "sounds right." The conviction such an explanation carries may range across a wide area, from the ascription of opium's sleep-producing properties to its soporific character to accounting for the sun's apparent motion by invoking the rotation of the earth. It appears to be an invariable human desire to have some statement made about the causes of or reasons for an event. Smith (1951), in an extensive treatment of the psychology of explanation, maintains that the need for explanation grows out of the observation of an event which does not fit an established belief.

> It would appear to be a characteristic feature of the human mind that it should be provoked by some experience which remains unrelated to the experiences which comprise the system of knowledge currently held. . . . The provocation in some cases might be reduced by some form of general statement . . . the task of explaining would at least consist in finding some phase of the subject's previous experience to which the present experience could be related. (Smith, 1951, p. 3 and p. 25.)

Whether one follows this or an alternative view of explanation, there seems to be little doubt that explanations have the effect not only of providing a way of making predictions but also of resolving or reducing a feeling of unease set up by the occurrence of an unusual or unexpected event. Moreover, there is oftentimes a tendency, particularly among academicians and other professional explainers, to seek out general statements for the usual and expected. The satisfaction which plausible explanations frequently evoke is of interest in our treatment of laws in psychology largely because it is useful to separate the success of a theory in making people feel comfortable or at ease and success of a theory in making correct anticipations of events. This may seem a point so obvious as to be insulting to the careful researcher, but an example of plausible explanation may illustrate the subtlety and ubiquity of this unsystematic kind of conviction. Suppose a four-year-old is observed to suck his thumb and to say frequently, "I don't suck my thumb any more." Presented with this protocol narrative, a number of plausible explanations can be invented. For example:

"The operation of the pleasure principle is restricted at this age not only by the reality danger of the parents' disapproval, but also by the appearance of incorporated prohibitions. Nonetheless, primitive oral gratifications are reinforced in this case by a tendency to restitute the lost mother in thumb-sucking."

"This is a typical double approach-avoidance conflict. If the child sucks his thumb, he is reinforced by the secondary reinforcement of mouth stimulation learned in the feeding situation, but he is also fearful to the degree that thumb-sucking has been punished. On the other hand, if he does not suck his thumb, he will be socially reinforced, but the learned drives supporting thumb-sucking will increase in strength. The resolution is similar to locomotor oscillation in the rat."

"Fours will often still suck their thumbs, particularly when tired or upset, but this is also a time when an attempt is made to act 'grown-up' and to give up babyish habits. One may expect that by five, the child will have reduced his thumb-sucking considerably."

These are imitative explanations, and it is doubtful that they would ever appear in just this form, but it is more than likely that a haphazard selection of child psychologists would vary widely in their choice of the most "reasonable" explanation of the phenomenon. Part of this variation may be ascribed to a careful assessment of the evidence supporting each explanation but there remains an element of habitual commitment to using certain kinds of words, whatever the evidence may be. It was such a habitual use of standard sentences which made the scientific revolution of the sixteenth and seventeenth centuries so dramatic; no longer would verbal commentary suffice. The emphasis on empirical test which defined that revolution is relevant to the appraisal of the satisfactions of present-day psychological theories; although most valid explanations tend to be satisfying or to reduce a discrepancy between the expected and the obtained, the contrary does not hold. Satisfying plausible explanations can be wrong, and the only method of judgment we have is the submission of the explanation to empirical test. Perhaps the force of this argument can be increased by an illustration drawn from the writings of a brilliant scientist. When Galileo reported his discovery of the moons of Jupiter, the astronomer Kepler expressed his doubts, writing: "If indeed four planets move around Jupiter at varying distances and periods, one may ask for whose good, as there is no one there whose eyes may take in this astonishing variety" (Kepler, 1610, p. 21).

The reminder that empirical tests are the means of separating valid explanation from merely plausible commentary leads us to the second important characteristic of explanatory systems in twentieth-century psychology. Whether current theories are susceptible of precise deductive statement or not, they play a crucial role as *ways of summarizing data.* We have necessarily gone far afield from the world of objects and events in our discussion of psychological language, but it should not be forgotten that the superstructure of theory is built upon and depends for its stability on the occurrence and observation of lawful regularities in the world. Granting that limitations exist on the use of any language system in science, it remains the case that a scientific discipline depends for its growth on the accumulation of reliable generalizations in the protocol language. Food-deprived rats will eat more than well-fed rats, psychotics will show test performances different from nonpsychotics, ten-year-olds will use more words than five-year-olds—all regardless of the theories proposed to account for these findings. It is one of the functions of explanatory systems to assist our recall of such reliable generalizations. For example, the statement "${}_SE_R = f({}_SH_R) \times f(D)$" not only operates in a deductive system, but also serves to call the psychologist's attention to a host of empirical observations.

Explanatory systems, however unconvincing they may be when subjected to a close scrutiny of their deductive status, function as sets of index cards or as tables of contents to a proliferating research literature. There may be no great predictive power in a statement like "The anaclitic relationship is necessary to normal ego development," but to an informed reader, such a sentence serves as a tag to the literature on institutionalization, just as the sentence "Synaptic resistance increases immediately after the passage of an impulse" calls up a group of studies on repeated stimulation. This mnemonic use of explanatory systems is by no means inconsequential to the development of a science; in the absence of fully explicit deductive explanations, quasi-explanations that keep in view the chief results of empirical research are more useful than empty speculation on one side or unorganized reporting of individual bits of data on the other. An analogy may be drawn to the postulation of planetary epicycles to prop up a staggering Ptolemaic theory of celestial orbits. It was recognized to be an inadequate repair, but it was better than scriptural astronomy and it clarified the search for a more adequate formulation. Plausible explanations are only way stations to the goal of accurate prediction, but so long as they jibe somehow with research findings, they serve to summarize and codify relevant empirical data.

Plausible explanations play a third role in the development of a science, a role which frequently more than compensates for the formal weaknesses of such explanations. It is as a *goad and guide to further research* that plausible systems take their place in the scientific scheme. The general empirical thesis demands, in the words of Pavlov's motto, "Observation, and then observation." As has been noted earlier, this movement from test to test requires some organizing principle on the part of the researcher, whether or not he chooses to announce it publicly or in detail. The steps taken between one empirical observation and the next may be nondeductive in the formal sense—they may even be silly by normal criteria—but insofar as they lead the researcher to revealing new information, they are of incalculable merit. The witticism about cognitive rats in California and mechanical rats in Iowa illustrates this point nicely. The "theory of the organism" may be different, quite beyond the formal deductive systems which represent it, and the variation in point of view can suggest variation in experimental procedures which lead to new data and sharpen old theoretical discriminations.

It goes without saying that this use of explanation falls short of the ideal case by a good distance, but it would be unwise to underrate the usefulness of plausible, even personally idiosyncratic, theories in a developing discipline. Kepler may serve once more as a case in illustration. He was led, throughout his career, by the conviction that the relationship between the planets' period of revolution and their distance from the sun was some simple harmonic function. The first result of his enthusiasm was an absurd speculation based more on geometrical superstition than on the evidence available, but the desire to show an underlying simplicity kept him at labor over Brahe's observations for seventeen years, trying first one, then another mathematical solution until "the unveiled sun [of discovery] burst out upon me" (quoted in Hart, 1923, p. 91). The laws of motion which came of this discovery were the heart of Newton's synthesis, and perhaps Kepler was not too vain in maintaining that God had waited 6000 years for an observer. The astronomer was carried by his commitment to a rudimentary "theory" that could scarcely be called rigorous, but it would be difficult to overestimate the scientific utility of such a plausible explanation. The biographers of science can cite a large number of similar instances in which incorrect, private, or fanciful explanations have moved us closer to accurate prediction and control.

Plausible systems of explanation will continue to be used in psychology, either as mere verbal commentary on data or in the more important ways of providing a framework for summarizing empirical results and as guides to fruitful new research. The workaday researcher will profit from his investment in plausible explanation to the degree that it furthers his achievement of the fundamental scientific goals—the observation of reliable relationships among events and the explicit statement of deductive theory.

THE SOURCES OF EXPLANATORY SYSTEMS

Any treatment of scientific explanation must at some time come to grips with the most frustrating and the most fascinating questions of all. Where do general principles come from? What are the conditions for the creation of a useful formulation? In what has gone before, we have taken for granted the existence of initial statements, predicating our discussion on the proper statement and use of them. But behind each theory or speculation, there is a human being, the inventive researcher or thinker who first cuts through confusion or doubt to state the illuminating principle. These are the men who are, in Freud's phrase, "obliged to build [their] way out into the dark" (Freud, 1900 [1954, p. 549]), and any construction of the language of psychology would be truncated indeed were this aspect of the scientific endeavor left out of consideration. It would be foolhardy to claim that a prescription can be written for scientific creativity, or a pamphlet issued on "how-to-build-a-Newton-yourself," but the overbearing importance of original thought in refreshing the course of systematic study requires that, at the very least, we review some of the scattered evidence on the sources of explanatory principles. This review will be a case of phenomenology revisited and will take us straightaway to the writings of creative scientists. In using this material, it is well to remember that ". . . out of false modesty, pride, lack of inclination or psychological insight, very few of the great discoverers have revealed their own mental processes; at the most, they have described methods of work—but rarely their dreams, urges, struggles and visions" (Dubos, 1950, p. 369). The noteworthy exceptions to this reticence—for example, Poincaré on mathematical invention or Loewi on experimental insight—provide an intimate and convincing glimpse at scientific creativity, but they present only the beginnings for a psychology of invention.[1] For the moment, no more than a plausible view of creativity can be proposed, held together largely by a collection of biographical anecdotes.

The Occasions for Scientific Creativity

Quite apart from his ingenuity in setting up explanatory systems, the creative scientist seems to have a peculiar sensitivity to discrepancy, a nose for the unexpected or disconcerting event. Most human beings, as has been noted earlier, are content to fit the world of reality to whatever prototheories they accept; the freakish occurrence is consigned to some special category of sports and accidents or else it is not perceived at all. Such seems not to be the case for the man who will twist established formulations; instead of putting the discrepancy out of view or assigning it to "error," he takes the odd event as a starting point for his thought and his research. Cannon (1945) tells of his annoyance at the variations in stomach contractions he observed among his animal subjects. For him, they served at first only to limit his research on gastric motility, yet out of this "error variance" grew his classic studies on the bodily effects of emotions. Similarly for Pavlov, the "psychic secretions" of his dogs interfered seriously with the accu-

[1] Cohen's (1956) study of Newton and Franklin is a model for biographical treatment of scientific thought. Careful work of this order may well lead to more comprehensive and more accurate accounts of creativity among scientists.

rate determination of physiological salivation, but instead of controlling this effect out of his experiments, he changed the entire course of his research career to study it. Over and over again in the biography of science this phenomenon is met with—what for the layman or even the merely competent scientist is an irritating discrepancy becomes for the creative researcher the beginning of a search. Cannon was remarkably optimistic about the generality of this characteristic and in speaking of "gains from serendipity," he suggested that such good luck is possible for anyone. The evidence, insofar as one can assay it, is against this egalitarian view. To cite only two cases, *Penicillium* mold was freely discarded before Fleming had the flexibility to examine its curious properties, and fluorescence of exposed materials had been noted over and over again before Roentgen made his studies of X-radiation. Chance or serendipity may play an occasional role in the work of science but in general Pasteur's dictum seems unassailable: Chance favors only the prepared mind.

It is on this point that an important difference can be noted between scientific creativity and the related behavior of poets, novelists, and metaphysicians. There can be no sudden illumination for the empirical worker who is not prepared by the hard and often dull labor of learning techniques, prior research, and prior theory. The very recognition of discrepancy requires that he know the expected; Pasteur, among others, argues effectively for a view of science which emphasizes the long reaches of meticulous and precise observation, interrupted only infrequently by the revealing insight. Histories of science, like histories of nations, point up moments of drama and sudden change, but this device does poor justice to the work of preparation.

A side light on the occasions for scientific creativity reveals a problem for the psychologist which can only be stated and left unanswered. What accounts for the apparently vast individual differences in the ability to "see" discrepancies? The lesson of many discoveries that might have been made earlier than they were teaches us that all men are not equally endowed or equally well trained in this regard, and it is one of the several open questions for a study of creativity to determine the antecedents of this central skill.

A Peculiar Condition of Creativity

Once a problem has been detected, or a discrepancy observed, the work of scientific creativity can proceed. It is not always easy, however, to throw the originality switch and let a rich flow of new ideas arise. As Miller remarks in his notes on scientific invention:

> When the mind is set free to allow any ideas to come up, including new and original ones, suppressed or repressed anxiety-arousing thoughts (irrelevant to the specific problem at hand) may come up. This anxiety motivates (and its reduction rewards) returning to trains of thought that are so thoroughly rehearsed that there is little chance of frightening associations to intrude. One might speculate that this is why certain highly intelligent and informed people never give themselves the freedom necessary for truly imaginative work. (Miller, 1950, p. 6.)

Although one may disagree with this particular theory of interference, its major argument is seconded by almost all commentators on scientific creativity. The shift required from a setting in which everything is well organized and stable to one in which ambiguity is dominant does not occur readily in human beings, and it is doubtlessly this fracture of conventional and comfortable ways of thinking that makes creativity difficult and rare.

When the limitations of customary thought are somehow put aside, the creative thinker enters a truly peculiar state. Troublesome though it may be for our image of the scientist as unbendingly rational and sensible, the biographies of scientists recount over and over again the occurrence of phenomena of creativity which are always puzzling and at times eerie. Freud's speculations about human thought made possible, and Poincaré's (1913) great prestige made respectable, the study of the *irrational* and *undirected* in creativity by scientists and their biographers.

One of the most dramatic illustrations of the odd circumstances of scientific originality can be drawn from Loewi's account of his research on the chemical transmission of nervous impulses, and his report highlights in its detail the psychological problems posed by the activity of the creative researcher.

> In the night of Easter Saturday, 1921, I awoke, turned on the light, and jotted down a few notes on a tiny slip of paper. Then I fell asleep again. It occurred to me at six o'clock in the morning that during the night I had written down something most important, but I was unable to decipher the scrawl. That Sunday was the most desperate day in my whole scientific life. During the next night, however, I awoke again, at three o'clock, and I

> remembered what it was. This time I did not take any risk; I got up immediately, went to the laboratory, made the experiment on the frog's heart . . . and at five o'clock, the chemical transmission of nervous impulse was conclusively proved. (Loewi, 1953, p. 33.)

This story demonstrates, in a more-or-less typical way, the characteristic of creative thought which can be found in almost all such testimony: the operation of two processes—inspiration and elaboration—and the associated suddenness of solution. Poincaré called the dual nature of inventive thinking ". . . the working methods of the two egos," and it has received a succinct statement from the poet Valéry:

> It takes two to invent anything. The one makes up combinations; the other one chooses, recognizes what he wishes and what is important to him in the mass of the things which the former has imparted to him. (Quoted in Hadamard, 1945, p. 30.)

As the Loewi story shows, these two activities need not always be separated in time; what is essential to the "hypothesis of two processes" is that, in original thought, something goes on quite different from the ordinary ways of thinking, restricted as they are by reality, logic, and consistency. Kris, in one of the few serious attempts to theorize about these phenomena, related the inspirational or first phase of creativity to "the facility with which id impulses, or their closer derivatives, are received" (Kris, 1952, p. 313), and he notes, as does Miller, the oscillation between the work of inspiration and the work of elaboration. The scientists themselves, in writing of their acquaintance with unconscious influences on their thought do not always present hypotheses about the conditions for such cooperation from the depths, but with varying degrees of clarity, their accounts support the postulation of two conditions for inspiration. The first has been noted earlier; startling solutions to research problems occur only after the most intense preparation, a preparation which usually consists of attempts to solve the problem by review of data, by careful thought of the ordinary conscious variety, and by the successive rejection of alternatives. Paradoxically, the second condition is that the thinker be in a state of relaxation or distance from the problem. Archimedes in his Syracusan tub is prototypical of the cases in which the solution appears after the problem has been left aside for a while, or the researcher has in some way relaxed his rational attack on it by sleeping or drinking or dreaming.

It is not difficult, on considering the evidence, to understand why men who have had such experiences are struck to amazement and tend almost invariably to see the process as near magical. Gauss writes of his victory over a mathematical puzzle, "Like a sudden flash of lightning, the riddle happened to be solved. I myself cannot say what was the conducting thread which connected what I previously knew with what made my success possible" (Hadamard, 1945, p. 15). In an almost embarrassed and certainly more constrained manner, Darwin relates much the same kind of event when he hit on the notion of natural selection: "I can remember the very spot in the road, whilst in my carriage, when to my joy the solution occurred to me" (Darwin, 1899, p. 69). The role of the unconscious is so strong in these cases that the poetic fancy about the voice of the Muse occurs in one form or another rather frequently. It is as if someone else were doing the work, and the thinker himself had only to listen. This is obviously a disconcerting experience for men who have devoted their lives to an explicit and rational understanding of natural phenomena, but the evidence is too detailed and too consistent for us to doubt the working of undirected thought in scientific creativity.[2]

The job of going behind the awe and mystery of scientific creativity to a systematic account of its determinants must be listed high on the agenda of a future psychology. Poincaré's "working of the two egos" is not a magical process, but it is, for the time being, a peculiarly resistant nut for the empirical hammer to crack.

It would be inaccurate to maintain that all original thinkers in science agree with the hypothesis of two processes. Magendie, for example, called himself "a mere street scavenger of science. With hook in hand and basket on my back, I go about the streets of science collecting whatever I find" (Dubos, 1950, p. 363). The man at the apogee, Newton, when asked how he came to discover the universal law of gravitation, replied, "By thinking about it ceaselessly." It is a task for the psychologist of creativity, restricted by anecdote and severely limited in number of cases, to take us beyond the guesses reviewed here to a systematic treatment of the phenomena of discovery. The central problem which he must face is to account for the fact that, with more-or-less the same information available to them, most men shrug or give up after trying conventional attacks, while others use the information in novel and effective combinations. The lives of

[2] Hammond (1923), Hart (1923), Cannon (1945), and Dubos (1950) present a large number of reports of these phenomena in scientific creativity.

great scientists make beguiling reading, but for the psychologist or teacher, it has depressing overtones. It seems fair to say that one cannot make a Newton; one can only hope to find him.

Creative thought is in many ways akin to what were called "private events" in Part I—it is in this sense that we are revisiting phenomenology. The private thoughts of the creative scientist, often clothed in a private language, are the first steps he takes toward building a theory. Psychology in particular has gained much from the phenomenal experience of the creative investigator; as much as it was seen to be unspeakable and useless as the data language of psychology, it has just as much been the primary source of fecund hypotheses about behavior. The personality theorist as well as the animal researcher find it useful to ask "What would I do?" or "How would I feel?" in order to arrive at fruitful hypotheses. If answers to these questions can be translated into the public language of science, then the phenomenal experience can take its proper place in the development of a language of psychology.

"Observation, and then Observation"

If he is talented and flexible enough to be truly creative, the scientist comes nearer the poet during his peculiar condition than at any other point in the scientific endeavor. But the conjunction is a brief one; after the tour of the unconscious which seems so frequently involved in the genesis of new ideas, the research worker must return to his laboratory to continue the usual business of test, revision, and test. In most of the popular snipes at psychology as a science, this point has been overlooked. Shakespeare and Dostoevski may be "better psychologists than the psychologists" in their ability to touch closely and movingly on some widely held prototheory of behavior; they may even provide a prodigality of plausible initial statements in their building of convincing portraits, but they and the nonempirical psychologists in general, apparently never feel the sharpest goad of the research psychologist—to find out by looking whether or not he is right. It should be clear from our excursion into the field of creative thought that the scientist comes to his germinal ideas in ways not altogether different from the ways of the poet. The defining characteristic of the scientific approach is by no means some special kind of "scientific thought," but rather the insistence, endlessly repeated, on demonstration and test in the world of reality. One of the incidental advantages of a familiarity with empirical data is the possibility it provides for "implicit test." The researcher can try out his novel postulates in a preliminary way by seeing whether they subsume what he already knows to be the case. If he has a set of statements which fit the existing body of data, he can turn to new empirical tests with greater assurance. Pavlov, with the fervor that pervades his writings on the scientific attitude, presented the following summary for his students.

> Train yourself to reserve and patience. Learn to do the heavy work that science involves. Study, compare, accumulate facts. Be the wing of a bird never so perfect, it would never bear her aloft without the support of the air. Facts are the scientist's air, without which he would never be able to fly. (Frolov, 1937, p. 258.)

Many of the copybook stories of scientific success neglect the empirical tail on the creative dog. Among Cannon's serendipitous cases is the account of von Mering and Minkowski's discovery of a sugar-control function in the area of the pancreas. They had, in the course of studies of this organ, removed the pancreas from several experimental animals. A laboratory assistant called his chiefs' attention to the curious fact that flies in abnormally large numbers were attracted to the urine of these subjects, and on the basis of this clue, von Mering and Minkowski revised their procedures and research goals. No doubt this was a break, a bit of good fortune, but a bald version of the story leaves out the two conditions that make it part of the history of science—the preparation of the experimenters which permitted them to recognize the importance of the observation, and the tedious and detailed research which was required to confirm what it suggested to them.

In order to complete a sketch of the creative scientist, we should note two further characteristics which appear with scarcely an exception in available biographies—the courage to be different and a commitment to long hours and hard work.

Certainly not all imaginative thinkers have been pilloried for their deviation from conventional explanatory schemes, but a compendium of the dangers, physical and emotional, of being a creative researcher would include many names in the hagiology of science. Gumpert has defended the thesis of necessary courage by presenting "a group of human documents from the domain of science with a view to demonstrating the ineradicable opposition to genius" (Gumpert, 1936, p. v), and although his examples are not always fully convincing, they demonstrate vividly the reluctance of human beings to be shaken from their comfortable error. One anecdote from many will serve as an illustration of Gumpert's contention. When Vesalius recognized with something akin to horror that Galen, the unimpeachable authority, had never dissected a human body, he hesitated for some time before he published his collection of Galenic mistakes. His teacher Sylvius, an anatomist of great stature, spoke for the scientific community when he argued, as part of a violent and personal attack on Vesalius, that if meniscuses are now present in our joints, they were absent in ancient times, because Galen did not describe them; therefore men must have changed, since Galen was infallible (Gumpert, 1936, p. 55).[3] With the evidence of such treatment, certainly common enough in the history of science, we must respect not only the vision of the trail blazers but their impressive tenacity as well. A psychological analysis of the courage to be creative may, in fact, show the importance of aggression in the make-up of the original thinker. Creative thought always involves the overturning of the *status quo* and the creative act, by its destructiveness, puts the innovator in the role of aggressor.

It is more difficult to document the generality of hard work and long hours as correlates of scientific creativity, for rarely can one find reliable information on work routines of famous researchers. What data are available, however, are repetitious in their reference to persistence, a refusal to be deterred by everyday demands, and quite often, a rigid regularity in the allocation of time for work. Once more, the psychologist of creativity is without the evidence that would permit a clear formulation of the part dedication plays in inventive thought, but there is a substantial collection of reports which suggests that for the innovators scientific work is no casual affair. In his eighty-sixth year, the Russian government built for Pavlov a laboratory which fit all his research requirements. It is reported that he sighed with regret that this opportunity had not been offered him twenty years earlier when, it is worthy of note, he would have been a mere sixty-six (Cannon, 1945, p. 187).

THE EVALUATION OF THEORIES

Explanations of natural phenomena have human sources, and we have detoured around a discussion of the proper statement and test of

[3] This story could be told, with hardly more than a change of names and subject matter, of debates in the Soviet Academy of Sciences on the infallibility of a Marxist psychology. Academic rigidity, whatever its sources, is not bound by century or place.

theoretical systems to examine some of the conditions for scientific invention and discovery. The complexity and interest of the phenomena of creativity should not, however, distort the fact that an explanatory scheme, when it has been made public, takes on a status independent of its originator. Whatever circumstances determine the invention of initial statements, their elaboration and test are matters of general concern, and no knowledge we have about the theorist will modify the utility of his theory. Once in the public domain of science, an explanatory system is evaluated according to its effectiveness in anticipating events. This statement of criterion brings us back to an examination of the grounds for accepting or rejecting a theoretical formulation. Apart from the functions of plausible systems described earlier, there are several aspects of explanation which warrant further consideration. The difficulties which face the researcher interested in the evaluation of explanatory systems can be treated under three headings—the need for a criterion of triviality, the need for a criterion of systematic power or parsimony, and the need for a criterion of weighting positive and negative instances.

Were there at hand a rigorous criterion for triviality, the psychological community could agree with confidence on the study of genuinely important issues, the ones that "really matter." Unfortunately for the researcher who needs reassurance that his work is not trivial, no such criterion of exclusion can be stated. The polemic use of terms such as "inconsequential," "limited," "far from reality," and so on, when applied to theories of behavior, misses the fact that science has no dead-end markers. We can look back into the past and see with relatively high acuity the junctures at which a line of theory went awry, but no satisfactory method can be proposed for making a similar judgment about contemporary systems of explanation. A responsible scientist may choose to work on whatever problems interest him but he is fooling himself if he claims to *know* that he is on a more direct route to some future truth than his colleagues. Franklin and Faraday were both asked "What good is it?" by curious and puzzled friends who were watching the demonstration of a new device. Franklin's famous reply "What good is a newborn child?" was a pointed recognition of our ignorance of future utilities, but Faraday expressed more accurately the disdain of the pure scientist for questions of applicability when he responded to Gladstone, "Why, sir, there is every probability that you will soon be able to tax it" (Hammond, 1923, p. 2). Much the same answers can be made to attacks against psychological theories on grounds of triviality; their ultimate contribution to knowledge is determined by so many unknown considerations that it seems wisest to recognize that attacks of this order cannot be justified by reference to an unambiguous criterion. A line of research may be judged trivial because it is not among a group of traditional problems, or because there is no effective theory to direct it, or because it has no immediate application to critical human problems, but judgments of this stamp, important as they may be in the motivation of researchers, are insufficient for predicting the future course of science.

The need for a criterion of systematic power or parsimony cannot be treated so summarily. It is a timeworn tradition in science to ask how efficient a set of general principles is in accounting for the relevant data, and it would seem that some way of deciding the question is essential to systematic study. Certainly the issue can be stated in a very broad fashion—at one end there is the handbook of all available generalizations, an unparsimonious solution; at the other are the general principles so inclusive as to be useless in predicting anything (e.g., "All behavior is motivated"). Somewhere between these extremes lies the band of effective explanations, those which have a high evidence-to-principle ratio. In evaluating a theory, it would seem that we would have to make a count of confirmed predictions and compare this, preferably in some mathematical way, to the number of principles necessary to derive the predictions. This is a very attractive line of argument, but it omits several considerations which make it somewhat less winning.

In the first place, an evidence-to-principle ratio can be established only for explicitly stated theories. Unless the initial statements of an explanation are out in the open and their implications drawn with reliable precision, it is manifestly impossible to count either principles or instances of confirmed predictions. It is not parsimonious to have a two- or three-principle theory which demands a host of auxiliary or *ad hoc* assumptions to produce a single prediction. Nor is it parsimonious to use one particular interpretation of explanatory principles to generate one prediction and a slightly different interpretation to get to a second prediction. Disagreements about parsimony will have the flavor of disagreements about triviality so long as the theories under consideration remain partly a matter of the theorist's ingenuity in selecting and using premises.

More weighty difficulties in establishing probabilities for systematic power have been raised by Hempel and Oppenheim. Even granting the existence of explicit deductive systems, there remain logical problems which bar "a significant application of [a theory of systematic power] in . . . the methodology of science" (Hempel and Oppenheim, 1948, p. 173). Many of the issues they discuss are beyond the scope of the present treatment, but one of their examples will indicate the complexity of the problem.

> Kepler's laws, K, may be conjoined with Boyle's law, B, to [form] a stronger law K.B; but derivation of K from the latter would not be considered as an explanation of the regularities stated in Kepler's laws; rather, it would be viewed as representing, in effect, a pointless "explanation" of Kepler's laws by themselves. The derivation of Kepler's laws from Newton's laws of motion and of gravitation, on the other hand, would be recognized as a genuine explanation in terms of more comprehensive regularities, or so-called higher laws. The problem therefore arises of setting up clear-cut criteria for the distinction of levels of explanation or for a comparison of generalized sentences as to their comprehensiveness. The establishment of adequate criteria for this purpose is as yet an open problem. (Hempel and Oppenheim, 1948, p. 159.)

It is impossible to predict whether the philosophers of science will be able to untangle the knots which surround a theory of systematic power, but it is unhappily clear that, for the present, discussions of relative parsimony must remain in the arena of common sense, with only the most insensitive comparisons carrying conviction.

If we lower our sights from the goal of a precise value for systematic power and turn to a consideration of less demanding grounds for the evaluation of an explanation, the problem of weighting positive and negative instances comes to the foreground. Again, the general issue can be stated in a deceptively easy way. The ideal case is surely that in which all predictions are confirmed, i.e., the case of all positive instances. Contrariwise, the case of all negative instances is easily resolved. But what of the much more frequent occasions when an explanation handles some of the available data, but is insufficient or wrong for the rest? The decision is even more barbed when it is remembered that an evaluation of this kind is usually required in a *choice* between alternative theories. It is not unlikely that one set of explanatory principles will account for a range of data which does not overlap neatly with the successful range of the other theory. On what grounds can we compare the explanations?

One possible answer has already been eliminated. There exists no mechanical way of evaluating relative success and thereby determining the more effective theory. A fully automatic technique permits only two conditions of a theory—it is correct so far or it is wrong. The first case is the one in which all predictions tested to date have been confirmed, but it should be added at once that even this pleasant condition does not permit us to stamp "True" on the explanatory system. The best summary that can be justified is "This theory *to date* is a member of the infinite set of explanatory systems which could be invented to encompass these data." Although this may seem an unnecessarily strict statement of the status of a confirmed theory, it would be fallacious to maintain that a theory is true when one of the conditions of its strength is that nobody has yet proposed an equally successful alternative. The shock to physicists of Einstein's revisions derived in part from the opinion, frequently expressed in the nineteenth century, that nothing new could be said about celestial mechanics. One of the ways of protecting a discipline from sterile rigidity is to emphasize the open nature of even the most highly confirmed theoretical system. This caution should not be swallowed whole by the practicing researcher. Clearly, if there is available an effective theory, i.e., one which handles existing data well and which is fruitful of further research, it is not to be despised because there may be unstated alternatives of equal merit. For the scientist attempting to comprehend a set of phenomena, an explanatory bird in hand is worth an indeterminate number of explanatory birds in the bush. It need not blunt the search for powerful explanation to note the absence of a criterion for labeling a scientific system "The one and only."

We are, paradoxically enough, on somewhat surer ground when a theory generates a wrong prediction, for in this case, it is possible to be *certain* that an error is present somewhere in the explanatory scheme. To deal with it, the theorist must revise some part or all of his system, and it is at this point that the caution expressed earlier about partial and unconsidered revision becomes important. In disciplines without agreed-on general theories, there may be a tendency to make *ad hoc* changes in an explanation without reviewing their full implications; the result of this maneuver is the compounding of "theories." If this mistake is avoided and the theory patched to show no obvious flaws, then it enters once more the class of explanations which are satisfactory *so far*.

The firm character of a failure of confirmation—a negative instance—has led to a view of science as a business of successive approximations to a stable truth. As more and more explanations are eliminated by the occurrence of negative instances, it is felt that we close in on the last formulation left—the true one. This picture of scientific pursuit is a tempting one; it is not inconsistent with the accumulative character of science that Conant has emphasized and, one may suspect, it is a part of most scientists' private credo. Yet with all this support, it is not possible to state a warrant for the argument with conviction. The number of alternative explanations for a set of data is not finite, to be chipped away one by one; getting rid of a single member of an infinite set does not substantially reduce the number of alternatives remaining. Scientific theories may become more comprehensive, that is, they may encompass more and more data, but unless we adopt a belief in terminal theoretical truth, there is little support for the thesis that we can achieve accuracy by elimination.

The apparently endless search for an unattainable goal which the rejection of the elimination criterion seems to impose upon the scientist is not, however, quite futile. While any given set of findings is explainable by an infinite set of general statements, there is also another infinite set of statements which fail to account for the available data. Thus class A does account for the present data, class B does not. Whenever new findings are added to the corpus of knowledge there will be a subset A′ of A which will fail to account for what is now available evidence. The class A″ which still covers the data remains infinite but we may safely discount all statements which fall into classes B, A′, and so forth. Elimination thus tells us what classes of statements will not provide a solution.

There is another aspect of the elimination argument which deserves mention. Although the objections to the possibility of reducing the size of infinite sets of explanations appear irrefutable on purely formal grounds, it may be that we move toward explanations which are terminally *satisfying* to human beings. For example, if we consider the following double set of numbers:

x:	1	2	3	4	5
y:	1	4	9	16	25

we can imagine a large number of equations which would represent the functional relationship between x and y. Yet it would be very unusual for anyone to propose a solution other than $y = x^2$. It is not unlikely, as a result of shared human experience or even as a result of the way the organism is constructed, that rules of simplicity or parsimony can be stated on psychological grounds.

This last consideration is related to another problem of weighting positive and negative instances which comes closer to the realities of a developing science. Researchers do in fact hold strong opinions about the relative power of different explanations and do not give up a theory even when it has been shown to be wrong. Moreover, there may be occasions when a theorist may prefer an explanation with a large number of negative instances to one with only a few. These observations make sense if it is recognized that positive and negative instances not only influence the formal status of a theory, but also are weighted by the scientist's *degree of belief*. His willingness to abandon a theoretical position or to accept an alternative is determined in part by the effect of bits of evidence on his commitment to an explanatory system. For some researchers, the occurrence of a single negative instance may be sufficient for him to scuttle the system which generated the erroneous prediction; for another, although it may weaken his commitment, the negative instance can be weighed lightly against the confirmations he has found for his theory. Just as in the problem of induction, these are questions in the psychology of confirmation, and their study, as was noted in Chapter 11, is only in its infancy. Bruner et al. (1956), among others, have presented evidence on the variety of responses to the occurrence of negative and positive instances of a generalization, and it is reasonable to believe that this approach may fruitfully be expanded to investigate the relationship between empirical evidence and a researcher's commitment to a particular explanatory system.

As has been seen so often in the discussion of explanation in psychology, problems in the psychology of scientists run alongside problems in the philosophy of science. No aspect of this intertwining deserves more careful investigation than this issue of the grounds for acceptance of explanatory systems. The practicing researcher, in order to go about his work at all, must accept less demanding criteria for acceptable theories than the philosopher of science can justify for him, but the hope may not be altogether pious that their shared interest in the issue will be fertile to the growth of more effective explanations.

THE GOOD THEORY

After having sought along several paths for a relatively simple way of characterizing the "good theory," and having come to sobering conclusions each time, it should be apparent that a facile specification of this desirable state of affairs would be little more than an abbreviated distortion. Certainly the good theory should be explicit, it should be relevant to the data for which the theorist wants to account, and it should be highly confirmed. But explanations have important functions in a developing discipline even when they are not comprehensive and when they display negative instances—they help the researcher to keep an optimal amount of data in view and, of critical importance, they provide a stimulus to the design of further research. One of these several functions may on occasion have a greater weight in determining utility than another; in our present stage of knowledge about theories and theorists, we can at best only outline the requirements for effective maps through the world of objects and events. It may be that a good theory, like a good painting, can be recognized only after the fads and prejudices attending its creation have been put in perspective by the passage of time.

SUMMARY

Explanation in science can be properly understood only after a consideration of its sources and uses. Plausible theories do not measure up to the requirements of fully deductive expression, but they may play an important part in the accumulation of reliable statements of relationships among events.

Theoretical systems arise not in a mechanical or magical fashion, but from the creative thought of informed men. Some of the phenomena of scientific creativity suggest the operation of unconscious processes, but the resulting proposals must always be subjected to the scrutiny of public test.

When we come to the evaluation of an explanatory system, it is possible to state several criteria for "the good theory," and a reasonable judgment of explanatory effectiveness can be made only by considering the degree to which all of these criteria are fulfilled.

chapter fourteen

Special problems in the language of psychology

SCIENCE CANNOT BE DISSECTED INTO NEATLY isolated disciplines, and in treating of the language of psychology we have often put under examination issues relevant to the languages of other systematic specialties. Most, if not all, scientific discourse depends on the resolution of general problems such as the posit of reality, characteristics of a basic vocabulary, and the nature of explanatory systems, to cite but three. In addition to these questions of broad impact, there is another group of problems which either are idiosyncratic to a science or else take on a special importance for a particular field of study. Psychology, perhaps because of the variegated character of its ancestry, seems liable to "special problems" in unusual number. Among the group of puzzles which are especially irksome in gaining an understanding of the language of psychology, three have historical roots and a present-day prominence which warrant their consideration in some detail. Two of them—the relation of psychology to other biological sciences and the nature of clinical insight—are vividly and polemically argued in the psychological court, and have generated a remarkable degree of academic heat. The third problem—the use of models and analogies—has had a less controversial hearing, but demands attention on grounds of its persistent appearance in discussions of research strategy.

PSYCHOLOGY REDUCED

It was noted in Chapter 9 that one of the recurrent themes in the history of psychology has been a concern with the relation of the study of behavior to other biological disciplines. More often than not, this concern has expressed itself in attempts to determine the physiological foundations of psychological phenomena, i.e., to *reduce* the regularities observed in behavior to a set of statements in the language of physiology. In Pratt's unequivocal statement of the position,

> The principal task of theoretical psychology in making a scientific portrait of human nature is to discover the immediate antecedents of initial descriptive data. These antecedent conditions are located within the biological organism. All psychological explanation must therefore move in the direction of physiology. The theoretical importance of psychological descriptions, as contrasted with any practical significance they may conceivably possess, derives almost exclusively from the light they throw on physiological mechanisms. (Pratt, 1939, p. ix f.)

This definition of the place of physiology in the explanation of behavior has not gone unchallenged, with Skinner (1931, 1932) making a forceful attack in his analysis of the reflex concept, and with a number of behavior theorists, notably Spence (*passim*), arguing against the demand for a physiological reduction of psychological laws. In 1948, the issue was reawakened by MacCorquodale and Meehl's proposal of a distinction between two classes of theoretical words—those "which merely abstract . . . empirical relationships" (intervening variables), and those which "involve the supposition of entities or processes not among the observed" (hypothetical constructs). The succeeding decade saw their proposal tied to the older reductionist controversy in a spate of papers on the nature of constructs in psychology. MacCorquodale and Meehl's differentiation was never clearly free of the reductionist argument, for the authors appended to their proposal the following requirement on the use of hypothetical constructs.

> Their actual existence should be compatible with general knowledge and particularly with whatever relevant knowledge exists at

> the next lower level in the explanatory hierarchy. (MacCorquodale and Meehl, 1948, p. 107.)

It is the expression of commitment to the "next lower level in the explanatory hierarchy" which has in recent psychological history started another round in the battle between the reductionists and the "pure psychologists" (for example, see Krech, 1950).

There are many knots in this psychological ball of yarn, and we will attempt to loosen only a few of them. The central concern of the present discussion will be the general thesis of reductionism—that psychological explanations can and should be expressed in the language of some more basic science—and the thematic question will be "Why reduce?" [1]

In part, the pressure to make psychology a biological discipline is a legacy from the philosophical disjunction of the mental and the physical. So long as a basic distinction was made between mind, a nonmaterial entity, and body, the nineteenth-century psychologist was cut off from the main line of scientific study and found himself put in the same compound as philosophers and theologians. One resolution of the disturbing dualism was the assertion that the psychologist's proper *scientific* study was of cerebral and other organic functions as they manifested themselves in behavior. With academic precursors in both philosophy and physiology, the first generation of systematic psychologists often allied themselves with the physiologists. Watson's later rejection of introspective evidence cemented the union; the psychologist's study of muscle spasms and glandular secretions was clearly a subdivision of the larger biological endeavor. If consciousness was no longer to be a fit subject for scientific study, then Titchener's dream of a psychology independent of physiology would have to be abandoned. From these sources, and in a search for a material foundation for their science, one important group of twentieth-century psychologists is committed to the eventual collapse of psychology into a more fundamental statement in physiological or other biological language. For them, the escape from the ambiguities and soiled reputation of "mind" led directly to the study of organ function.

Side by side with this development, there has grown up another tradition of approach to the study of behavior. It appears to be compounded of two elements—one which emphasizes the independence

---

[1] This fourth treatment of "reduction" represents an extension of the general problem outlined in Chapter 9.

of psychology on empirico-descriptive grounds, another which maintains that theoretical statements about behavior can be made in any language so long as adequate prediction and control result. Rather than escaping the problems of "mind" along the physiological road, psychologists of this persuasion have attempted to build a language of description and explanation which avoids the metaphysical pitfalls, but remains more-or-less independent of other scientific languages.

In the rational scientific community, one might hope that considerations of historical sources and academic prejudice would have little to do with research strategy and tactics. Comforting as this hope may seem—that only the layman is tied to his prototheories of behavior—the extent and intensity of the reductionist debate suggests that it remains haunted by the buried but not dead issue of whether the proper study of psychology is "mind" or "body."

There is another basis for the reductionist controversy, which relates closely to our earlier discussion of the functions of plausible explanation. When a psychologist tries to explain a phenomenon, he must necessarily call on whatever resources of training and ingenuity are available to him. For some students of behavior, this work of explanation will be more easily achieved in the language system of physiology or anatomy or biophysics; for others, the establishment of tentative explanations will be carried on in the language of a behavior theory; for still others, the work of hypothesis formation may be more readily advanced by the language of mythology, or probability functions, or science fiction. For reasons of the psychologist's specialized training, or his personal commitment to a senior colleague, or some misty idiosyncratic technique of problem solution, the phenomenological grounds for the invention of explanations will vary from one psychologist to another. The resulting public statement of an explanation will almost certainly carry the marks of such private sources.

Under these circumstances, it should be no surprise that researchers with similar views of the nature of psychology tend to cluster into "points of view" about psychological explanation. In our present state of knowledge about behavior, the sharing of an explanatory language, even if it is at a low level of deductive power, provides important supports to the planning and execution of research. One of the major dimensions along which such *compagnons de l'esprit* have arrayed themselves is the emphasis given to physiological reduction of behavioral phenomena.

The problem of reductionism in psychology goes beyond discussions of the philosophical roots of behavior study and the personal style of creative thinking; there are grounds for the disputation within the domain of adequate explanation for behavioral phenomena. One of the more convincing positions taken in support of the reductionist thesis can be based on the criteria for a stable vocabulary described in Part I. If it is the case that the language of physiology or anatomy has a reliable and consistent usage, then it is reasonable to maintain that this language is to be preferred to the ambiguous terms of non-reductionist theories. For example, a neuron can be made visible, the frontal lobes are palpable rather than inferred, and so on. Terms like "habit," "drive," or "libido" cannot be given an analogous assignment in the world of objects and events, and this deficiency has been a major point of assault for the psychobiological theorist. It should be noted that if degree of palpability or visibility were the sole criterion in this dispute, the nonreductionists would be in a very bad way.[2] Psychology, as delimited by Skinner or Spence, has no entities of this order.

It is well to recall, however, that the criteria for a scientific vocabulary do not demand that "actual existence" underlie terms in the sense that tables and dogs exist. Rather, the basic requirements turn on the reliable usage of terms in particular observational circumstances and in the sentences of a theory. On the first criterion, there may be in the language of physiology a group of terms which, for reasons of their systematic history, have a high level of reliability of usage, but there seem to be no defensible reasons why "drive" may not come to be as reliably applied as "synapse," or "libido" as reliably applied as "association area." Of much more weight is the consideration of theoretical status; there is no clear and present evidence that the initial statements and rules for manipulation of physiological theories of behavior produce more accurate predictions than do the initial statements and rules for manipulation of "purely psychological" theories. It is this last point that brings us to an examination of how reduction fits into the explanation of behavior and of the steps necessary to achieve it.

Even assuming that the language of physiology contains a vocabulary of high reliability, it is clearly not commensurate with the reductionist

---

[2] In Chapter 4 we discussed some of the sources of the search for palpability or tangibility. Psychology was seen to be physicalistic to the extent that "entity" characteristics are restricted to objects and events for which there are reasonable theoretical or prototheoretical "physical" justifications. "Mental" entities, whether souls or reflexes, cannot claim such dispensations.

thesis merely to substitute physiological words for psychological words. This kind of verbal juggling does not change the explanatory status of a theory, and it accomplishes no more than would a substitution of legal or chemical words. What then does physiological reduction require? The most straightforward answer to this question lies in considering the function of any explanatory system. As was pointed out in Chapter 12, the demand for an explanation is a demand for a system of general principles which will permit the deduction of the phenomenon to be explained. Viewed from this angle, the reductionist thesis may be reformulated in the following way: The laws of psychology can and should be deducible from explanatory systems in the language of physiology. This characterization of the proposal has the estimable advantage of cutting away the encumbrances of implicit prototheories, and of putting the issue in a form which permits less perfervid evaluation.

Let us suppose, somewhat unrealistically, that there exists a set of reliable protocol sentences about behavior, *Psi,* and a corresponding set of statements about physiological functions, *Phi.* For the purposes of this example, let us suppose further that there is a "good theory" in the language of behavior theory, *T-Psi,* which permits deduction of *Psi* and an equally "good theory" (*T-Phi*) which handles *Phi* (Table 7). In these idealized circumstances, where does the reductionist proposal lead?

Table 7

THE REDUCTIONIST PROBLEM

(See Text for Explanation)

T-Phi	T-Psi
↓	↓
Phi	Psi

There are several plausible answers, and each of them touches on a slightly different aspect of the problem. First, and of most ambitious character, is the establishment of a superordinate theory, *Super-T,* which either through *T-Phi* and *T-Psi,* or without mediation of prior theories, permits the deduction of both *Phi* and *Psi* (Table 8).

This is a solution with which no psychologist, regardless of his strategic stripe, would argue; it represents the usual scientific goal of increasing comprehensiveness of explanatory systems. However, this sort of solution requires several comments. We have already noted

Table 8

Two Solutions of the Reductionist Problem

(see Chapter 12) that psychology is without an explicit and comprehensive theory on the model of *T-Psi* which will encompass what we know of behavior. Moreover, physiologists seem to be in much the same tentative and argumentative stage. On these grounds, the proposal of *Super-T* becomes so unrealistic as to be outside serious consideration within the foreseeable future. It is also worthy of note that the language of such a supertheory cannot be predetermined. In order to encompass a wider range of phenomena, it may be necessary for the Newton of *Super-T* to use chemical, or biophysical, or even quite original terms in the construction of his system.[3] It then will be a matter of taste and a matter of history whether or not *Super-T* is called a physiological or "lower-level" theory.

Another possible expression of the reductionist claim would be that the only proper terms for *T-Psi* are those drawn from *Phi* or *T-Phi*. This is probably a more-or-less accurate representation of the point made by Pratt in his evaluation of psychological theory, i.e., that the explanatory language of psychology must have physiological import. Unfortunately for this variation of the reductionist thesis, the criteria for adequate explanation hinge on predictive efficacy, and a theory about behavior in physiological language must be evaluated on precisely the same grounds as a theory in any other style. If a psychophysiological explanation does a better or more comprehensive job of accounting for *Psi* than other theories, then it will take an important place in the explanation of behavior. But what must be recognized is that it is not a better theory merely because it is in physiological dress; it remains a matter of empirical test whether psychological theories based on physiology will meet the predictive require-

[3] One of the incidental ironies of the reductionist controversy is its variation with position in the so-called hierarchy. Psychologists opposed to physiological reduction seem to see no inconsistency in their own attempts to reduce sociology to psychology; on the other hand, physiological psychologists do not always seem happy about the potential reduction of their discipline to biochemistry or biophysics.

ments better than their competitors. It is not an issue for decision by fiat either for or against the reductionist proposal. Two questions will show how deeply rooted this problem is in empirical rather than in formal or extrascientific grounds.

What physiological principles or laws are to be used in setting up a theory of behavior? The reductionist argument seems to suggest that physiologists are more secure in their theories than psychologists are, yet the innovations and discoveries of recent years would seem to belie this assurance. Certainly, a psychologist who several decades ago designed a theory of behavior based on then-current physiological principles would not be able to claim much merit for his reduction or translation today. Physiology is a growing and contentious science just as psychology is, and the pressure to conform with contemporary physiological explanations can easily leave the theorist of behavior with an explanation of little relevance to the next advance in physiological research.

The second question to put to the reductionist solution based on a borrowing of constructs is: What is the appropriate procedure in cases where the psychologist is interested in phenomena which have no present place in the language of physiology? Clearly, he will not stop his research or theorizing until physiologists come abreast, and Pratt's suggestion that he invent quasi-physiological explanations is an invitation to advertise ignorance without advancing the efficacy of prediction. Demanding that the psychologist predict the future course of physiological research seems an unreasonable requirement.

There remains for examination one last formulation of the reductionist thesis, which may be called "the weaker hypothesis." This variation, which seems to be reflected in MacCorquodale and Meehl's presentation, would require only that no principle used in a psychological theory be contradictory to established generalizations in other sciences. Insofar as contradiction can be detected, this requirement is eminently reasonable; the psychological theorist certainly will be unsatisfied with an explanation which he knows to be wrong. However, the rub comes in determining the presence of a contradiction. If the theory implies a statement which is empirically incorrect, then it is to be charged with a negative instance, and the theorist is under some obligation to revise his explanation. But MacCorquodale and Meehl appear to make a broader demand, namely, that theories using hypothetical constructs must be free of contradiction with current physiological theory. They use as a bad example Freud's quasi-hydraulic theory of libido, commenting that "the central nervous-system does not in fact contain pipes or tubes with fluid in them, and there are no known properties of nervous tissue to which the hydraulic properties of libido could correspond" (MacCorquodale and Meehl, 1948). This reinterpretative device misses the function of explanatory systems. Freud's theory has as its range of intent certain responses of human beings, e.g., reports of fantasies and dreams, sexual behavior, and so on. If the libido explanation leads to testable and confirmed statements about such behavior, then it has met the central requirement of a good theory. If it achieves this function at a very high level, then discussions of the "reality" of libido in pipes become as irrelevant as discussions of the "reality" of electrons in orbits.

Once again, it is highly commendable if a theorist can make so general a statement of premises that he can predict over a wide range of data, but the only defensible requirement that one can impose on the construction of theories is that they permit accurate predictions over their range of intent. The failure of libido theory to predict neural functioning is precisely analogous to the failure of theories of cortical functioning to predict the content of fantasies or dreams. Someday, the creation of a more general theory may illustrate dramatically the fruitless character of the reductionist controversy, but in the meantime, it seems unwise to legislate the invention of explanations. A theory of dreams, or of thinking, or of animal learning which makes confirmed predictions and which is the basis for the design of informative research is a good theory, regardless of whether or not it is possible to reinterpret its premises into statements consistent with current physiological theory.

In reviewing the literature of the reductionist contention, we are led to the conclusion that the issue resolves down to a statement of preferred strategies. On one side are the psychologists who are convinced that the future language of psychology will be closely akin to the future language of physiology, and that current theoretical attempts should aim for this meeting; on the other side are the psychologists who maintain that any language system can be used in the explanation of behavior, and that present-day theories will be useful to the degree that they lead to accurate prediction and fruitful research, regardless of developments in other language systems. There is no presently available evidence which will permit a decision between these alternatives; the reductionist controversy in psychology is an excellent example of the wisdom of Wittgenstein's injunction against speaking when there is nothing meaningful to say.

THE USE OF MODELS AND ANALOGIES

In their attempts to understand novel or unusual phenomena, men are often forced to draw on explanations which are appropriate to well-understood phenomena. They use what they are confident about in order to comprehend what is still unclear. This sort of theorizing by extension of the old to the new may be called *explanation by analogy,* and its common occurrence in science at large and in psychology suggests the importance of its function in the work of explanation.

Analogical treatments can be seen at a simple level in the pedagogy of elementary science. In order to get across the notion of "valence," chemistry students are told to imagine that each atom has a specified number of hands or hooks which determines the proper combination with other atoms; electricity is often discussed in analogy to hydraulic systems; the mathematical laws of electron activity are set in a comprehensible model about the planetary orbit of particles; and so on. If the student goes beyond the fundamentals expressed in such analogical fashion, he is usually weaned away from this primitive kind of presentation, and slowly taught the system of general principles which is appropriate to the subject matter under study.

As we have noted earlier, the road from the vernacular to the scientific language is of gradual slope, and the use of analogies is an important guide and crutch. Piaget's theory of adaptation is an elegant expression of the fact that we can assimilate or use only what can be fitted somehow into an earlier "theory" of natural phenomena. The choice of analogy is of course dependent on the prototheories which a human being brings with him—e.g., the analogy in explanation of electrical phenomena given a five-year-old will usually be quite different from that given a college freshman—but there is doubtlessly systematic variation in what will be a popular form of analogy at any particular time in the history of science. From the Newtonian reconstruction in the seventeenth century until well into the twentieth, analogies based on the movement of particles—billiard balls, planetary systems, molecules of gas—have dominated the field. More recently, analogies based on quantum theory and on "field" effects have begun, as they grow more familiar, to take a place among the popular models of explanation. Fruitful scientific theories seem to show a regular progression from incomprehensibility and rejection through acceptance and test to an uncritical extension beyond their original range of intent. This "extension" usually takes place through the technique of analogical reasoning.

The use of models and analogies in science is by no means confined to the classroom; there is ample biographical evidence that they frequently appear in the creative work of scientific theorists. Newton, for all his reluctance to invent hypotheses, was led to a wave theory of color by an extension of his observations on sound. He anticipated that color would depend on vibration "much after the manner, that in the sense of hearing, nature makes use of aereal vibrations of several bignesses to generate sounds of divers tones; for the analogy of nature is to be observed" (Birch, 1757, p. 262). The fact that he was on the right track has added another gem to the Newtonian crown, but the "analogy of nature" is not always so kind; Titchener's mental chemistry was not too unlike Newton's generalization from sound to color.

The place of models in scientific explanation can perhaps best be typified in Maxwell's handling of electromagnetic induction. In an early presentation and commentary on Faraday's results, he developed an ingenious model with cylinders and spherical balls, turning and rolling against one another in a way which permitted him to account for the empirical results. In a later exposition, the mechanical model gave way to a hydrodynamical one, in which he drew his analogy from notions of lines of flow in an incompressible fluid. Side by side with the hydraulic model were the mathematical equations containing his theoretical principles, from which so much of modern physics derives. The nonmathematical analogies served two purposes; they provided Maxwell with instructive leads to a formal theory, and they made possible the presentation of his results in forms comprehensible to his colleagues. But, as Einstein has noted, he took none of his mechanical constructions very seriously; "it was clear that the equations themselves were all that was essential" (Thomson et al., 1931, p. 70). Maxwell himself had a remarkably clear view of what analogies were good for and his comments are relevant to scientific explanation today.

> If we adopt a physical [i.e., analogical] hypothesis, we see the phenomena only through a medium, and are liable to that blindness to facts and rashness in assumption which a partial explanation encourages. We must therefore discover some method of investigation which allows the mind at every step to lay hold of a clear physical conception, without being committed to any theory

> founded on the physical science from which the conception is borrowed. (Quoted in Thomson et al., 1931, p. 99.)

It is the partial character of analogical treatments that makes them of ambiguous value in the work of scientific explanation. For the very reason that a model is drawn from a different area of discourse, it is likely that its extended application will at some point break down. The "valence-as-hooks" analogy cannot meaningfully be broadened to include all that is known about hooks; the water-in-tubes model for electricity provides no way of dealing with phenomena of magnetic induction; the planetary model for electrons is limited in its handling of modern discoveries of subatomic phenomena. To take examples from psychology, the theory of Oedipal conflict does not include the prediction that a son will be driven to blind himself or a mother to hang, regardless of the Sophoclean solution. Nor does the generalization about ontogeny recapitulating phylogeny entail the growth of feathers in children during the birdlike stage of their development. Analogies or models often go too far and land in absurdity or they do not go far enough to account for the phenomena under examination. These devices can be seen as special cases of plausible explanation, and they have both the advantages and disadvantages of other plausible systems. Analogies may serve to facilitate communication of novel ideas, and they almost certainly are important aids to the creative scientist, but like their vernacular cousins, the prototheories, they often fall short of producing a consistent set of general principles which lead to the prediction of confirmable outcomes. Frank has noted, for the special study of physics, a change in the scientific climate which may be applicable to other disciplines as well.

> The rise of twentieth-century physics, of relativity and the quantum theory, was closely connected with a new view of the basic principles. It was no longer taken for granted that the principles from which the facts had to be derived should contain a specific analogy, either to an organism or to a mechanism. Nothing was required except that the observed phenomena could be derived from the principles in a consistent way and as simply as possible. The words and symbols that occurred in the principles, and the way these were connected, could be invented according to their fitness as bases for deriving the phenomena discovered by the experimental physicist. (Frank, 1949, p. 252 f.)

From the point of view of the psychology of thought, this is undoubtedly overoptimistic. Human beings, scientists as well as laymen, will continue to find their way toward new conceptualizations by means of old ones, and the analogy will continue to serve didactic and heuristic ends. Nonetheless, Frank correctly emphasizes the absence of a priori restrictions on the language of explanation. Science is indissolubly tied to its groundings in reliable observation, but the superstructure of theory has surprisingly few limitations on its language beyond the bounded ingenuity of creative men.

Analogical reasoning in psychology can often produce a group of problems which closely resemble the ones raised in the discussion of reductionism. If the human organism is assumed to behave "just like" a hydraulic or a thermodynamic or a chemical or a neurophysiological system, the use of the appropriate analogy may provide the explainer with a feeling of having a "more basic" theory. Surely, if he turns to highly developed scientific systems, he will find well-confirmed principles and a rich source of interlocking theoretical relationships. This wealth is not easily claimed, however; until his system is so revised and edited that it permits accurate prediction of behavior, it remains analogical, with whatever virtues and encumbrances this mode of explanation brings with it.

There is another somewhat more elusive relationship between analogical explanation and the reductionist controversy. Much of MacCorquodale and Meehl's argument for a dichotomy of theoretical words depends on the notion of "actual existence," and this criterion for hypothetical constructs parallels the older demand in the physics of wave phenomena for what Maxwell called a "physical hypothesis." Both positions imply strongly that good explanations are those which draw on well-established, or at least well-accepted, theories for their basic constructs. The argument from "actual existence" is one of the thorniest problems in the philosophy of science, but the experience of physicists, who some time ago gave up such a prototheoretical commitment, should be a warning to psychologists not to be cheered too much if their theories are "existential." The analogy from other sciences would seem to support with heavy underlining that "the equations themselves are all that is essential."

Thanks to an unhappy development in psychological argot, a group of theories of behavior which are almost antithetical to analogical treatments have also been called "models." These explanatory systems—the so-called mathematical models—are of interest in the present context precisely because they have so few of the disabilities attached to analogical reasoning. The stochastic theories (see Bush and Mosteller, 1955) have as their central theoretical terms certain mathematical operators which, unlike almost all other psychological explanations, do not have any obvious relationship to the language of the vernacular or to the language of other empirical disciplines. The initial statements of the explanation are chosen only with regard to their mathematical consistency and their usefulness in producing meaningful descriptions of observed phenomena in the field of learning. The result of this strategy is twofold. In the first place, there results a calculus of explanation and a set of rules for its manipulation which, on grounds of explicitness and clarity, is unrivaled in present-day psychology. Moreover, such a system can be manipulated quite independently of any specific empirical interpretation, and the work of theoretical revision and addition can be carried on without contamination from "physical" or archaic analogies. Mathematical "models" are free from any taint of surplus meaning in the sense either of prototheoretical associations or of the reductionist contention.

The nature of this achievement can be illustrated by comparing the stochastic theories with earlier attempts to set up mathematical treatments of behavior. Hull, for example, carefully chose association-free symbols (e.g., ${}_SH_R$, D, r) in his theoretical principles, but his textual discussion of the theory and its use by other researchers quickly demonstrated the infiltration of associations to "habit," "drive," and so on. Similarly, Lewin's attempt to build a topological explanation of behavior was soon overlaid with extratheoretical associations to terms like "force" and "valence." To the present date, the mathematical theories of behavior have remained relatively clear of this kind of increase in "meaning." It is, of course, a matter for the future testing and refinement of the theories to determine their utility in the explanation of behavior, but they have the apparent advantage of being disconnected in their public statement from the "analogies of organism and mechanism" which have characterized psychological theory in the past.

If we except the mathematical "models," the function of analogies and models in psychology can be seen as largely that of plausible explanation. They often promote communication, particularly between teacher and student, and they frequently serve as guides to creative researchers in the construction of formal theories and in the design of research, but the value of analogical reasoning in the explicit statement of deductive theories is not so clearly demonstrable. The gain in vernacular comprehensibility that comes from the exposition of an apt analogy may be more than offset by the illusion of having achieved a genuinely deductive explanation.

CLINICAL INSIGHT AND CLINICAL INFERENCE

The psychologist in his attempts to understand behavior must frequently make decisions for which he has no clear theoretical warrant. In devising an apparatus for the study of animal learning, for example, or in the construction of an experimental room for observation of social interactions, he will proceed only in part as his principles of behavior direct; quite a few details must be determined by hunch or best guess. Although these addenda to explicit theory are apparent in all areas of psychology, they have been noted in greater detail and with more self-consciousness in the field of clinical psychology, and have given rise to extended discussions of clinical insight, clinical inference, and clinical prediction.

In the typical example, a clinician is presented with or obtains for himself a collection of information about his subject. This may consist of anamnestic material, projective-test responses, intelligence-test scores, interview reports, and so on, from which the psychologist develops an evaluation. For the highly specialized case of psychotherapy, such an evaluation is compressed in time and the therapist must make almost instantaneous decisions about what he will do or say next in response to the patient's behavior. At first glance, the techniques of the clinician seem far indeed from the kind of theory construction we have discussed earlier, but an examination of the apparent contrast will provide leads for a better understanding of clinical theorizing.[4]

At the outset, it is obvious that the work of the clinician is not a "game on paper," that is, a precise derivation of theorems from an explicit set of general principles. Even leaving aside the psychotherapeutic exchange, where the need for immediate action precludes such deductive manipulation, there is no mechanical system into which the clinical psychologist can plug his data and come out with a unique solution. On the other hand, the clinician is performing the central task of a theory—predicting or anticipating behavior—and doing so at a rather rapid rate. It is the predictive character of the clinical inter-

---

[4] More-or-less explicit theories of personality or of the nature of psychotherapy are not relevant to the present paragraphs; rather, it is the practicing clinician's making of everyday professional decisions which is under study.

action which brings it under observation as a variety of theorizing. Whether he is attaching a diagnostic label, or making statements about etiology, or recommending disposition of a case, the clinician is behaving like a theory. On the basis of data available to him, and these are analogous to the Conditions sentences of Chapter 12, he makes statements of expected behavior, i.e., predictions. Clearly what is missing from the picture of the clinician as ambulatory theory is the set of general principles which normally bridges the gap between conditions and predictions. But unless one is willing to disavow the evidence of Chapter 11 that inductive inference, clinical or otherwise, does not simply arise out of collections of evidence, there is left only the deductive analogy. A plausible conclusion is that clinical inference is based on a group of principles which somehow affect the making of predictions, but which are not always given public expression. Such a "black-box" or "empty-organism" portrait of the clinician raises several questions which are relevant to the language of psychology.

Of great interest to psychologists, whether clinicians or not, is the question of validation. Does clinical prediction work? Does the clinical psychologist make predictive hits above chance expectancy? Meehl (1954), in a keen analysis of this problem, has summarized the empirical evidence available on the success of clinical prediction and has concluded that we are far from any certain answers to this basic question. Although the validation issue has been raised often enough over the last several decades, there is a surprising paucity of pertinent investigations on the effectiveness of the clinical "black box." While almost all psychologists are well disposed toward the proposition that the skillful clinician does a better job of predicting than could be achieved by random guessing, there is little evidence to show the degree of his superiority, or the amount of information and time needed to reach a certain level of predictive success, or even how to go about selecting "good clinicians" for more detailed study. These gaps in our knowledge cannot be filled by polemic, and Meehl has built a very strong case in support of the need for a systematic empirical study of clinical prediction. The practicing clinician, faced with his increasing professional burden, cannot wait for the researchers to tell him how successful he is likely to be before he attempts answers to the immediate practical problems which confront him. But "there is a difference between veridical knowledge and purported knowledge, between knowledge which brings its credentials with it and that which does not" (Meehl, 1954, p. 138); neither the occasional brilliant success nor the confidence of the clinician in his instruments and his interpretative scheme is a legitimate substitute for the attested demonstration of predictive effectiveness.

Even if the effectiveness of clinical inference is conceded, there remain questions of its relation to the more conventional kind of theorizing in psychology. Following the analogy to deductive procedures suggested earlier, it would seem likely that the clinician operates with a set of implicit general principles relating various aspects of human behavior and that, presented with a statement of conditions—that is, particular values for the variables in his "system"—he proceeds to a series of manipulations which produce the terminal prediction. Some of this work can be made public—scoring techniques, unusual signs in projective records, profiles of characteristics associated with diagnostic categories, the relative importance of age or sex, and so on. But the fact that no simple automatic technique will normally produce the same results indicates the addition to the solution of something peculiar to the human deducer.

If the deductive analogy is to be maintained, clinical inference must be seen as a system with unverbalized premises. So long as the principles in the clinical machine remain private, the "theory" remains incomplete, and falls into the larger group of partial explanations which may be convincing to their holders, and even creditably accurate, but which suffer from the serious disadvantage of being incommunicable. The clinician, no matter how successful he may be even in a demanding test of his procedures, faces the job of educating his students and colleagues in the use of his principles; if he is unable to transmit his system, his art remains as mysterious as the poet's. Another disadvantage of the private character of the clinician's theories resides in the hidden changes that these systems undergo. There is no guarantee that a particular set of premises used to explain a patient's behavior will not shift in unknown directions at the moment of explanation. A more attractive prospect for the place of the clinician in psychology is that his private "deductions" will serve the same functions that the musings of creative thinkers do. In this view, the phenomenology of diagnosis and therapeutic manipulation would form a source for publicly stated propositions, which could then be put through the familiar trial by research.

The problem of clinical inference is a reasonable miniature of the present state of psychology at large. There is the same mixture of vernacular prototheories, occasionally successful but poorly expressed explanatory schemes, a commitment to empirical verification, and a narrow but growing edge of reliable generalizations and adequately stated principles.

Last words

OUR EXPLORATIONS OF THE LANGUAGE OF psychology set out with the belief that a combination of empirical and logical analysis might prove rewarding. We have had occasion to range over a varied terrain; from the homeground of the science of behavior, we have strayed into areas usually assigned to the history and philosophy of science. The goal of this intermingling of psychological, philosophical, and historical analyses has been to reach an understanding of psychology as a scientific discipline. Just as Sarton defended the study of the history of science by insisting that "we shall not be able to understand our own science of today (I do not say to use it, but to understand it) if we do not succeed in penetrating its genesis and evolution" (Sarton, 1936, p. 4), so have we been led to the conviction that an examination of the psychologist's language provides a basis for understanding the status and development of contemporary psychology.

Examinations of this order have frequently been met by two apparently incompatible attitudes. On the one hand, commentaries on a science have been considered either presumptuous or fruitless by the man-who-does-the-work. The empirical researcher, deep in his own problems, may have little patience with abstract speculations about logic and language. On the other hand, there has been abroad a half-formulated hope that the philosophy of science might provide incontestable rules for achieving empirical progress. This longing has produced a search for the nostrums of "true concepts" and manuals for theory construction. However, neither the disdain of the former position nor the aspirations of the latter do justice to the interplay between the work of the scientist and the critical examination of his language. There is a middle ground, where the empirical psychologist may benefit from an understanding of the presuppositions his language brings to the laboratory, and where his knowledge of human behavior may help in the resolution of traditional problems in the philosophy of science. It is in support of an amalgamation of empirical psychology and the analysis of scientific language that we have attempted a survey of this middle ground.

In working toward this joining of forces, it is necessary to agree that the work of science is the systematic accumulation of knowledge. Reliable empirical relationships are codified in communicable general statements which permit the deductive inference of particular events. Scientific systems are, moreover, open systems in the sense that all statements in them are subject to revision—they invite the growth of knowledge. Given these assumptions, we have considered their implications for the behavior of scientists. The insistence on publicity and communicability is an outcome of the accumulative aspect of science. Publicity in its turn determines what is and what is not observable. Thus, there is no need to postulate that science is about observable events; such a conclusion follows from the more general considerations. Similarly, the systematic aspect of science is closely bound to the demands for communicability. The deductive requirement that theoretical statements must permit the prediction of concrete events requires a common system, that is, a common logic. Finally, the requirement of openness of the systems emphasizes the timebound nature of scientific statements; new knowledge changes what we know and what we thought we knew—"the present changes the past" (Boring, 1929, p. vii). It is the growing and changing nature of scientific knowledge that tempers the rigid demand for precision and clarity.

In a sense, this view of science is prescriptive. There is little place in it for trends in psychology which violate the public, deductive, and growth requirements of systematic study. But where we have argued for invariant terms, we have also argued for the value of vagueness and surplus meaning in the vocabulary of newly opened fields of study. And where we have argued for the advantages of explicit deductive systems, we have also defended the less rigorous generalizations and insights of the creative theorist.

In order to maintain this position, it has been necessary to collect and adumbrate what seemed to be reasonable hunches, hypotheses, theories of theories, and plain guesses. The plank-by-plank reconstruction of a scientific discipline like psychology is luckily restricted by the necessity of keeping the ship afloat while rebuilding it. These repairs will proceed slowly, not only because of the expanding horizon of logical analysis, but also because of the inadequate psychological knowledge available for sound empirical statements. But the unfinished nature of any contemporary treatment of the language of science has another source in the growing realization of modern philosophy that objective "truths" are not cheaply come by. The hope of the nineteenth century that science will provide objective appreciations free of value judgments is slowly being jettisoned. In a parallel development the old saw that a science of human behavior is impossible because any statement about other human beings always involves some moral or evaluative implication is no longer tenable. Paradoxically, this state of affairs has come about not because the archaic belief in valuation is false, but because it is trivially true—it applies to all phases of human activity. Choice and decisions and *weltanschauliche* frames of reference always intrude whenever theories are propounded, deductions tested, or inferences defended, no matter what the subject of the discourse.

The best, in fact the only, course available to us is to try to elaborate some of the pervasive assumptions behind our thinking, and to reduce the hidden influences of these basic tenets. Because all theoretical statements, whether about sticks and stones or about the languages of science, involve evaluative presuppositions, judgment of them must fall back on the prosaic criterion: How well do the theories work? In discussing the science of behavior, which itself lacks an integrative theoretical formulation, we have made use of an equally unfinished theory of science. It is the availability of this partial theory to empirical test which balances its formal deficiencies.

In treating of science as human behavior, we have argued that questions of fact about the behavior of scientists are relevant to an understanding of the philosophy or logic of the scientific endeavor. The research psychologist, impatient with "philosophical" and "metaphysical" intrusions into his empirical bailiwick, may agree with Boring that the slow development of psychology is ascribable in part to its "divided soul," its "inability to surrender its philosophical heritage" (Boring, 1929, p. 661). For philosophical problems which permit no empirical formulation these misgivings may be justified. However, many questions traditionally assigned to metaphysics have in recent years come within the purview of empirical analysis, and a psychology freed of irrational fears of metaphysics may competently address itself to the resolution of these problems. From this point of view, Campbell's cautious soundings in the philosophical deep present a challenge for the empirical psychologist.

> We are all interested in problems which the metaphysician attempts to solve. Metaphysics, like science, has developed out of the mass of common unorganized knowledge. . . . The world is not divided into those who do and those who do not hold metaphysical doctrines, but rather into those who hold them for some reason and those who hold them for none. (Campbell, 1920, p. 12.)

Our excursion into the world of philosophical warrants has assumed that the basis for at least some of these reasons may be found within the context of empirical hypotheses and theories. To the philosopher who may be perturbed by this turnabout—the invasion of his field of competence by the psychologist—we can only maintain that our hypotheses and conjectures are part of the more general attempt to extend our knowledge of human behavior. They will stand or fall in the light of evidence.

While we have, with some reservations, introduced a working distinction between the vocabulary and the theory of psychology, it should be clear that future developments in the vocabulary cannot be sought in a theoretical vacuum. Only theory will tell us what the important things in the world are and in what relations they stand to one another. The trend toward inclusive, global theories of behavior has abated in mid-twentieth century and creative thinkers in psychology are now concerned with building less pretentious theories about discrimination learning, psychophysical scaling, schizophrenia, activation, decision making, concept attainment, conflict, and so on. These efforts are developing the new vocabulary of psychology by pointing to important variables and by stating relationships among them. The integrative insight which combines fields and develops the basic postulates of a more general system neither springs from a patient perusal of instances nor does it develop without implicit testing of plausible hunches. The great innovator, whom psychology awaits all too passively at times, has usually been the competent and sophisticated traveler in well-trodden paths. Data at his finger tips and genius in his make-up, he can be creative only to the extent that science provides him with the proper background. The mosaic of psychological data which presents itself even to the casual reader of the psychological literature lacks, with some notable exceptions, the consistency and comparability that must be available for the testing of novel ideas. The lack of response to calls for standardized procedure and the readiness with which old notions are abandoned to give way to picayune reformulations both make for confusion. The persistence of a Freud in pursuing the free associations of his patients, of a Skinner in relating response probability to schedules of reinforcement, and of a Piaget in digging into the development of logical thought is too rarely recognized as providing the consistent vocabulary and theory which are necessary before another innovator can propose the integrative idea or general system.

"Research, and then research" is the minimum requirement for scientific progress, but it is necessary that the empirical scientist recognize the role of language in the planning and interpretation of his investigations. Words and sentences are not stable parts of the environment, to be used naively and without critical appraisal. The aim of an analysis of scientific language is to make the researcher as skeptical and careful about his manipulations of constructs and theories as he is in his dealings with laboratory equipment, statistics, and subject samples. The achievement of this aim leaves inviolate the work of laboratories and clinics, and it does not legislate the specific content of psychological theories. The informed and skeptical use of the language of psychology will resolve the conflict between uncomfortable disdain and irrational hope for the analysis of the language and logic of science.

References

A CONTEMPORARY STUDY OF THE LANGUAGE of psychology depends on an extensive literature in the philosophy of science, the history of psychology, and the exploding field of contemporary psychology. The reference list which follows represents these sources only fractionally and has been compiled under two general rules.

The first decision made was to cite only those works which are mentioned in the text; what follows therefore is a reference list rather than a bibliography of the language of psychology. A second decision was to cite whenever possible the most recent or most didactic statement of any particular position. This may result in the appearance of disservice to the originators of the basic ideas elaborated in the foregoing treatment. It is to be hoped that the reader who goes beyond the present study to discover the sources of the psychological language for himself will find the landmarks set up by Locke, Peirce, Dewey, Mach, Whitehead, James, Pearson, and the other architects of science to whom explicit reference has not been made.

Allport, F. H. (1955) *Theories of Perception and the Concept of Structure.* New York: Wiley.

Bacon, F. (1620) *Instauratio Magna. Novum Organum.* London: John Bill.

Bakan, D. (1953) "Learning and the Scientific Enterprise." *Psychol. Rev.,* **60,** 45–49.

Bergmann, G. (1944) "An Empiricist's System of the Sciences." *Sci. Mon.,* **59,** 140–148.

——— (1950) "Semantics." In V. Ferm (Ed.) *A History of Philosophical Systems.* New York: Philosophical Library.

——— (1951) "The Logic of Psychological Concepts." *Phil. Sci.,* **18,** 93–110.

——— (1954) "Sense and Nonsense in Operationism." *Sci. Mon.,* **79,** 210–214.

——— (1957) *Philosophy of Science.* Madison, Wisconsin: University of Wisconsin Press.

Bergmann, G., and Spence, K. W. (1944) "The Logic of Psychophysical Measurement." *Psychol. Rev.,* **51,** 1–24.

Birch, T. (1757) *The History of the Royal Society of London,* Vol. III. London: A. Millar.

Boring, E. G. (1929) *A History of Experimental Psychology.* New York: Century.

Braithwaite, R. B. (1953) *Scientific Explanation.* Cambridge: Cambridge University Press.

Brett, G. S. (1912–21) *A History of Psychology.* London: Allen.

Bridgman, P. W. (1927) *The Logic of Modern Physics.* New York: Macmillan.

Brown, R. W. (1956) "Language and Categories." In Bruner, J. S., Goodnow, Jacqueline J., and Austin, G. A. *A Study of Thinking.* New York: Wiley.

Bruner, J. S. (1957a) "On Perceptual Readiness." *Psychol. Rev.,* **64,** 123–152.

——— (1957b) "Mechanism Riding High." *Contemp. Psychol.,* **6,** 156.

——— (1957c) "Going beyond the Information Given." In *Contemporary Approaches to Cognition.* Cambridge: Harvard University Press.

Bruner, J. S., Goodnow, Jacqueline J., and Austin, G. A. (1956) *A Study of Thinking.* New York: Wiley.

Brunswik, E. (1952) *The Conceptual Framework of Psychology. Int. Encycl. Unified Sci.,* Vol. 1, No. 10, Chicago: University of Chicago Press.

Bucklew, J. (1955) "The Subjective Tradition in Phenomenological Psychology." *Phil. Sci.,* **22,** 289–299.

Bush, R. R., and Mosteller, F. (1955) *Stochastic Models for Learning.* New York: Wiley.

Campbell, B. A., and Kraeling, Doris (1953) "Response Strength as a Function of Drive Level and Amount of Drive Reduction." *J. exp. Psychol.,* 45, 97–101.

Campbell, N. R. (1920) *Physics: The Elements.* Cambridge: Cambridge University Press.

Cannon, W. B. (1945) *The Way of an Investigator.* New York: Norton.

Carnap, R. (1936, 1937) "Testability and Meaning." *Phil. Sci.,* **3,** 419–471; **4,** 1–40.

Carnap, R. (1937) *The Logical Syntax of Language.* London: Kegan Paul, Trench, Trubner.

——— (1938) *Logical Foundations of the Unity of Science. Int. Encycl. Unified Sci.,* Vol. 1, No. 1, pp. 42–62, Chicago: University of Chicago Press.

——— (1950) *Logical Foundations of Probability.* Chicago: University of Chicago Press.

Cohen, I. B. (1956) *Franklin and Newton.* Philadelphia: American Philosophical Society.

Cohen, M. R. (1931 [1953]) *Reason and Nature.* Glencoe, Illinois: Free Press.

Cohen, M. R., and Nagel, E. (1934) *An Introduction to Logic and Scientific Method.* New York: Harcourt, Brace.

Conant, J. B. (1947) *On Understanding Science.* New Haven: Yale University Press.

Condillac, E. B. de (1780) *La logique.* Paris.

Cramér, H. (1946) *Mathematical Methods of Statistics.* Princeton: Princeton University Press.

Cronbach, L. J., and Meehl, P. E. (1955) "Construct Validity in Psychological Tests." *Psychol. Bull.,* **52,** 281–302.

Dantzig, T. (1954) *Number: The Language of Science.* (4th ed.) New York: Macmillan.

Darwin, C. R. (1899) *The Life and Letters of Charles Darwin.* New York: D. Appleton.

Dollard, J., and Miller, N. E. (1950) *Personality and Psychotherapy.* New York: McGraw-Hill.

Dubos, R. J. (1950) *Louis Pasteur: Free Lance of Science.* Boston: Little, Brown.

Ebbinghaus, H. (1908) *Abriss der Psychologie.* Leipzig: Von Veit.

Eddington, A. S. (1928) *The Nature of the Physical World.* New York: Macmillan.

Feller, W. (1957) *An Introduction to Probability Theory and Its Applications,* Vol. I. (2nd ed.) New York: Wiley.

Ferster, C. B., and Skinner, B. F. (1957) *Schedules of Reinforcement.* New York: Appleton-Century-Crofts.

Frank, P. (1949) *Modern Science and Its Philosophy.* Cambridge: Harvard University Press.

Freud, S. (1900 [1954]) *The Interpretation of Dreams.* London: Allen and Unwin.

——— (1910) *Leonardo da Vinci.* London: Psychoanalytic Library.

——— (1949) *An Outline of Psychoanalysis.* New York: Norton.

Frolov, Y. P. (1937) *Pavlov and His School: The Theory of Conditioned Reflexes.* London: Kegan Paul, Trench, Trubner.

Galanter, E., and Gerstenhaber, M. (1956) "On Thought: The Extrinsic Theory." *Psychol. Rev.,* **63,** 218–227.

Gesell, A. (1954) "The Ontogenesis of Infant Behavior." In L. Carmichael (Ed.) *Manual of Child Psychology.* (2nd ed.) New York: Wiley.

Gibson, J. J., and Gibson, Eleanor J. (1955) "Perceptual Learning: Differentiation or Enrichment." *Psychol. Rev.,* **62,** 32–41.

Goodman, N. (1955) *Fact, Fiction, and Forecast.* Cambridge: Harvard University Press.

Gumpert, M. (1936) *Trail-Blazers of Science.* New York: Funk and Wagnalls.

Hadamard, J. S. (1945) *The Psychology of Invention in the Mathematical Field.* Princeton: Princeton University Press.

Hall, C. S., and Lindzey, G. (1957) *Theories of Personality.* New York: Wiley.

Hammond, D. B. (1923) *Stories of Scientific Discovery.* Cambridge: Cambridge University Press.

Harrod, R. F. (1956) *Foundations of Inductive Logic.* New York: Harcourt, Brace.

Hart, I. B. (1923) *Makers of Science.* London: Oxford University Press.

Hempel, C. G. (1945) "Studies in the Logic of Confirmation." *Mind,* **54,** 1–26, 97–121.

——— (1952) *Fundamentals of Concept Formation in Empirical Science. Int. Encycl. Unified Sci.,* Vol. 2, No. 7, Chicago: University of Chicago Press.

——— (1954) "A Logical Appraisal of Operationism." *Sci. Mon.,* **79,** 215–220.

Hempel, C. G., and Oppenheim, P. (1948) "Studies in the Logic of Explanation." *Phil. Sci.,* **15,** 135–175.

Hilgard, E. R. (1956) *Theories of Learning.* (2nd ed.) New York: Appleton-Century-Crofts.

Hovland, C. I. (1952) "A 'Communication Analysis' of Concept Learning." *Psychol. Rev.,* **59,** 461–472.

——— (Ed.) (1957) *The Order of Presentation in Persuasion.* New Haven: Yale University Press.

Hovland, C. I., Janis, I. L., and Kelley, H. H. (1953) *Communication and Persuasion.* New Haven: Yale University Press.

Hull, C. L. (1943) *Principles of Behavior.* New York: Appleton-Century.

——— (1952) *A Behavior System.* New Haven: Yale University Press.

Hume, D. (1748 [1939]) *An Enquiry Concerning Human Understanding.* In E. A. Burtt (Ed.) *The English Philosophers from Bacon to Mill.* New York: Modern Library.

Humphrey, G. (1951) *Thinking.* New York: Wiley.

Husserl, E. G. (1913) *Logische Untersuchungen.* Halle: Niemeyer.

James, W. (1892) *Psychology.* New York: Holt.

Janis, I. L. (1954) "Personality Correlates of Susceptibility to Persuasion." *J. Personality,* **22,** 504–518.

Jessor, R. (1956) "Phenomenological Personality Theories and the Data Language of Psychology." *Psychol. Rev.,* **63,** 173–180.

Jessor, R., and Hammond, K. R. (1957) "Construct Validity and the Taylor Anxiety Scale." *Psychol. Bull.,* **54,** 161–170.

Kaplan, A. (1946) "Definition and Specification of Meaning." *J. Phil.,* **63,** 281–287.

Kendall, M. G. (1948) *Rank Correlation Methods.* London: Griffin.

Kepler, J. (1610) *Dissertatio cum Nuncio Sidereo.* Florence: J. A. Caneo.

Klein, G. S. (1954) "Need and Regulation." In M. R. Jones (Ed.) *Nebraska Symposium on Motivation: 1954.* Lincoln, Nebraska: University of Nebraska Press.

Koffka, K. (1935) *Principles of Gestalt Psychology.* New York: Harcourt, Brace.

Krauss, R. (1952) *A Hole Is to Dig.* New York: Harper.

Krech, D. (1950) "Dynamic Systems, Psychological Fields and Hypothetical Constructs." *Psychol. Rev.,* **57,** 783–790.

Krech, D., and Crutchfield, R. S. (1958) *Elements of Psychology.* New York: Knopf.

Kris, E. (1952) *Psychoanalytic Explorations in Art.* New York: International Universities Press.

Leeper, R. (1951) "Cognitive Processes." In S. S. Stevens (Ed.) *Handbook of Experimental Psychology.* New York: Wiley.

Lewin, K. (1938) "The Conceptual Representation and the Measurement of Psychological Forces." *Contr. psychol. Theory Duke Univ.,* **1,** No. 4.

Loewi, O. (1953) *From the Workshop of Discoveries.* Lawrence, Kansas: University of Kansas Press.

Luce, R. D., and Raiffa, H. (1957) *Games and Decisions: Introduction and Critical Survey.* New York: Wiley.

MacCorquodale, K., and Meehl, P. E. (1948) "On a Distinction between Hypothetical Constructs and Intervening Variables." *Psychol. Rev.,* **55,** 95–107.

Marx, M. H. (1951) "Intervening Variable or Hypothetical Construct?" *Psychol. Rev.,* **58,** 235–247.

Meehl, P. E. (1954) *Clinical versus Statistical Prediction.* Minneapolis: University of Minnesota Press.

Melton, A. W. (1936) "The Methodology of Experimental Studies of Human Learning and Retention. I. The Functions of a Methodology and the Available Criteria for Evaluating Different Experimental Methods." *Psychol. Bull.,* **33,** 305–394.

Mill, J. S. (1843) *A System of Logic.* London: J. W. Parker.

Miller, G. A. (1951) *Language and Communication.* New York: McGraw-Hill.

Miller, N. E. (1950) Notes on Sources of Difficulty in Creative Thinking. Unpublished paper.

Moltz, H. (1954) "Resistance to Extinction as a Function of Variations in Stimuli Associated with Shock." *J. exp. Psychol.,* **47,** 418–424.

Moss, F. A. (1924) "Study of Animal Drives." *J. exp. Psychol.,* **7,** 165–185.

Murray, H. A. (1936) "Basic Concepts for a Psychology of Personality." *J. gen. Psychol.,* **15,** 241–268.

Newton, I. (1713) *Philosophiae Naturalis Principia Mathematica.* (2nd ed.) Cambridge.

Pavlov, I. (1927) *Conditioned Reflexes.* London: Oxford University Press.

Perkins, M. (1953) "Intersubjectivity and Gestalt Psychology." *Phil. phenom. Res.*, **13**, 437–451.

Peters, R. S. (Ed.) (1953) *Brett's History of Psychology*. London: Allen and Unwin.

Piaget, J. (1929) *The Child's Conception of the World*. London: Routledge and Kegan Paul.

—— (1930) *The Child's Conception of Physical Causality*. London: Kegan Paul, Trench, Trubner.

—— (1951) *Play, Dreams and Imitation in Childhood*. London: Heinemann.

—— (1953) *The Origin of Intelligence in the Child*. London: Routledge and Kegan Paul.

—— (1954) *The Construction of Reality in the Child*. New York: Basic Books.

Piaget, J., and Szeminska, Alina (1941) *La genèse du nombre chez l'enfant*. Neuchatel et Paris: Delachaux et Niestlé.

Pillsbury, W. B. (1916) *The Fundamentals of Psychology*. New York: Macmillan.

Poincaré, H. (1913) *The Foundations of Science*. New York: Science Press.

Polya, G. (1954) *Mathematics and Plausible Reasoning*. Princeton: Princeton University Press.

Pratt, C. C. (1939) *The Logic of Modern Psychology*. New York: Macmillan.

Quine, W. V. (1950) *Methods of Logic*. New York: Holt.

—— (1940, 1951a) *Mathematical Logic*. New York: Norton.

—— (1951b) "The Two Dogmas of Empiricism." *Phil. Rev.*, **60**, 20–43.

—— (1953) "On Mental Entities." *Proc. Amer. Acad. Arts Sci.*, **80**, No. 3.

—— (1957) "The Scope and Language of Science." *Brit. J. Phil. Sci.*, **8**, 1–17.

Rapaport, D. (1951) *Organization and Pathology of Thought*. New York: Columbia University Press.

Russell, B. (1905) "On Denoting." *Mind*, **14**, 479–493.

Ryle, G. (1949) *The Concept of Mind*. London: Hutchinson's University Library.

Salzinger, K. (1959) "Experimental Manipulation of Verbal Behavior: A Review." *J. gen. Psychol.*, in press.

Sarton, G. (1936) *The Study of the History of Science*. Cambridge: Harvard University Press.

Skinner, B. F. (1931) "The Concept of the Reflex in the Description of Behavior." *J. gen. Psychol.*, **5**, 427–458.

—— (1932) "Drive and Reflex Strength." *J. gen. Psychol.*, **6**, 22–37.

—— (1945) "The Operational Analysis of Psychological Terms." *Psychol. Rev.*, **52**, 270–277.

—— (1948) Verbal Behavior. Unpublished William James Lectures, Harvard University.

—— (1950) "Are Theories of Learning Necessary?" *Psychol. Rev.*, **57**, 193–216.

—— (1957) *Verbal Behavior*. New York: Appleton-Century-Crofts.

Skinner, B. F. (1958) "Reinforcement Today." *Amer. Psychologist,* **13,** 94–99.

Smith, F. V. (1951) *The Explanation of Human Behavior.* London: Constable.

Smoke, K. L. (1932) "An Objective Study of Concept Formation." *Psychol. Monogr.,* **42,** No. 191.

Snygg, D. (1941) "The Need for a Phenomenological System of Psychology." *Psychol. Rev.,* **48,** 404–424.

Spence, K. W., Farber, I. E., and Taylor, Elaine (1954) "The Relation of Electric Shock and Anxiety to Level of Performance in Eyelid Conditioning." *J. exp. Psychol.,* **48,** 404–408.

Standen, A. (1950) *Science Is a Sacred Cow.* New York: Dutton.

Stevens, S. S. (1936) "Psychology: The Propaedeutic Science." *Phil. Sci.,* **3,** 90–103.

——— (1939) "Psychology and the Science of Science." *Psychol. Bull.,* **36,** 221–263.

Thomson, J. J., et al. (1931) *James Clerk Maxwell.* Cambridge: Cambridge University Press.

Titchener, E. B. (1896) *An Outline of Psychology.* New York: Macmillan.

von Neumann, J. (1947) "The Mathematician." In R. B. Heywood (Ed.) *The Works of the Mind.* Chicago: University of Chicago Press.

von Wright, G. H. (1957) *The Logical Problem of Induction.* (2nd ed.) Oxford: Blackwell.

Watson, J. B. (1913) "Psychology as the Behaviorist Views It." *Psychol. Rev.,* **20,** 158–177.

Wertheimer, M. (1938) "Gestalt Theory." In W. D. Ellis (Ed.) *A Source Book of Gestalt Psychology.* New York: Harcourt, Brace.

Whorf, B. L. (1956) *Language, Thought, and Reality.* (Ed., J. B. Carroll.) New York: Wiley.

Wittgenstein, L. (1922) *Tractatus Logico-Philosophicus.* London: Routledge, Kegan Paul.

——— (1953) *Philosophical Investigations.* Oxford: Blackwell.

Woodger, J. H. (1939) *The Technique of Theory Construction. Int. Encycl. Unified Sci.,* Vol. 2, No. 5, Chicago: University of Chicago Press.

Wundt, W. (1874) *Grundzüge der physiologischen Psychologie.* 1. Band. Leipzig: Engelmann.

——— (1904) *Principles of Physiological Psychology.* (5th ed.) New York: Macmillan.

Zilsel, E. (1941) *Problems of Empiricism. Int. Encycl. Unified Sci.,* Vol. 2, No. 8, pp. 53–94. Chicago: University of Chicago Press.

Index of names

Index of subjects